F 2270.2 .C25 M33 1993
"So Wise were our Elders
McDowell, John Holmes

184702

DATE DUE

"So Wise Were Our Elders"

"SO WISE WERE OUR ELDERS"

Mythic Narratives of the Kamsá

JOHN HOLMES McDOWELL

THE UNIVERSITY PRESS OF KENTUCKY

I dedicate this book to the memory of three friends,
each of whom (in his way) made it possible:

taita Bautista and taita Mariano,
men of intellect and fine aesthetic sense;

and especially don Justo,
my field partner in the mythic quest.

Scholarly publisher for the Commonwealth,
serving Bellarmine College, Berea College, Centre
College of Kentucky, Eastern Kentucky University,
The Filson Club, Georgetown College, Kentucky
Historical Society, Kentucky State University,
Morehead State University, Murray State University,
Northern Kentucky University, Transylvania University,
University of Kentucky, University of Louisville,
and Western Kentucky University.

Editorial and Sales Offices: Lexington, Kentucky 40508-4008

Library of Congress Cataloging–in–Publication Data
McDowell, John Holmes, 1946–
    "So Wise were our Elders" : mystic narratives from the Kamsá /
John Holmes McDowell.
        p. cm.
    Includes bibliographical references and index
    ISBN 0-8131-1826-3 (alk. paper) :
        1. Camsa Indians—Religion and mythology. 2. Camsa language—
    Texts. 3. Camsa language—Grammar.
F2270.2.C25M33 1993
398.2'089'983—dc20   93-5083

This book is printed on recycled acid-free paper meeting
the requirements of the American National Standard
for Permanence of Paper for Printed Library Materials. ∞

Contents

Preface

Some fifteen years ago I came upon a treasure in the Sibundoy Valley of Colombia, an indigenous American mythology that was still largely unknown beyond its natal territory. As I listened in, initially to María Juajibioy, then to the master storyteller, taita Mariano Chicunque, I sensed that I was gaining access to something precious. Even during the first performances I witnessed, I could identify key substantives: these tales were about seductive bears, animal-people, celestial deities. Sometimes the storyteller would provide a brief Spanish gloss at the end of the performance: *esos perros ya son de, dicen que son de roca* ("those dogs are of, they say that they are of rock"). After each of those initial sessions, I would ply my host and collaborator, Justo Jacanamijoy, for Spanish versions of the tales. As my knowledge of the Kamsá language improved and as I continued exploring *antewa parlo*, ancient tales, with don Justo, I became a more competent audience member, though I would say throughout the process these stories were told primarily for the Kamsá audiences present and not for me.

What I didn't realize at the time was that the privilege of encounter with a living Native South American mythology would entail a serious responsibility, one that I am discharging only now with the publication of this book. Since 1978–1979 when a Fulbright-Hays Research Grant sustained me for a year in the Sibundoy Valley, I have been wrestling with the compromises involved in reducing spoken narrative to the printed page and in making these splendid tales accessible to readers from other cultural backgrounds. I have been guided by a cluster of convictions as I sought to fix these fleeting performances in viable textual representations. First, I wanted to present the stories in a manner that would reflect their stylistic integrity as spoken objects of art. Second, I wanted to convey the sense of them as the Kamsá themselves understand them. Third, and perhaps most important, I wanted to preserve in print the original language of the stories.

It seemed to me that the printed texts must capture as much as possible the rhythm and acoustic color of the original speech. The prose paragraph, which lumps discourse units into a barely differentiated mass, is hardly suited to represent a verbal medium composed of clearly marked utterance segments. The deliberate vocal articulations of Kamsá narrators, reinforced by grammatical and lexical patterns, are best represented in sequences of separate text lines. This is not to invoke all the conventions of poetry but rather to respond to a rhythmic tendency in Kamsá narrative discourse. The visual arrangement of speech into lines of text, these in turn grouped into chunks of lines, is my attempt to approximate the phonesthetic character of the original spoken performances.

I have introduced other devices to conserve stylistic nuances of the spoken narratives. The narrators extend certain vowels into tuneful interludes at moments of emotional intensity in the plots, and these junctures are underlined in the Kamsá text. I have indexed to the appropriate lines of text the significant gestures of the narrators as they mimicked in their own personal spaces the gestures and movements of story protagonists. More extended stylistic features such as passages of subdued or heightened pacing and intonation are registered in notes keyed to the relevant lines. These segments of the performances dramatize the narrator's involvement in the unfolding plot.

Translating the sense of these narratives is at least as complicated as representing their sound. In this effort I was aided by what might seem at first glance a further liability, the movement from Kamsá to English through an intermediary, the Spanish translations provided by my Kamsá consultants. I noticed that the Spanish translations did not attend carefully to each particle of meaning but sought to trace a more global sense of Kamsá words and phrases. The translations from Kamsá to Spanish impressed me for their simplicity and clarity, effects that I have sought to recreate in my English accompaniment. The English versions in this volume stick quite close to the sense of the Kamsá roots, but they do not "overtranslate" by making explicit every possible inflection of meaning. They are intended to be loyal to the original discourse yet viable in their own right as vehicles of a narrative experience.

The sense of the narratives is of course partially dependent on familiarity with the cultural setting, and on this score too I have tried to provide some assistance to the reader. Each group of narratives and each individual narrative is preceded by a commentary that traces the cosmological setting, points to especially interesting dimensions of the material, and locates the main plot structures in the web of cross-cultural parallels. Naturally, the narratives are saturated with the objects and practices of the Kamsá life. I have caught some of these details and explained them briefly in notes cued to lines within the stories. I am quite aware that the scope of this effort is not commensurate with the need; not nearly enough cultural background could be provided without substantially expanding the project at hand. In consolation, I refer the reader to my earlier publication, *Sayings of the Ancestors: The Spiritual Life of the Sibundoy Indians* (University Press of Kentucky, 1989), which contains a broader base of cultural data relevant to perceiving the sense of these mythic narratives.

Lastly, I appreciate the decision of the University Press of Kentucky and its editor-in-chief, William Jerome Crouch, to include the original language of these narratives. It may seem more efficient to publish only the translations, but too much of the texture of the original performances is lost with this procedure. In my experience, texts in translation are so denatured as to be practically useless. By including the Kamsá texts here, I have secured a resource for future generations of Kamsá people who may wish to consult these materials. Moreover, I make available the source materials for a range of ethnolinguistic and ethnopoetic treatments by interested scholars. To facilitate this process, I have included in chapter two a brief description of Kamsá grammar and a survey of major poetic devices employed by performers of Kamsá mythic narrative.

The interlinear presentation with Kamsá text in bold and the English translation underneath makes possible three different routes through the narratives. Those who know Kamsá may attend exclusively to the original language of the stories. Those who prefer to encounter the stories in translation may attend exclusively to the English translation. And those who wish to investigate the rich field of Kamsá narrative poetics can work back and forth between the two languages. I have found that people quickly adjust to the interlinear format even though it may appear odd at first. Here I must ask the reader to bear with me; with a little effort you will find your way into these texts, whatever your ultimate design may be.

I acknowledge here the encouragement and assistance of many individuals. My primary debt of gratitude goes to the Kamsá individuals, the storytellers and those who helped me process the stories, whose knowledge and cooperation is obviously essential to the project. I would make special mention of taita Bautista Juajibioy and taita Mariano Chicunque, both of them skilled artists in the tradition, both of whom shared their expertise with me in the closing years of their lives. I cannot overstate the gratitude I feel towards Justo and María Jacanamijoy and two of their sons, Juan and Angel, whose assistance at every step was invaluable. I have benefitted from many discussions of these narratives with my colleagues and students, and I thank them for helping me sustain this project over the years. Members of my family, both local and dispersed, gave me courage to persevere. At last I must thank my wife, Patricia Glushko for her patience when this work kept my head immersed for long periods of time in the magical world of the Kamsá ancestors.

1 The Making of a Mythology

achka kulta bngabe tangwanga
So wise were our elders.

Thus exclaims taita (father) Mariano Chicunque, himself an elder, in the course of narrating "About the Red Dwarfs" (m4). His exclamation assesses the role played by the elders of the ancestral period in vanquishing a residual cosmic menace but could just as well serve as a capsule summary of the broad thematics of Kamsá mythic narrative. Taita Mariano is making a very explicit point: in spite of the fact that the ancestors were not baptized in the Catholic faith, they commanded extraordinary spiritual knowledge and power:

> **krischanga chká are bngana anteona ndwabainungasa ch tangwanga**
> Like that our ancestors were not Christians, those elders were not baptized.

> **yojowenana ndwabainungaka**
> They understood even though they weren't baptized.

What emerges as a digression from the narrative action, in which the ancestors have devised a remedy to smoke the harmful Red Dwarfs out of their caves, is in fact a leap into the heart of Kamsá mythic narrative as the storytellers themselves understand it. These stories convey pride in the intrinsic value of Kamsá civilization, and they identify the elders and ancestors as guardians of its precious truths. By continuing to speak of the ancestors, storytellers keep alive an eternal model that remains the one sure guide to a healthy existence in this danger-fraught world. Awareness of the ancestors' doings converges with practical steps such as the blessing (a renewal of the social order) and the cure (a renewal of the cosmic order) to forge an indigenous South American survival plan (see McDowell 1989, 1992).

Kamsá mythology is a storehouse of knowledge about the exemplary and formative events of the ancestral period. It records the civilizing process in the Sibundoy Valley as that process has established proper forms of behavior with regard to human subsistence and reproduction. The body of mythology assembled here does not portray every stage in the evolution of Sibundoy civilization. Instead, we have access to only an intermittent account; it is as if we peer through a keyhole into a lavishly appointed room, but our vision is restricted to a series of glimpses, each of them suggestive in its own right but none of them conveying sure acquaintance with the whole. It becomes then a matter of conjecture to provide an overview of the ancestral world, yet there is some comfort in the fact that each of the mythic narratives gathered here contains a striking revelation of its own partial truth. And the mythic cycles, especially those centering on the culture hero Wangetsmuna, piece together significant portions of the mythology; in their case it is as if the door restricting our view into the world of the ancestors has been momentarily cracked open, affording us a quick impression of the room's contents.

Kamsá mythology, even in this incomplete state, can be read as an account of the genesis of the world as the Kamsá know it. It is a chronicle of the evolution of society and the natural world from a primary condition to its present condition. At the outset of the ancestral period, the first people interact directly with celestial deities in a universe defined by brute spiritual potential. The myths tell of the vanquishing of substrate populations and of their replacement with properly mannered people. The rampant spiritual potency of the earlier period is gradually tamed and channeled. One indication of this is the demise of the animal-people who populate the younger phases of the ancestral period. At a certain point the culture hero blows his horn, and from that day on people have remained as people, and animals as animals (see m3).

Another indication of cosmic change is the decreasing capacity of mortals to endure and profit from spiritual encounters. In the earlier phases these encounters bring vision, knowledge, and power; in the later phases they are more often destructive. Even so, the spiritual vitality of the ancestral period lives on in the spirit world, a parallel and transcendent reality of limited accessibility to contemporary Kamsá people. It is mainly in dreams and in drug-amplified visions that the modern people refurbish their lives through mediated contact with this ancestral power.

Kamsá mythic narrative exists within the framework of a Sibundoy big-bang theory of cultural evolution, a theory that explicates all subsequent history in relation to the pivotal example of the first people. All of the myths gathered here deal with this exemplary stratum of Kamsá ethnohistory, that is, the Kamsá account of their own ethnogenesis. The myths tell not only of the eradication and subduing of adverse spiritual presences, but also of the loss of an intended earthly paradise, of the curious dealings of animal-people who appear as suitors but are thwarted in their attempt to join the human family, of the powerful masters or owners of the natural elements, of the spiritual realm that persists into the modern period and can intrude at any moment on human consciousness.

In the absence of salient indigenous classifications, I have organized the texts into four groups reflecting the major thematic and chronological features of the collection. "The Raw Time" (m1) stands apart as a frame-setting prelude. Assignment of a particular myth to a particular group was at times rather arbitrary, though I advance the present scheme as a reasonable guide to the essential dimensions of Kamsá mythology. Each thematic grouping assembles a diverse set of myths possessing some important common feature. *The Wangetsmuna Cycle* is the most cohesive, each myth relating details from the life of the culture hero. *Tales of the Ancestors* includes myths set in the ancestral period and portraying the deeds and times of the original people. The mythic narratives gathered in the third unit, *Tricksters and Suitors*, remain within the ancestral framework but focus on the deceptive actions of animal-people as they interact with human beings, frequently in search of human spouses. *Tales of the Spirit Realm* contain many of the mythical elements found in the other branches, but these narratives are set within the modern period and involve protagonists very much like the contemporary residents of the valley.

In its totality, this corpus of mythic narrative possesses at least three distinct levels of resonance. In the broadest frame of reference, it stands as a vernacular rendering of a mythical ethos that is shared among all peoples of this globe. Many of the themes treated in the Kamsá corpus are present in the greater portion of the world's mythologies, both ancient and modern. European influence is detectable in many or most of these narratives, attesting to the intimacy between indigenous and imposed cultures in this section of the Andes. But equivalents to dozens of mythical themes and motives present here can be found in mythologies from every one of the earth's continents. The most prominent of these suggest a universal mythical heritage: the sequence of cosmic moments gradually approximating the present arrangement, the harsh judgment that eradicates an earlier creation, the substrate population that must be banished from the cosmic stage, the powerful deities and demigods establishing correct patterns of behavior, the loss of an intended paradise, the transformations across gender lines and from animal to human states. It is difficult to say whether these equivalences should be traced to the human brain and psyche, to a process of diffusion from a common origin, or to the dynamics of social life in human communities. Perhaps each of these has its place in an account of the continuity in human mythopoeisis.

Kamsá mythic narrative possesses a special resonance in reference to Amerindian mythology and, more particularly, to the mythologies of the peoples of the Andes and the adjacent northwest portion of the Amazonian basin. The contents of Kamsá mythic narratives define recognizable variants of a common American, and especially South American, mythological bedrock. Major statements of Amerindian mythology, for example the Mayan *Popol Vuh* (Tedlock 1985) or the *huarochirí* manuscripts from colonial Peru (Salomon and Urioste 1991), as well as a wealth of more local and partial mythological records, all attest to a common Amerindian mythical vocabulary that is given a particular expression in the mythic narratives of the Kamsá people. A distinctly Central Andean flavor emerges in this mythical universe featuring powerful ancestors who move the world through a series of cosmic stages culminating in a syncretic spiritual paradigm that manages to incorporate Christian elements. Characteristic elements include a hunting complex involving an exchange of human for animal souls (widespread in the Northwest Amazon), a generalized sky god who acts as a sponsor to the culture hero (widespread throughout the Andes), ancestors who became powerful doctors through the acquisition of spiritual vision, and many others.

In the final analysis, the Kamsá corpus stands as a definitive treatment of the civilizing process within the confines of the Sibundoy Valley. The topographical features of the valley and its peripheries serve as the setting for the cosmological drama played out in the mythic narratives. The deities and ancestors establish customs that remain familiar in the contemporary ethnic repertoire of the Sibundoy peoples. These mythical figures speak Kamsá, they share the concerns of modern Kamsá families, they eat, drink, and even party as the Kamsá people do. It may be that global and regional mythical themes flourish in this mythology, but these themes are given a Kamsá inflection in the narratives assembled here.

The assimilative capacity of the tradition is especially salient with reference to narrative resources of probable European origin. Several international tale types (see Thompson 1961) can be located in this collection, most convincingly, 327A, "Hansel and Gretel," in m11, "The Tale of the Two Little Children"; 175, "The Tarbaby and the Rabbit," in m14, "About the Rabbit"; 301, "The Three Stolen Princesses," in m26, "Juan Oso"; and 676, "Open Sesame," in m31, "About the Thief." In addition, several other myths contain motif clusters (see Thompson 1955–1958) that are strikingly familiar from the international corpus. It is possible, in a few cases probable, that tale types and motifs entered Kamsá tradition through contact with Spanish narrative resources. After all, Spanish missionaries and settlers have been present and presumably swapping stories with Sibundoy Valley natives for several centuries.

But positive identifications of European components are hindered by two considerations. For one, the European paradigms are so thoroughly absorbed into the Kamsá ethos that their origin in a foreign narrative tradition seems inconsequential by comparison. Robert Laughlin (1988, 17) notes that less than 20 percent of his Zinacantán corpus exhibits an "obvious" European influence and that "nobody, presented with two collections of tales, one from Zinacantán, the other from Spain, could confuse the two." Much the same could be said of the present collection of Kamsá mythic narratives. Less than a third of the corpus exhibits a decisive European influence, and in those instances the familiar plot structures are indelibly stamped with the aura of life in the Sibundoy Valley. Instead of enchanted princes and princesses who return to their human form after the curse is lifted, the Kamsá corpus is populated with powerful doctors who take on animal form when it suits their purposes and with resolute animal-people who retain aspects of both incarnations. It appears that the European materials derive from a different moment of mythopoeisis.

Another problem arises in describing a European origin for Kamsá mythic narratives. Parallels are as abundant in the Native American as in the European corpus. The very myths that proclaim an affinity with European models also demonstrate fidelity to Amerindian prototypes. If analogues can be found in the European märchen, they can also be found in the Mesoamerican *Popol Vuh*, in ethnohistorical documents from colonial Peru, and in countless other collections of Native American mythology. The evidence suggests not so much a mechanical process of borrowing as a dynamic process of narrative convergence, a fortuitous blending of indigenous and imported elements at the juncture of two tale-making traditions.

I have provided sample annotations of the mythic narratives included in this collection through reference to the two standard international indexes, especially Stith Thompson's enlargement of Anti Aarne's index, published as *The Types of the Folktale: A Classification and Bibliography* (1961), and to a more limited extent to Thompson's *Motif-Index of Folk-Literature* (1955–1958). Of greater utility in tracking parallels are the indexes and collections featuring Spanish and Latin American narrative, in particular Ralph Steele Boggs's *Index of Spanish Folktales* (1930), Terrence Hansen's *The Types of the Folktale in Cuba, Puerto Rico, the Dominican Republic and Spanish South America* (1957), Américo Paredes's *Folktales of Mexico* (1968), and Stanley Robe's *Index of Mexican Folktales* (1981). The four-volume treatise on mythology by Claude Lévi-Strauss has served as a handy resource for spotting kindred narratives in native South and North America, and the fine work of Susan Niles—*South American Indian Narrative: An Annotated Bibliography* (1981)—has also proved quite useful in ths endeavor. It should be readily apparent that I have not sought to produce systematic accounts of types and motifs, versions and variants, but rather that I draw on these resources to indicate a significant cross-cultural and cross-linguistic presence of the mythic narrative repertoire of the Kamsá.

Who Wrote These Myths?

James Clifford (1986, 118), arguing for a revision of what he calls "ethnographic authority," poses the following question: "Who, in fact, writes a myth that is recited into a tape recorder, or copied down to become part of field notes?" I think it important to provide a description of the process that has converted words spoken in the Sibundoy Valley all those years ago into the mythic narrative texts presented in this volume. These texts result from a collaborative effort involving in every instance a cast of at least three individuals: a performer, a native interpreter, and an ethnographer. They are surely mediated, processed, polyvocal. At the same time, I hope readers will be convinced that the methods employed in collecting, transcribing, translating, and presenting these materials have worked to insure texts with a high degree of fidelity to the mythic tradition they claim to represent.

Let me describe now the sequence of events and the lines of cooperation that have produced the texts included in this collection. I had managed a few brief visits to the Sibundoy Valley, home of the Ingano and Kamsá indigenous communities, but the opportunity to work extensively with the folklore of these peoples arose in the fall of 1978, when I arrived in Colombia with a Fulbright-Hays Research Abroad Grant. Alberto Juajibioy, then a curator of the ethnological museum at the Universidad de Antioquia in Medellín, had graciously provided me with a letter of introduction to his father, the highly respected elder taita Bautista Juajibioy, six times governor of the community, and it was this courtesy that facilitated my initial contact with the Kamsá community in 1974. I was determined to return to the home of this remarkable elder, but this time for a prolonged visit. As before, I made my way to Pasto, a provincial capital in the high Andes of Southwestern Colombia, then across a first mountain rim and down into the valley that houses La Cocha, a vast body of chilled Andean water. At last our heroic bus crossed another rim of the *cordillera* to enter a high plateau of perpetual drizzle, the *páramo;* from there we descended to the western edge of the Sibundoy Valley, which stretched out beneath us like a silent green jewel.

After spending the night in Sibundoy's lone hotel, I walked out into the Indian *veredas* (hamlets) and eventually found the thatch-roofed cottage of taita Bautista and his wife, Concha. Taita Bautista received me once again, and within a few days I met almost all of the extended family that radiates from that apex, including Justo and María Jacanamijoy, son-in-law and daughter of the elderly couple. I was drawn from the start to Justo and María. They were friendly, polite, lively, *disinteresados*, to use that wonderful Spanish word that refers to people who seek no immediate personal gain. Moreover, they had constructed a rather substantial house, with an upstairs rarely used now that their oldest children were in high school in the town of Sibundoy. I proposed moving in with them, but they were at first hesitant. "You would not like my Indian cooking," said María, and Justo objected, "The fleas would drive a white man like you crazy." But these objections yielded rather quickly to my insistence, and after the deal was settled and I had become a fixture at the Jacanamijoy home, Justo would claim me as "our eldest son."

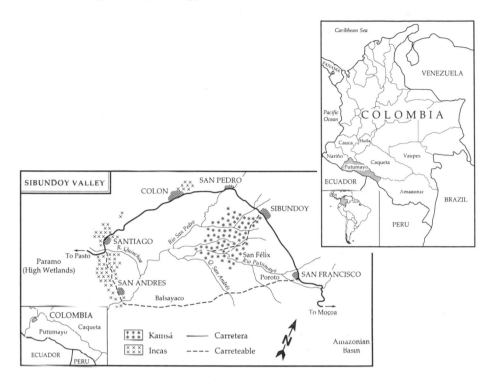

I arrived as a cultural (and linguistic) neophyte, and the Jacanami-joy family took me under its wings. I recall with fondness our sessions in the kitchen after dinner each evening, when the outlines of Kamsá cosmogony first became visible to me. These sessions lasted one or two hours; they would often start as a language lesson, or an inquiry concerning some Kamsá tradition, and evolve into freewheeling exchanges in the cool Sibundoy evening. I found that my hosts were as curious about my world as I was about theirs, and after a while we spent as much time talking about world history and geography as we did about Kamsá tradition.

The language lessons were daunting. Though we shared a non-native Spanish, I was anxious to learn the Kamsá language. Kamsá is a complicated tongue, famous for its ability to defeat outsiders who would learn it. The nearby Ingano people refer to Kamsá as *coche*, it was explained to me by my Kamsá hosts, meaning pig language—that is, "unintelligible gibberish"—in testimony to its difficulty. Even if this etymology can be challenged, it nonetheless attests to the perceived difficulty of the language. I often heard it said that Inga (a dialect of Quechua) can be learned by outsiders, but not Kamsá. Problems abound in both the phonology and grammar of the language, radically divergent from Indo-European models. I recall asking early on how to say that something is *tasty*, so that I could praise María's fine cooking in her own Kamsá tongue. But the answer was not a simple one: Kamsá adjectives take on nominal qualifying suffixes depending on the type of object involved. Thus, to praise María's corn and bean soup I would have to say *tamnaye*; the delicious *naranjillo* (a local fruit) would be *tamnabé*; the wonderful roasted corn would be *tamnatxe*; and so forth. It turned out there would be as many as a dozen different words used, each built on the root *tamná*, but appending the appropriate nominal classifier.

But in spite of such difficulties, we made progress, and my hosts remained at all times gracious instructors. Reciprocity developed as I worked with their children on their English lessons, and helped them figure out the words to English-language songs they were hearing on their transistor radios. Somewhat later I was pleased to administer to Justo and María their first lessons in the writing of Kamsá. As the weeks wore into months, our exchanges became more substantial, and we began to explore in earnest various facets of Kamsá tradition. Foremost among these was a tradition of mythic narrative that flourished, although increasingly displaced from the center of activity, in the Kamsá *veredas*.

The corpus of Kamsá mythic narrative assembled here could never have come about without the assistance of Justo and María and their older sons, especially Juan and Angel. Justo and María were active in almost every phase of the project, as narrators, as field assistants, as consultants in the processes of transcription and translation. Justo became a partner in the investigation. A handsome man with mixed Indian and mestizo features, Justo had listened well to the *antewanos*, tales of the first people, and had developed his own curiosity about the times of the ancestors. He had good connections with many local elders, including taita Bautista, his father-in-law, and taita Mariano Chicunque, a talented storyteller whom he addressed as *compadre*. Justo provided a crucial link by arranging for well-known storytellers to perform in my presence. Without this initial assistance, it is unlikely I would have secured the cooperation of these individuals.

But the contribution of Justo and of his family goes much further. María performed for me the very first Kamsá mythic narratives that I had the privilege to hear, and some of these performances are reflected in the texts assembled in this volume (see m12, m19, m22, and m23). Moreover, in some recording situations, Justo and members of his family constituted the Kamsá audience for the tellings, and, without such an audience, it is unlikely that the tellers would have performed with such verve. Most Kamsá elders were uneasy speaking Kamsá to me, sensing my imperfect mastery of the language. But they were delighted to address their stories to Justo and other Kamsá people present, often providing for my benefit a brief synopsis in Spanish. The importance of an informed, competent Kamsá audience cannot be overestimated, and many details in the texts assembled here—for example, the wonderful impersonations of speaking protagonists in the stories—would never have emerged if I had been the sole auditor of the performances. In some cases, I sensed that we had tapped into a natural channel of Kamsá communication, in which an elder explains to people of lesser age and wisdom the continuing importance of the ancestors and their deeds.

Justo and members of his family also played a central role in helping me transcribe and translate the Kamsá of the original performances. When I settled into Justo and María's home as their adopted son, I had only a distant acquaintance with the Kamsá language, extracted from the very limited published materials on the subject. Travelers had produced a few word lists (Mosquera 1853; Rocha 1905; von Buchwald 1919), but these disagreed in most details with one another. The scholarly literature afforded consensus neither on the name of the language and its speakers (known to outsiders variously as Mocoa, Coche, Cebundoy, Sibundoy, Quillasinga, Camsá, and Kamsá over the years), nor on its proper linguistic affiliation. Daniel Brinton (1901, 200) mentioned the Mocoas, noting that "we have a very imperfect knowledge of their language." In 1912 Paul Rivet showed that Mocoa was related to Sibundoy on the basis of small published vocabularies in the two languages. Later the same author provided a brief and surprisingly accurate description of what he referred to as the Coche language family (Rivet 1924).

Cestmir Loukotka (1967) listed the Mocoa family of languages as an independent stock in his taxonomy of South American Indian languages. Jijon y Caamaño (1938) proposed a Chibchan affiliation, locating Quillasinga-Sibundoy in his Chicha-Aruaco grouping and suggesting a close affinity with Muisca. Sergio Ortiz (1954) disputed this linkage, arguing that the language must be classified as an isolate for the time being. John Mason (1950) in his article in the *Handbook of South American Indians* took note of this controversy but did not try to resolve it. He listed the Mocoa or Coche family as a language of doubtful Chibchan affiliation. Joseph Greenberg (1960) avoided the issue by organizing his discussion along geographical rather than genetic lines.

These and other data allowed me to piece together a loose account of the ethnohistorical setting. I surmised that the archaic Quillasinga federation, which occupied much of the current state of Nariño and territory of Putumayo, included peoples known as Coche, Mocoa, and Sibundoy. The Sibundoy survive to this day and are located in the intermountain valley of the same name; Coche appears to be an alternative name for them, perhaps derived from the place name La Cocha (Quechua for "laguna"), located just west of the Sibundoy Valley. The Mocoans were dispersed at the eastern edge of the Andes; they might have been a lowland extension of the Sibundoy societies. Kamsá acquires additional importance in this light as the sole surviving dialect of the otherwise extinct Quillasinga language.

The only source of serious linguistic description had been carried out in association with the Summer Institute of Linguistics: Linda Howard published a very useful study of Kamsá phonology (1967) and a preliminary study of Kamsá morphology (1977), and Alberto Juajibioy collaborated with Alvaro Wheeler (also of the Summer Institute of Linguistics) to produce a handy little volume, *Bosquejo etnolingüístico del grupo Kamsá de Sibundoy, Putumayo, Colombia* (*Ethnolinguistic Sketch of the Kamsá of Sibundoy, Putumayo, Columbia*, 1973). Lacking entirely then (as now) were a dictionary and grammar of the Kamsá language.

Under these circumstances, my attempt to study the mythic narrative of the Kamsá people would have been fruitless without the cooperation, indeed, the dedication, of intelligent native speakers and members of the community, and in this role Justo, María, and their older sons made a very important contribution. Over time we developed the following method: I would play back the recorded narration, pausing at each break in the flow of words to allow Justo or one of his sons to repeat to me slowly the words spoken by the narrator. With my consultant's deliberate re-uttering of each phrase I was able to write down the Kamsá text line by line. We even developed a technique for managing the most sensitive phonological matters, for example the sorting of two closely related phonemes, the /x/ and /sh/: when a sound like one of them appeared, I would ask Justo, "Is that as in *kex* (dog) or *shema* (woman)?" I asked Justo to repeat exactly the words heard on the audio tape, and he made an effort to do so, though I find in reviewing his work that on occasion he interjected his own "corrections" of the original. In some cases I have retained these corrections; I have replaced them with the narrator's original words when these seemed more fitting.

During these sessions on the porch of Justo's house, occasionally interrupted when María would bring up a bowl of soup for lunch, we struggled as well with the problems of translation. Once I was convinced that I had accurately written the Kamsá words in a given utterance, I would inquire about its meaning. Using our common medium, the Spanish language, we would explore possible translations of the Kamsá into Spanish. I found that Justo was quick at producing fullblown translations but less disposed to provide definitions of specific grammatical forms. The result of our efforts is a pairing of lines from the original Kamsá performance with translations that have traveled from Kamsá into Spanish, and from there into the present English versions. Our leisurely process of consultation guarantees an accurate representation of the native speaker's understanding of the original Kamsá narrative phrases rather than an intensely faithful rendering of linguistic nuance.

I owe a special debt of gratitude to the talented individuals who performed the mythic narratives assembled in this collection. Among the Kamsá almost anyone can tell a handful of mythic narratives. Best known and most popular are the trickster cycles clustering around the figures of rabbit, squirrel, and bear. I heard versions of these stories from young children, adolescents, young adults and elders. But certain individuals were recognized and appreciated for their mastery of *antioj palabra*, ancient words. These tended to be middle-aged to elderly men who had heard the old stories as youngsters and had kept them alive in performance settings such as evening gatherings after *mingas* (collective work parties), or around the family hearth. I was fortunate to spend several hours with the late taita Mariano Chicunque, who has contributed the majority of the tales assembled here. Performances by four other storytellers, taita Bautista Juajibioy, Francisco Narváez, Estanislao Chicunque, and María Juajibioy, are also represented in this volume. Let me provide a brief sketch of each of the narrative artists who has left a mark on this collection.

Mariano Chicunque

Taita Mariano Chicunque was a kindly elder, perhaps some eighty years of age when I met him in October 1978. With Justo as mediator, we worked together intensely through the last months of that year. I was distressed to learn of taita Mariano's untimely death in early January 1979. At least there is the consolation that some portion of his knowledge and skill had been captured on a series of audio tapes before he left this world. In all we spent some four afternoons together, and the catch was twenty-three outstanding mythic narratives. Taita Mariano was proud of his ability to render the deeds of the ancestors. He told me that he could hold forth for five straight days, and once let on that he had enough stories to keep us working together for months. It seemed to me that he was thrilled to find an appreciative audience at that late moment in his life.

Taita Mariano was wizened and slightly bent from a long life of labor, but his eyes held the sparkle of an unmitigated love of life. He explained his familiarity with the old myths as follows: "I used to hear them talk like this when I was a little boy, and I have kept these things in mind." He said that as a boy he would sit around the hearth and listen to the old men well into the night; sometimes he would drift into sleep, and when he did, "they would scold me for sleeping while they spoke." If taita Mariano was born just before the turn of the century, as seems likely, he was a young fellow in the first decade of the present century. Indeed he tells us as an anecdote in one of his performances, m13, "The Judgment," that he grew up under the harsh dominion of the Capuchin fathers, who came to the Sibundoy Valley at the turn of the century to impose upon its native peoples their idea of progress. The elders during his youth would have been around since the early part of the nineteenth century, well before the Capuchin Order arrived and transformed the traditional life of the Indians. In those insular days, the Sibundoy Valley was accessible only by foot, the lineages were still matrilocal residential entities, and the deeds of the ancestors held sway within a living traditional religion.

Taita Mariano had been rich in lands as a younger man, but through misfortune had lost his assets and now found himself in a lonely and impoverished old age. I heard stories of unscrupulous priests who cheated him of title to his lands, and of taita Mariano's days as a lively high-stepper, generous with women and with his pals, but not judicious in managing his lands. His later years were spent working in the fields for a pittance and weaving straw fans to be sold for whipping up the embers in the hearth. But his years on the chicha (maize beer) circuit made of him an accomplished flautist, an alluring conversationalist, and an unsurpassed performer of Kamsá mythic narrative.

Taita Mariano's performances were characterized by a conceptual completeness, by a leisurely progress through the plot, by engaging impersonations of the story protagonists, and by the use of vocal shifts to enhance the drama of the moment. He made considerable use of hand, arm, and head gestures and was not above breaking into laughter in the midst of especially humorous episodes. It seemed to me that he lived in those stories more than in the paltry existence old age had allotted him.

Bautista Juajibioy

Taita Bautista was a genial elder, very proud and articulate. I would catch glimpses of him laughing out loud as he gazed into the flowering bushes around his cottage. He was an important elder in the community, six times governor, the owner of much land, and the patriarch of a large and important extended family. In earlier visits to the Sibundoy Valley I had heard taita Bautista perform mythic narratives. His son, Alberto Juajibioy, has published some of these in two volumes, in the *Bosquejo etnolingüístico* (1973) I have already mentioned, and in a more recent volume, *Relatos y leyendas orales* (*Oral Tales and Legends*), released by Servicio Colombiano de Comunicación Social in 1987. By the time I returned to the valley in 1978, taita Bautista had become more devout in his Catholicism, and he now dismissed the myths as *cuentos pajosos*, foolish stories; he would narrate only sacred history from the Bible. In one of our last meetings, I passed a note to him, since he was having trouble hearing me, pleading the importance of the traditional stories: "I ask you to remember all the old stories you can, in order to conserve this beautiful legacy of the Kamsá people." He received the note, read it carefully, and placed it inside his copy of the Bible. But he remained silent with a perplexed look on his face.

Luckily, I had made a few recordings in previous visits and I have drawn on one of them, "The Raw Time" (m1), to launch this collection of Kamsá mythic narrative, and on another, "The Gold Mine" (m32), to close it. There is no doubt but that taita Bautista was formerly a fine performer of Kamsá mythic narrative. One of the stories recorded by his son and published in the 1973 volume, "La Comadreja," tells how the weasel obtained fire from the culture hero Wangetsmuna and how the mouse obtained corn from the same source. These episodes trace in a vital segment of the comprehensive mythology. Taita Bautista liked to talk about the legendary *cacique*, Carlos Tamoabioy, and his legacy of lands willed to the descendants of the people of Santiago, Sibundoy, and Aponte. He was a personable and knowledgeable representative of his community, a man of strong intellect who could match wits with missionaries, ethnographers, and government agents.

Francisco Narváez

Francisco was working on a field crew when we arrived at the home of Justo's sister. When Justo mentioned *antioj palabra*, Francisco was sent for, and members of the work crew assembled to hear his stories. Francisco was a crusty middle-aged man, probably some sixty to sixty-five years of age at the time. He told his stories with clarity and good dramatic effect, eliciting at each turn the keen interest of his audience. Included here are m25, "About the Lively Bear"; m26, "Juan Oso"; and m30, "The Tale of the Father-in-Law," the last one re-performed for me by my host, Justo Jacanamijoy, due to a failure on the part of my recording equipment to pick up the original performance.

Estanislao Chicunque

Estanislao was a sprightly man, sixty-five years old at the time, and a nephew of taita Mariano Chicunque. He told me that he learned all of his stories from his grandfather, who apparently lived to be a very old man. Estanislao was a handsome man, resplendent in his traditional garb, soft-spoken but very effective as a storyteller. His stories are well-composed, performed with deliberation, and less peppered with special effects than those of his uncle. Estanislao uses a whispered delivery to great dramatic effect.

María Juajibioy

Gentle and shy, María had listened to her father, taita Bautista Juajibioy, and knew the old stories well. Because a married woman's role among the Kamsá precludes her taking on public attention, María was reluctant to step into the limelight at social gatherings. She once told me she couldn't drink chicha and dance like other people, for if she did, "Who would take care of the children?" When she did perform mythic narratives in my presence, she seemed at first very self-conscious but, as the session went on, her voice became firmer, and her control over the material became quite evident. María concentrates on the moments of conflict between story protagonists. She is drawn to the emotional and dramatic core of the stories, and her performances are more personalized, less imbued with cosmological detail, than those of the other narrators. I see them as moving in the direction of folktale, yet she too expressed a conviction that the events she narrated really did happen in the days of the ancestors.

2 Kamsá Mythic Narrative

A myth is a sacred story; it encodes religious beliefs and practices into narrative discourse. Beyond this pragmatic assignment, myths are utilized as instruments for thinking through the fundamental mysteries, ambiguities, and contradictions posed by human strivings in the web of social convention. Imaginative works of art, myths capture our fancy and delight our sensibilities even as they help us envision the cosmos. The myths of the Kamsá people retain a religious function, particularly as embodiments of ancestral wisdom, but they are evolving toward a folktale corpus as entertainment and moral instruction take precedence over the manifestation of religious truth.

I use the words "mythic narrative" to refer to specific realizations of prototypical or relatively constant narrative structures, which I refer to as "myths." The myth, then, is a fairly constant chronology of events, the mythic narrative its realization in a specific verbal performance. In this light, myths are the *langue*, the collective dimension of mythopoeisis, whereas the narratives are the *parole*, its manifestation in specific versions and variants (Saussure 1935). Another term, "mythic cycle," will be used to denote clusters of mythical elements that migrate and recombine within the corpus of mythic narratives. In this scheme of things a mythology is composed of several myths and mythic cycles that emerge in diverse mythic narrative performances.

In addition, I intend that the term "mythic narrative" allow for some drift toward the secular. The adjective form, "mythic," signals a dissolution of myth's essence. Kamsá mythic narrative presents a mythology in transition, one that might well take on the appearance of a folktale corpus as the community becomes increasingly less connected to its traditional cosmology. The present narrative corpus possesses attributes of both myth and folktale, though I would argue that it tilts for the moment in the direction of myth. Stith Thompson (1929, xvii) is probably on target when he states that "attempts at exact definition of 'myth' as distinguished from 'tale' seem futile." Nonetheless, a broad guideline for distinguishing myth from its kindred narrative forms is proposed by Erminie Vogelin (1950, 778): "A myth remains properly a myth only as long as the divinity of its actor or actors is recognized; when the trickster becomes human rather than divine, when the hero is a man rather than a god, myth becomes legend, if explanatory or limited to some specific location, or folktale, if more generalized." A mythology is imbued with actual religious precept. Folktale and legend, on the other hand, are essentially secular in character, illustrative perhaps of profound community values but divorced from explicit religious observances. Mythic narratives (like folktales) may well be appreciated for their narrative suspense, or for their humor, but in addition they necessarily encompass the spiritual identity of their communities. Folktales commonly exhibit certain remnants of previous religious belief, but they exist outside the framework of an active religious system.

Kamsá mythic narrative operates within a religious framework, if religion is understood liberally to be the spiritual edifice of a people. The situation is complex, for the Kamsá Indians are devout Catholics, yet within and around their Catholicism lurks a synthetic religious orientation that I have referred to as Sibundoy folk religion (McDowell 1989). I argue that Sibundoy folk religion is a lively and still-evolving religious system composed of indigenous Andean and Amazonian elements adapted to the imposed Christian overlay. Or perhaps it would be more accurate to say that the Christian elements are assimilated into an indigenous religious orientation. This syncretic amalgam features Andean celestial deities and Amazonian visionary shamanism in some sort of loose accommodation to elements drawn from folk and orthodox Catholicism. Thus Our Lord, who appears frequently in the mythic narratives, is simultaneously the sun, the culture hero Wangetsmuna, and Jesus Christ.

The central tenet of Sibundoy folk religion is the civilizing process of history, which has gradually established in the Sibundoy Valley conditions favorable to human society. In order for this to happen, the brute spirituality of earlier cosmic moments had to be tamed and harnessed, and this task fell into the hands of the *anteonga*, the ancestors. Kamsá mythic narratives depict the exemplary deeds of the ancestors, who possessed or acquired ample reserves of spiritual power and employed this power to remove obnoxious substrate peoples, to rearrange existing subsistence and reproductive customs, and to establish precedents for appropriate forms of behavior.

By the close of the ancestral period, human life is recognizable and now situated in the world as we know it today. This world is seen as composed of an outer and an inner layer. The outer layer, the world of routine sensory experience, is derivative and illusory. Within it is a spiritual reality that conditions the events that we witness. Kamsá native doctors specialize in breaking through to this inner reality in order to negotiate more favorable arrangements. The central object of their practice, and indeed of much Kamsá thought, is *binyea*—literally "wind," but understood to mean "spirit" or "evil wind" or "spirit sickness." The Kamsá believe that by following the example of the ancestors, and by communing with them through dreams and spiritual visions, it is possible to lead the charmed life conferred by spiritual health.

To this end, every Kamsá imbibes once a year the visionary remedy, *yagé* (genus *Banisteriopsis*), as a kind of physical and spiritual purge. Those who experience misfortune or ill health are likely to make more frequent use of the remedy. It is thought that the visionary properties of the drug activate a return to the ancestors and thereby bring about a kind of spiritual realignment. In addition, people consult their dreams and interpret them in reference to a set of traditional *sayings of the ancestors* in the attempt to monitor their vulnerability to spiritual sickness.

In this context the myths about the ancestors retain a significant religious aura, for it is through the mythic narratives that the elders acquaint younger members of the community with the days and deeds of the ancestors. Frequently I heard claims about the truth value of these narratives. For example, in one of the most popular myths (see m19) a bird-woman appears in ancestral days as a messenger of the gods. Because of a human misunderstanding, she fails to deliver her message, which would have enabled humans to make *bokoy*, the corn-based chicha that lubricates social life in the valley, out of only a few grains of corn. The story goes that the bird-woman sat combing her hair in the patio; later she plunged into a barrel of chicha. The modern-day bird referred to has smooth hair feathers and ruffled body feathers. As Justo exclaimed: "So you can see that this really happened; when she dipped into the chicha, she ruffled her body feathers but her head feathers remained smooth." A similar claim was made about m23, "About the Rainbow," in which a young woman follows a suitor into the river; they emerge as the two rainbows, one clear and the other faint, that can often be observed straddling portions of the Sibundoy Valley.

The Sibundoy folk religion does not possess much in the way of a sacramental life. Generations of priests were largely successful in replacing the indigenous rites with their orthodox Catholic rites. I was told of elders who still light a candle at noon to Our Father the Sun, but for the most part such observances have vanished from the valley. Moreover, there is evidence that the younger generations are increasingly enculturated into a mainstream Colombian consciousness. The name of the Kamsá culture hero, Wangetsmuna, is becoming obscure as his children forget him. Some Kamsá families have taken up evangelical forms of Christian worship, even more hostile to indigenous tradition than the Catholic church. These developments tend to recast Sibundoy folk religion as an esoteric residual system increasingly confined to the elderly and to ritual specialists. The continuing importance of these traditional curers offers perhaps the best hope for the persistence of the traditional worldview.

Internal evidence as well points to a pattern of change. Within this mythic narrative corpus there is a tendency to create episodic and personalized versions of the myths. Episodic renditions stitch together a series of loosely related narrative events clustering around some central figure such as Our Lord or Wangetsmuna. The premium is on entertainment rather than fidelity to prototypes in these mythic narratives. Episodes are piled upon one another with intent to entertain rather than to studiously conserve, and in some cases episodes will be drawn from a number of different myths to coexist in an eclectic mythic narrative. These episodic narratives demonstrate the remarkable fertility of a mythology in transition, which offers numerous avenues for personal interpretation of traditional narrative resources. Personalized versions emerge as the performers extract compelling moments of drama from their cosmological settings. The narrator seizes on, for example, a tense conflict between two individuals and leaves out details establishing the ancestral identities of the protagonists and the cosmic significance of their encounter. A mythology in transition is no longer tethered in cultural space by ritual observances; it becomes an open storehouse of narrative potential as people find personal inspiration in the old stories.

Both dimensions of Kamsá mythic narrative will be evident in the assembled texts, its roots in the folk religion and its tolerance for episodic and personalized adaptations of the myths. It is too early to pronounce a verdict on the drift of the corpus, since a rebirth of previous vitality is always possible, and folklorists are generally premature in proclaiming the "death" of endangered traditions. Yet it is safe to say that prevailing sociopolitical conditions are not auspicious for the continuation of the Kamsá traditional way of life, and Kamsá mythic narrative, an ideational heritage, is perhaps more at risk than ethnic attributes grounded in cultural praxis. The Kamsá people have mostly lost contact with their culture hero, Wangetsmuna, though for the moment they continue to value a generalized concept of "the ancestors" and to locate an abiding communal investment in tales about these influential first people.

The Verbal Habitat

Verbal art performances are inherently ecological, rooted in the soil of their native linguistic environments. The great majority of Kamsá mythic narrative in my possession was performed in the Kamsá language. I do have a few versions reported in Spanish for my benefit, one of them included here (see m32), but there was never a doubt that Kamsá was the appropriate vehicle for the performance of these narratives. The Kamsá define their mythology as one important item in a collection referred to as *bngabe soy*, "our things," carefully set apart from *xkenungabe soy*, "white people's things." The native mythology stands out in clear relief from other narrative traditions known to them—for example, biblical stories and folktales such as those in the Pedro Urdemalas cycle, cultivated among the non-Indian segment of Colombia's rural population. The Kamsá refer to their mythic narrative as *antioj palabra*, "ancient words," and stipulate that it dwells on the ancestors of the present-day Sibundoy people. These categorical distinctions became clear when someone would insist: "Stick to the *antewanos* (the old stories) friend."

As the Kamsá language is an isolate, no contemporary linguistic relatives have been positively identified. It is now accepted that Kamsá is the sole surviving dialect of the archaic Quillasinga, the language spoken throughout the Quillasinga federation at the time of first Incan and then Spanish incursion. Ethnohistorical documents indicate that the Incas were skirmishing at this northern fringe of their empire just before the arrival of the Spaniards. With the advent of Benalcázar and the other Spanish captains, the territory of the Quillasingas, a swath of the Andes bridging the modern border between Colombia and Ecuador, came under the control of Spanish lords and priests.

The Sibundoy Valley was a remote outpost of the Quillasinga federation, a region famous for its placer gold, for its abundant food production, and for the prowess of its spiritual experts. When the federation succumbed to Spanish invaders, the Kamsá periphery remained largely untouched, and it is this accident of geography and history that has preserved this lone-surviving dialect of Quillasinga. So remote is its setting, the Kamsá language (as previously noted) has been known to the outside world by a number of inappropriate names. Only in recent years has the correct label gained currency. But even on this score there is a serious problem: "Kamsá" is apparently a modification of some original label. Sergio Elías Ortiz (1954, 217) credits Fray Marcelino de Castellví, the most learned among the Capuchin missionaries, with introducing to the outside world the term "Kamsá," used by the members of this community to name their own language. Ortiz notes that people gave the meaning of this term as *así mismo,* "just like this." This observation suggests to me that the root for this label might be *ka mntxá,* the Kamsá equivalent of "just like this"; a more fanciful (but unsubstantiated) hypothesis would identify the source as *ka mwentxá,* which could be translated "(we the people of) this place." In any case, the term "Kamsá" is evidently a dilution, perhaps adjusted to the Spanish ear, of some underlying indigenous label. In social gatherings I often heard elders insist, with emphasis on the elusive phoneme: "We are not the Kamsá, we are the Kam*txá.*" I understand that Kamsá bilingual teachers are promoting yet another version of this label, *camëntsá.* I have opted to stick with *Kamsá* for the moment, since this label has gathered a degree of external acceptance, and the community's will on this matter is as yet far from evident.

As I have noted, the Kamsá language has not yet been the object of comprehensive linguistic analysis. There is no full-scale dictionary of the language, though the glossary provided by Juajibioy and Wheeler (1974) is useful. Also lacking is a sustained treatment of Kamsá grammar; Linda Howard (1977) has produced an analysis of paragraph structure, and Juajibioy and Wheeler (1973) provide a helpful sketch of

Table 1. Phonemes of the Kamsá language

Consonants	labial	alveolar	retroflex	palatal	velar
stop (voiceless)	p	t			k
obstruent (voiced)	b	d			g
affricate		ts	tx	ch	
fricative	f	s	x	sh	j
nasal	m	n		ñ	
lateral		l		ll	
vibrant		r			
semivowel	w			y	

Vowels	front	central	back
high	i	ë	u
low	e	a	o

Kamsá morphology. Only in the area of phonology has the language received careful linguistic scrutiny, in Linda Howard's "Camsá phonology," published as part of an anthology on the phonological systems of Colombian languages in 1967. Her research isolates the Kamsá phonemes and identifies many prominent allophones. It has served as the basis of my own transcriptional system for Kamsá, a system I have developed to provide a broadly accurate rendering of Kamsá sounds while making use of familiar orthographic symbols.

Kamsá phonology presents much difficulty to the ears of outsiders. Linda Howard (1972) identifies the following as "special features" of Kamsá phonology: the retroflex consonants, the large number of fricatives and affricates, the contrast of alveolar and palatal laterals, the free fluctuation of bilabial consonants and of front vowels, and the multiplicity and complexity of consonant clusters, all syllable initial. She identifies twenty-eight segmental phonemes, twenty-two consonants, and six vowels. The consonants include: voiced obstruents /b d g/, voiceless stops /p t c/, voiceless affricates /ts tx ch/, voiceless fricatives /f s x sh j/, nasals /m n ñ/, laterals /l ll/, vibrant /r/, and semivowels /w y/. Table 1 shows how these twenty-six consonants and the six vowels can be charted.

Howard notes a number of consonant variants that acquire importance in a faithful rendering of the sound of spoken Kamsá, and one of these must be mentioned here: the semivowel /y/ has a voiced alveolar affricate allophone [dž] after [n]. Recurrent words such as *nye*, *nyetxá*, and other less common words with this feature are all pronounced with the affricate [dž], approximately like the consonant that begins the second syllable of the English word *engine*.

Stress in Kamsá tends to fall on the penultimate syllable, though this prescription is subject to a number of qualifications. Thus, the addition of verbal suffixes causes the main stress to shift forward as it remains attached to the syllable it would normally mark in the absence of suffixing. Longer, compound words reveal complex patterns of primary and secondary stresses that cannot be examined here. I have opted to place accent marks only on those lexemes that violate these rules by exhibiting a routine stress on the final syllable (e.g. *nyetxá*, "completely") or on a syllable prior to the penultimate (e.g. *yébuna*, "house").

It should be noted that the weakness of final, unstressed vowels is a key factor in the accentual regularity of Kamsá. I have chosen to eliminate the weak interconsonantal final vowel that Linda Howard and some other scribes of Kamsá locate in words like *inamna* ("once upon a time there was"), according to them, *inámena*. If these constructions are heard as containing two discrete final syllables instead of one (*-mna*), then the stress in many Kamsá verbs could be said to shift forward to the syllable before the penultimate. But my ears detect one syllable rather than two in these subdued word endings, and this hearing also preserves the rule of routine stress falling on the penultimate syllable.

I have introduced only a few modifications in creating from Howard's analysis the present transcriptional system. I have dispensed with the /ë/, which can either be eliminated or represented by /u/ or /e/ in the Kamsá speech that I heard. I write the velar stop as /k/ rather than /c/, in conformance with the current consensus in the scholarly literature. I go along with Howard in rendering exotic phonemes through combinations of familiar letters rather than through unfamiliar diacritics. The two most prominent examples are the /ts/, a voiceless alveolar affricate (like the consonantal part of English "its"), and /tx/, a voiceless retroflex affricate involving a whistling sound that has no precise equivalent in English.

I have striven for a transcriptional policy that is neither broad nor narrow, one that does justice to the sound of the language but does not unnecessarily complicate the reading of its texts. The result is a system that captures all phonemic distinctions and gives some play to variable features, but doesn't attempt to render every nuance of articulated sound. To cite one illustrative case, there is in spoken Kamsá considerable variability in the realization of vowels, and I have chosen to give this variability some play in the transcriptions. Thus readers will find many instances of the same word presented with different vowels between the consonants, for example, *xexon* and *xoxon* ("child"); and *remidio* and *remedio* ("remedy"). I felt that some degree of fidelity to phonological variation should take precedence over a premature canonization in the orthography. But other audible features have been eliminated from the texts in order to create readable, approximate transcriptions of the sort encountered in most literary languages. For example, spoken Kamsá includes the occasional glottal stop, usually wedged into a space bounded by a syllable-initial stop (usually a /t/) and a subsequent stop or nasal. Since these effects are neither regular nor phonemic they have been removed from the transcriptions.

The architecture of meaning in Kamsá depends primarily on the elaboration of the Kamsá verb, a very technical matter that can only momentarily detain us here. Kamsá features both aggutinating and inflecting grammatical processes. Sentences are composed of a single word or a few words, these in turn consisting of a root, a group of from two to a dozen prefixes, and the occasional suffix. Verbal roots attract the greater number of affixes; nominal roots are rarely prefixed at all but do tend to attract one or a few suffixes. Affixing involves the conjoining of morphemes in such a way that individual morphemes sometimes retain, and sometimes lose, their identity.

In lieu of a more thorough treatment, let's inspect a few of the more productive grammatical processes that shape utterances in the language. I draw on Juajibioy and Wheeler (1973) as well as on my own experience with Kamsá to develop this commentary. Kamsá nouns are either animate or inanimate, and different morphemes attach to either class of noun. They are marked for number (singular, dual, plural), function (instrumental, benefactive, comparative, possessive, locative, narrative, etc.), and form. The narrative function suffix, -na, plays a significant role in segmenting narrative discourse into manageable chunks of utterances. There are a dozen or more nominal classifiers, suffixes that specify the physical shape and size of the nominal referent. Some of these have been "frozen" into the lexicon, but the following nominal classifiers appear routinely in adjectives and articles tied to Kamsá nouns, and indeed can be found throughout the Kamsá texts to follow:

-bé	"a round object"
-fja	"a rigid, cylindrical object"
-jwa	"a flexible object"
-shá	"a hairy object"
-kwa	"a body part"
-ye	"a liquid"
-she	"something dry, old, ruined"
-txe	"something oval in shape"

Performers of mythic narrative sometimes exploit certain of these to enhance the dramatic effect of their utterances and to signal an authorial attitude toward the story in progress. For example, in m25 the bear-person is referred to as *chabé* (*cha* is "he"), meaning "that round person." This is a clue that the bear-person here is the humorous oaf of the trickster's world and not the fierce suitor who appears in other mythic narratives. Among the most prevalent nominal affixes in Kamsá speech and storytelling are the suffixes marking object scale but encoding nuances of speaker attitude. The diminutive *-tema* is used both to mark a small object and also to reflect a positive emotional bond between speaker and referent. The suffix *-jema* can also be thought of as a diminutive, but it carries a strong sense of speaker empathy. The third morpheme in this category is *-yema*, which signifies something large and ugly. This set of suffixes plays an important expressive role in defining the speaker's stance with regard to particular moments and characters in the narrative. For example, in m8, "About the Poor Scabby Girl," the narrator maintains a constant empathetic refrain through the insertion of *-jema* in virtually every reference to the story protagonist; even the title retains this feature. The poor scabby girl, it turns out, is the earth's fertility.

As I have intimated, the structure of the Kamsá verb is far more challenging. Verbal roots are typically preceded by as few as two or as many as a dozen affixes, and they may take on one or a few suffixes in addition. Part of the difficulty with the Kamsá verb lies in the adjustment of the roots themselves to their morphological environment. Different constructions appear in transitive and intransitive verbs, and the structures vary as well depending on the type of clause in which the verb appears: independent, dependent, declarative, interrogative, etc. Moreover, the prefixes attached to verbal roots may appear in variable order, and they may be partly assimilated to the morphophonemic environment. In spite of these complications, a canonic verbal paradigm can be extracted from the maze of variant forms. Verbal roots are generally marked for mood, aspect, reference, circumstance, and participation. The typical Kamsá verb assembles these semantic markers in the following sequence:

mood: displays the speaker's attitude or intentions with regard to the utterance.

ke-	negative, interrogative, conditional
ka-	reportative
kwa-	certainty
m-	imperative
tai-	conjectural

aspect: depicts the character of the action.

t-	completed action
i-, y-	legendary discourse (remote past)
ts-, s-	progressive
cha-	future intention
nd-	negative
n-	narrative

reference: indicates the objects and subjects.

tsi-	first-person subject
xo-	first-person object
ko-	second-person subject or object
mo-	third-person subject or object
xko-	second-person subject, first-person object
xmo-	third-person subject, first-person object
kmo-	second-person subject, third-person object

participation: defines the speaker's participation in the events.

n-	affirmative (speaker as participant)
k-	affirmative (speaker as witness)

verbal marker

j-	marks the construction as a verbal one

circumstance: defines relationships between the events and persons, places, or time.

tet-	repetitive action
b-	movement towards speaker
ets-	movement away from speaker (or from protagonist)
is-	transitory action
fts-	movement away from speaker in order to do something else
en-	reciprocal
bo-	benefactive

preverb

a-	indicates collective action
o-	indicates actor's initiative
i-, e-	indicates that the site of the action receives attention

ROOT

post-verb

-ye	indicates complexity of the situation
-ma	indicates purpose to the action
-na	indicates narrative succession

Two independent morphemes play an important role in the construction of verbs in Kamsá mythic narrative, the sequential marker *-se, -s,* which indicates temporal juncture between two clauses, and the quotative *-ka,* which routinely attaches to clauses of reported speech but can appear elsewhere with the impact of, "they say that. . ."

As indicated above, the rules for co-occurrence and sequencing of these morphemes are complex and beyond the scope of this exposition. I have attempted to provide some idea of the structure of the Kamsá verb so that the more ambitious readers might discover for themselves the joys of Kamsá syntax. The most characteristic marker of Kamsá mythic narrative is the legendary prefix, *y-, i-*, indicating that the action belongs to a remote temporal frame, typically (but not always) the period of the ancestors. All narrative clauses in our corpus of mythic narrative, that is, clauses that advance the plot, make use of this marker, which locates the action in the formative period of Kamsá civilization. Those clauses that transpire as reported speech evade this morpheme, for they are presented in an embedded narrative present. Digressions of course may feature any of the tense markers. The conscious recognition of mythic narrative as a separate category has its analogue in this obligatory marker of ancestral discourse.

The contrast between mythical and historical discourse appears clearly at the outset of m24, "About the Bear." When the narrator tells of his own experience, he uses the preterite marker *t-*: *tijoftsesente*, "I myself experienced it." A few lines further on he launches the narrative proper with the word: *inaishanya*, "In the times of the ancestors they were looking after the house." This movement from historical to legendary past, from personal experience to myth, signals the placement of subsequent plot details in the civilizing period of Kamsá cosmogony.

Finally, a word should be provided concerning the multi lingualism of the texts. There is some borrowing from the neighboring Inga (a dialect of Quechua), but most remarkable is the blending of Spanish linguistic elements into this Kamsá mythological discourse. Spanish speakers will recognize numerous lexical roots in the Kamsá, and they will probably fail to recognize others that have been thoroughly assimilated to Kamsá phonology and morphology. Both nominal and verbal Spanish roots appear in the Kamsá lexicon, and a few Spanish-origin roots have entered the host-language morphology. Moreover, Kamsá speakers switch into Spanish from time to time, further expanding the presence of Spanish in Kamsá speech. In general, the proportion of Spanish within the discourse mirrors the proportion of narrative material bespeaking a European heritage—somewhat less than a third in either case.

Let's examine one typical sentence (line 198 from m11, "The Tale of the Two Little Children") in order to pinpoint the confluence of linguistic resources in this "creolized" speech:

i cho*rka* yoja*ordena* <u>eso sí</u> ndetxebeka <u>lo que se pueda</u> jutsatechnunganjan*
And then he told them, yes sir, to throw rocks, as many as possible, at her.

The matrix code is clearly Kamsá, but Spanish enters the locution in the form of relatively assimilated and unassimilated bits. The utterance is launched by a (largely assimilated) Spanish connective; the next word incorporates a Spanish borrowing *-or-* (from *hora*, "hour, time") that

---

*Note: assimilated elements are placed in italic; unassimilated elements are underlined.

serves as a temporal marker in Kamsá morphology. The third word in the utterance includes a verbal root of Spanish origin, *ordena*, meaning "to order, to command," placed within a Kamsá morphological structure. Thereafter the speaker switches into Spanish twice, to exclaim (*eso sí*) and to intensify (*lo que se pueda*). It can be seen that the intersection of the two languages is far from casual, but also that Kamsá remains the organizing linguistic code. In the transcriptions I have adapted the assimilated Spanish bits to Kamsá orthographical conventions but retained Spanish orthography for unassimilated bits.

Poetics of Mythic Narrative Performance

The Kamsá language, with Spanish incrustations, is the verbal habitat of the mythic narratives assembled here; the performances are made effective through exploration of poetic conventions associated with this particular speech genre. The Kamsá speech repertoire includes several stylistic options (McDowell 1983). Its most specialized speech variety is the "singing to the spirits" performed by the native doctors in curing ceremonies. Kamsá native doctors chant, whistle, and sing in an attempt to traverse the gap between surface and underlying realities. Their performances are only partially verbal, and these verbal elements are not always transparently semantic in character. Kamsá ritual language is another speech variety, whose central mission is procuring a blessing for human encounters and activities (McDowell 1990). Its linguistic profile is closer to the familiar cadences of conversational Kamsá, but several features mark it as a distinctive use of the language. Conversational Kamsá is broadly accessible and largely devoid of special linguistic effects, though it too has its specialized adaptations, for example, in the teasing routines that often occur when men drink chicha together, or in the stylized lamentations of the women.

The mythic narrative employs a speech variety that departs from conversational Kamsá in certain respects but is less divergent than the ceremonial and ritual varieties of the language. The neighboring Ingano people maintain a narrative speech variety that is audibly distinct from ordinary speech, a hurried monotone that approaches chanting. Kamsá mythic narrative is performed in a more conversational style; it doesn't really stand out that much from the characteristic hum of conversation. True, there is a tendency for discourse to fall into parallel phrases, especially when the narrator wishes to dwell on a particularly important detail. But the movement toward parallel structure is only intermittent and partial in the narrative discourse style.

Still, there are special linguistic features in this narrative discourse, features that derive from the attempt to present a clear narrative structure and from the attempt to dramatize particular moments in the narratives. The performances were often framed by brief introductions and conclusions exhibiting a small dosage of Kamsá ritual language. The storytelling occasions activated a Kamsá etiquette requiring a show of deference between interlocutors. Justo, who was often present at the performances, stood in a relationship of formal respect toward many of the narrators. My presence too, as a distinguished outsider and companion of Justo, entailed some special recognition. Many of the performances are bounded by discourse that takes stock of the performance occasion. Some years ago (see McDowell 1973) I labeled such discourse *metanarrative,* in the sense of "external to the narrative plot." The tonality of Kamsá ritual language flashes briefly in opening gambits but is most evident in closing gambits like these:

chkase atxena tstatxumbo
Just like that I know the story.

nyetxá xmopasentsia
Please forgive me.

nyetxana tijenoyebwe i respeto tijenoperdey
I have told it all without losing respect.

The request for forgiveness is formulaic in ritual language speeches, where it often provides for a smooth transition from one phase of a speech to another. The disclaimer of disrespectful behavior is also standard in ritual language speeches where it expresses fidelity to the example of the ancestors.

The storytellers frequently supplied a tag, summary, or evaluation in Spanish at the beginning or end of their performances, presumably for my benefit. Here is one of the more elaborate cases, from m6, "About the Hunters":

chan i ch conversa del casador hasta allí no mas
That's the story about the hunters, that's all there is to it.

ese es corto
That is a short one.

ese es de los perros que hay esos chiquitos
That's about those dogs that exist, those little ones.

esos perros ya son de dicen que son de roca
Those dogs are of, they say that they are of rock.

una cosa así pues del volcán sabemos decir
Something like that, well from the volcano as we say.

de las rocas de las piedras sí de esos
From the rocks, from the stones, yes, from those.

The narrator signals the end of his story by switching into Spanish to announce its conclusion. He characterizes the story as a short one. He then elaborates in Spanish the central mystery of this mythic narrative,

the formation of the small dogs from the very rock of the volcano. He
dwells on this curious detail for the next four lines. This ending, then,
contains both metanarratve reference and a brief recapitulation of the
main point of the story, what Labov (1972) would call its "evaluation."
More commonly the narrators terminate a performance by using some
variant of a conventional closing formula:

> **ndoka remidio nyetxana tstatxumbo**
> So be it, that's all I know of it.

Here we encounter one of the least translatable phrases in Kamsá,
the ubiquitous *ndoka remidio*, composed of the Kamsá word for "without" and a borrowing of the Spanish word for "remedy," thus literally
"without remedy." This phrase is symptomatic of the presence of Kamsá
ritual language, where it punctuates the discourse, recurring with a
rhythmic monotony. It plays an important role as well in narrative discourse, where it signifies the narrator's conviction or acceptance of
destiny.

In this closing formula it partakes of the formality of ritual language,
since terminating (and initiating) a tale performance in this community
most often involves the display of ritual delicacy. In ritual contexts,
ndoka remidio can be translated "so be it," indicating its semantic vague-
ness but a strongly affirmative quality. In narrative clauses it has something like the effect of "it happened that" or "as it happened." It will be
noted that I have experimented with a variety of English renditions of
ndoka remidio in the pages to follow in an effort to provide some indication of its functional plasticity. The closing formula can be expanded to
encompass reduplication:

> **nye nyetxá tstatxumbo**
> Only like that do I know it.

Other less formulaic endings reinforce the authority of tradition that
pervades these narratives:

> **pero ya tijatsekwentana como koftsekwentanga**
> But now I have told you about it just as they told me.

Opening gambits are often metanarrative in character but tend to be
less expansive. Often the narrator will provide a handle or title to the
story. These are constructed on two patterns, either with the suffix
-biama, *-biana*, an ablative form roughly equivalent to "about"; or
through the use of the Spanish borrowing, *parlo*, "story." This handle
might be spoken to launch the performance:

> **koskungobiama mntxá**
> The one about the owl is like this.

In order to stay as close as possible to the native perspective, I translate these titles with the casual phrase, "About the. . ." Thus, *koskungobiama* as title becomes "About the Owl." Titles presented with the word *parlo* create a more formal result, "The Tale of. . ." Thus *uta xexonatemabe parlo* is translated as "The Tale of the Two Little Children."

These handles can be embedded in metanarrative phrases:

murselakobiana morna mo chjatenakwentá
The one about the bat, now let's speak of it among ourselves.

xkwatsparla iyendonena
I will surely speak of squirrel.

The first example makes use of the future marker, *ch(a)-*, as well as of the reciprocal marker, *-en*, to locate the performance in a context of intended social intercourse. The second example introduces the intensifier *kwa-* to lend a sense of determination to the narrative act.

Another strategy involves launching the story with a snippet of personal recollection before moving into the framework of mythic narrative (see m31):

anteo atxena serta basajema tijoftsabwatmana jashajanaka bastoy
In the old days, truly as a child I knew the high wetlands on the way
    to Pasto.

The place that was familiar to the narrator as a child becomes the site of mythical events to be related in the narrative performance. This topographical continuity reinforces the veracity of the narration and is an important corollary to mythic narrative's claim to describe the actual civilizing process in the Sibundoy Valley.

But let's turn to the narrative discourse itself and the narrator's task of providing a clear chronological structure. Notable for their presence in narrative are words and morphemes signifying the progress of the plot design. These components are used to chunk the discourse into series of utterances and also to mark transitions of major importance within utterance chunks. The most salient of these is the Spanish word *bueno*, "fine" or "well," which is often set apart from the surrounding discourse by a sustained pause. Occasionally the narrator says *pero bueno*, "but fine." These devices generally signify a major discontinuity in the exposition of the plot, a movement from one constitutive story unit to its sequel. They provide a tangible reference point as the narrative takes a turn in another direction. By implication they close off one large narrative section and open up another.

Within these chunks a number of temporal transition markers orient the hearers to the progress of the story. Most important are a series built on the form, *chorna*, which can be parsed as follows: *ch-ora-na*, that-hour-narrative morpheme. The meaning is, "at that moment." This formula is subject to modification in forms such as *chore, chora, chorkokayé*, the latter implying a sense of immediacy or urgency. A similar formulaic system is built on the root *as* or *ase*, meaning "and then." This system can also incorporate the narrative morpheme, *-na* to produce *asna*. The two roots can enter into combined phrases such as *ase chor*, "and then at that moment." Additional but less common markers of temporal transition include *mor, more, mora*, "now," and *tempo, tempna*, from the Spanish word for "time," used by Kamsá narrators to mean "right then" or "right away."

These markers crop up regularly within the larger chunks of narrative utterances, usually at the beginning of transcribed lines. They guide the audience from one action sequence to another, drawing our attention to mid-level structural units larger than the utterance but smaller than the utterance chunk. As far as I can tell there is a degree of free variation within this system, though the forms that include a temporal word plus the narrative morpheme generally mark the more important turning points within the utterance chunk.

Kamsá has three morphemes that mark narrative structure within the utterance: the narrative morpheme *-na*, the quotative *-ka*, and a sequential morpheme *-se* or *-s*. The narrative morpheme has already been encountered as an adjunct to temporal transition markers. Within the utterance it is used to isolate focal points in the narrative's local design. A new actor on the scene or a new twist in the action will be foregrounded through the use of the narrative morpheme. The quotative appears periodically throughout mythic narrative discourse, marking episodes of reported speech but also attaching to narrative clauses to provide emphasis on particular words and phrases. The sequential marker appears on verbal contructions to clarify the chronology of events or actions related in adjacent clauses.

All of these devices operate at their respective levels to organize the narrative discourse, setting off chunks of utterances, identifying points of narrative juncture within the chunks, and marking specific focal points within the utterances. This structuring equipment is present in ordinary Kamsá, but its employment is far more casual or automatic there. In narrative, and specifically mythic narrative, these devices work together to create an ordering of the discourse into a coherent narrative design. This ordering is not always systematic, for Kamsá mythic narrative lacks the rigid formal organization of ceremonial and ritual discourse. But the narrative transition markers appear in a sufficiently consistent manner as to allow for a quasi-poetic rendering on the printed page.

In recent years students of verbal art have directed considerable attention to the necessary evil of representing spoken performances on the printed page, arguing convincingly that representational formats conceal significant ideological persuasions (Hymes 1989; Tedlock 1972; Swann 1992). In the transcripts to follow, I have sought to capture the feel of Kamsá mythic narrative discourse by observing and marking palpable aspects of performance technique. But I have also accepted the literary medium as the inevitable environment for these transcriptions, and I find that the impulse to devise readable texts places constraints on the accurate representation of speech. I have attempted to strike a balance between divided loyalties, to the narratives as spoken objects of art and as texts designed for literary consumption. My approach to the dilemma of transcription stops short of both Dell Hymes' quest for the poetic essence of narrative discourse and of Dennis Tedlock's quest for aural reproducibility, though it profits from the methods developed by each of these leading figures in the ethnopoetic movement.

My transcriptions are intended to convey the feel of Kamsá mythic narrative discourse as quasi-poetic, quasi-conversational speech, coinciding with Jan Mukarovsky's category of "esthetically coloured speech" (1964). I have set utterance chunks apart by placing a blank space between them. Organization within these chunks is signaled through line breaks marking the minimal complete utterances, often set apart in the performances by a falling intonation and pause at the end. The resulting marks on the pages of this volume will hopefully convey the impression of a discourse style that leans toward consistent phrasing but still allows the narrator considerable flexibility in pursuing local narrative effect.

Having previewed some of the poetic devices serving the narrator's obligation to clearly order the progression of narrative utterances, let's turn to the process of dramatizing the narrative, whereby the narrator moves beyond recounting an experience and stimulates or simulates a reliving of it. I have elsewhere characterized such moments as "narrative epiphany," by which I mean a breakthrough from discourse into experience in a way that illuminates key dimensions of the story (see McDowell 1985). Kamsá narrators make use of several devices to plunge the audience into the very heart of the events being narrated.

There are techniques to enliven performances, some of them conventional, others more idiosyncratic. Moments of significant action will be foreshadowed by the word *ndeople* or *ndeolpne* (with the narrative suffix added), apparently from the Spanish expression *de golpe*, meaning "of a sudden" (literally "as a blow"). Moments of key dramatic interest are often preceded by unattached exclamations that implicitly reveal the narrator's own rising involvement in the story: *aray* (from the Spanish, *caray*, "damn"); *ndeombre* (from the Spanish, *de hombre*, "by my word"); *an de la warda* (from the Spanish, *dios le guarde*, "God preserve you"). These exclamations are delivered in a somber, awe-saturated tone. At times it is unclear whether they should be treated as reported self-address on the part of a story protagonist or as the narrator's emotive response to a forthcoming twist in the plot. Also prevalent are the emotive markers *oh* and *ay*, often intoned on extended and tuneful vowels.

Narrators make extensive use of iconic expressive devices within emotionally charged utterances. These techniques involve a mirroring effect between the diction of the narrator and the event or action that is being depicted. Conspicuous throughout much of the corpus are the lengthened vowels that signify intensity or complication within the narrative frame. The word *mallajkta*, meaning "very much" or "extreme," almost always occurs with a lengthening of the intermediate /a/. But any of the vowels can be prolonged in step with the emotional progress of the narrative. The period of such extensions ranges from approximately one to three seconds. These vowel elongations, often shaped into tuneful pitch contours, stand as vocal gestures pointing to the extreme character of some action or object currently being described in the narrative discourse. They often project the intensity of the protagonist's experience at that moment in the plot. I have underscored these extended vowels throughout the transcripts.

Another iconic effect involves the repetition of clauses to coincide with a repetition of action within the narrative frame. Consider this segment from Mariano Chicunque's "About Wangetsmuna" (m2), which occurs as the protagonist unsuccessfully seeks to return to his masculine form. He has been told to lie still by the river so that all the animals can pass by and lick him; but one with sharp claws comes last and causes him to cry out and throw the beast off:

ooh chora nyetska bayunga limpe imojishekona
Oh, then all the beasts came back,

chora jabjonana ndoñese
now not to take a lick,

jwentsanan jwentsanan jwentsanaye
to take a bite, take a bite, take a bite.

imojtsepochoka bestxabé ko ndoñeka
They finished him off, leaving only his head.

The iconic line here is the third one (line 151), which repeats the phrase "to take a bite" three times. The narrator makes the repetition stick by pausing between each statement and giving each phrase a similar intonational contour. In this way the repeated action of the animals is made graphic in the words of the narrator. Note also the lengthening of vowels in the first line quoted above as the narrator prepares us for this peripety. Narrators also produce, in varying degrees, special vocal effects that contribute to a reliving rather than just a recounting of experience. The two most prevalent strategies are a *heightened* delivery, with accelerated pace of articulation and higher vocal pitch levels, and a *sub-dued* delivery, which often collapses into a whisper. The heightened delivery occurs at moments of rash action, especially if there is some irony or major implication attached to the event. It simulates the presumed excitement of the protagonist in that situation; in this vein, the narrator's arousal becomes emblematic of the protagonist's presumed arousal. The subdued delivery marks topics and events that are especially awesome; it simulates the presumed caution of the protagonist as he or she confronts a disconcerting circumstance.

Among the most effective means of introducing drama into a performance is the use of reported speech, especially if the narrator makes an effort to impersonate the speaking protagonist. Kamsá mythic narrative becomes an anthology of Kamsá ways of speaking as other speech styles find a place in the performances. Conversational Kamsá abounds in the narratives, for many of them represent ordinary speech situations even if the interlocutors are ancestors, animal-people, or celestial deities. In these episodes the narrators affect the casual tonality of everyday speech, what Dwight Bolinger (cited in Ladd 1979) refers to as "informative utterance," with its "constant subtle ups and downs of pitch." Narrators accurately display the sound, syntax, and lexicon of routine talk in the Kamsá speech economy.

The ceremonial and ritual forms of Kamsá are also heard in Kamsá mythic narrative. One is never far from the sound of Kamsá ritual language in the Sibundoy veredas, since it occurs not only in formal gatherings but also in casual conversations when speakers wish to entreat or honor their interlocutors. And its presence is palpable in the mythic narratives as well. Several of these embed fully marked ceremonial speech acts, some of them bordering on complete ritual language speeches. Narrators strive to convey the chant-like intonational design, the rapid pacing, the required morphologies, and the canonical universe of reference that distinguishes this specialized mode of spoken Kamsá (McDowell 1983, 1990).

One mythic narrative, m16, "The Tale of the Weasel," presents a portfolio of Kamsá speech varieties. The story exhibits narrative Kamsá in the discourse that presents the plot elements. Conversational Kamsá appears in the words exchanged between the deer and his father toward the end of the story. The ritual language enters in this exchange between deer and the native doctor, weasel:

achka tkmojoftselisentsia shnanatem kwabwatemaka
"As it happens, God has bestowed upon you the knowledge of the good medicines.

chama tsabo mal tsepasa tseshnamaka
For this I have come, I am not feeling well, I need a treatment."

ar señoraka
"By Our Lord."

Kamsá ritual language appears in attenuated form in order to enhance the prospects of an entreaty. Native doctors are regarded with respect and their services must be appropriately solicited. Taita Mariano Chicunque produces a very accurate representation of the language used in such entreaties. The attribution of human prowess to God, the use of the diminutive on the word *shnana*, "remedies," the use of kinship terms to accomplish personal address: all of these bespeak the presence of ritual language. What cannot be gleaned from the printed representation of this speech are its performance features: the leveling of intonation to approximate the chanting tone of ritual language, and the noticeable acceleration of the pace of delivery, also characteristic of ritual language speech variety. This same mythic narrative portrays the speech of the native doctors, though this time in a humorous, not a serious vein. The weasel sets about doing all the things native doctors normally do: she takes out her curing branches, brushes the patient with them, and begins to circle around him. She even sings to the spirits, but instead of calling the spirit helpers, she calls on a set of culinary helpers:

ah tsetxá tsetxá tsetxá seboyuxe seboyuxe tamó tamoka
Ah, "Sauce, sauce, sauce, onion, onion, salt, salt."

Even if the mood is humorous, the narrator correctly portrays the native doctor's invocation of spirit helpers through intoned repetitions of their names.

The narrator's impulse to simulate the voices of protagonists extends to the animal figures as well. The ancestral period is characterized by a spiritual fluidity that would allow animals to take on human qualities, most notably the ability to converse as humans do. Narrators focus this central Kamsá postulate by pausing over the remarkable fact that in the old days the animals were speakers like us, *biyanga*, not mute like the beasts, *bayunga*. But the animal-people are also animals, and the narrators underscore this inherent duality by giving the animals their voices. The small dogs of the volcano cry in the distance: *kwe kwe, kwe kwe, kwe kwe* as they come down from the mountains to pursue the wild burros. The squirrel boasts from his safe perch in the trees: *chuj chuj chuj chuj chuj chuj chuj*. The hawk-man, after he has reverted to his animal form, calls from the branches overhead: *ko ko ko*. This same animal-person picks at the snails he has collected into a pile: *pex pex pex pex*. In stories involving animal suitors the imitation of their voices is a powerful device to keep us mindful of their dual identities.

All of these impersonations ultimately confound the voice of the protagonist with that of the narrator and thereby collapse the frame of the performance onto the frame of the story. When this happens, we experience narrative epiphany, a transitory illusion that we have penetrated the narrative world itself. If such effects are skillfully accomplished, the narrative comes to life as the audience engages the story events from this more intimate perspective. The impersonations, along with the other devices used to dramatize the narratives, draw us into the story's web and enable us to experience vicariously the adventures of the first people as they activated the civilizing process in the Sibundoy Valley.

3 Prelude

In the epoch of the raw time, the sun, the moon, the stars, the thunder, the rainbow, the flora and fauna of the region had special powers to transform themselves into human beings.
—Alberto Juajibioy (1987, 64, my translation)

It was a late afternoon in November in San Felix and several Kamsá companions had gathered in the thatch-roofed cottage of Bautista and Concha Juajibioy, as doña Concha readied the fire to prepare soup for that evening's supper. I joined the group inside the kitchen area and listened as taita Bautista explained to the younger men (most of them in their fifties) how things used to be in the old days. My presence was partially a catalyst for this talk, yet it unfolded with such passion and direction as to signal a natural causeway for discourse about former times and the present falling away from grace. Taita Bautista spoke at length of the Ingano taita Carlos Tamoabioy and his Kamsá counterpart, Leandro Agreda, native leaders who some centuries before had sought to guarantee the land rights of indigenous peoples of the valley. Here is a sampling of the discourse, translated from Kamsá and Spanish into English, that I witnessed that November afternoon; it prepares for our first mythic text a context of concern with accurate knowledge of the past and how things came to be. It is worth noting that Carlos Tamoabioy has been mythologized in Kamsá oral tradition as a solar deity who arrived, provided for his people, and departed all in the course of a single day (Friede 1945; Bonilla 1972).

This place is Carlos Tamoabioy's . . .
One has to know how things were.
This is our land; he left it to us.
He delivered the papers, signed by his hand.
The will and testament is housed in Quito,
the deed in Popayán . . .
Later this place became a reservation,
the property of the Indian.
This land, from the Patascoy Volcano to the Tortuga,
from doña Juana (a volcano) to,
what is the name of that river?
It borders on Los Laboneros.
The people of this place are the owners,
the true owners.

The people of this place didn't know how to hold it.
But Carlos Tamoabioy provided for us.
Because we didn't heed him,
we have been thrown off our own land.
And then we sought help from a native lawyer,
Leandro Agreda, like this, a very small man.
He fought hard for us,
he defended the Indian well.
The people of this place must respect him.
One of the missionaries told me:
"What if you people had said:
'Five days warning and all whites must leave,
because there is a law.' "
But due to our ignorance,
they have stolen our land. (laughs)
We, the people of this place, being the real owners.
And the writing is housed in Quito,
the deed in Popayán.

Thus spoke taita Bautista in the hushed chill of late afternoon sunshine in the Sibundoy Valley. A key word, indicative of the intimate focus of this discourse, kept surfacing—*mwentxenunga*, "we, the people of this place." A small cup of *aguardiente* was repeatedly filled and emptied as it passed from hand to hand around the room. The younger men nodded respectfully and occasionally ventured supportive comments.

In the midst of this talk taita Bautista brought forth the account of raw times that is reproduced below as our first mythic text. His mood at this moment was one of reminiscence, bemusement, a hint of the irony that engulfs human affairs penetrating his voice. His words on that distant afternoon, though not deeply narrative in their own right, are the appropriate place to begin our walking tour of Kamsá mythic narrative. In measured, deliberate phrases that occasionally slid off into calm laughter, he produced a skeletal account of a largely forgotten Kamsá cosmogony. The constant shifting from Spanish to Kamsá and back again to Spanish is likely an attempt to include me, a novice in this recondite tongue, in the conversation. The names of each epoch, along with brief descriptions, are given in Spanish for my benefit, but taita Bautista clearly savors the resonant Kamsá lexemes, and *kaka tempo* asserts itself as the persistent motif of this stretch of talk.

(m1) kaka tempo
The Raw Time

As performed by Bautista Juajibioy, in Kamsá and Spanish, December 1976

cuentan, ¿no?
They tell it, see?

tiempo de la oscuridad yibets tempoka
The time of darkness, the dark time.

y ya tiempo de luzna binyen tempoka
And later the time of light, the dawn time.

**y ya otra kaka tempoka tiempo crudo comían todo crudo kaka
tempo**
And later another, the raw time, the time of rawness, they ate every-
erything raw, the raw time. (laughs)

todo tiempo crudo que comían crudo pues todo
All the raw time they ate everything raw.

toda fruta, todo crudo, crudo, crudo como antes no había candela
Every fruit, everything raw, raw, raw, since before there was no fire.

por eso se llama kaka tempo tiempo crudo
That's why it is called the raw period, the time of rawness.

después ya que hubo candela entonces ya aprendían a cocinar
Later when there was fire, then at last they learned how to cook.

antes que sabía gustar como habían muchos
Earlier I used to like it, since there were many,

habían estado conversando los mayores
the elders would be conversing

uno estaba allí oyendo todo
one was there hearing everything.

antes de la llegada de los misioneros
Before the arrival of the missionaries.

We begin not with a story but with a story about stories, a native synopsis, as taita Bautista recalls talk of the elders about the string of cosmic ages leading from the dawn of creation to the modern period. Taita Bautista, now an elder himself, remembers as a child hearing this talk, which has since largely faded from his memory, leaving behind only a few mythic narrative fragments along with this overview of cosmic evolution. He was a child at the turn of the century, so it is reasonable to suppose that talk of this cosmic sequence harks back to at least the middle of the previous century and thus takes us back to a moment when the Sibundoy Valley was still a remote outpost and still nourished a vital South American Indian religion.

The inventory of cosmic ages provided by taita Bautista is as close as we are likely to come to a traditional Sibundoy creation myth. The Catholic missionaries struggled long and hard to eradicate Sibundoy "idolatries," and over the centuries a great deal of indigenous tradition vanished, went underground, or experienced a transformation into apparently harmless "folktale." We know from historical documents that the first *doctrinero* (Catholic religious teacher) entered the Sibundoy Valley in 1547, shortly after the conquest of this north-central Andean region (Bonilla 1972). Since then a succession of religious orders gained permission to evangelize in the Sibundoy Valley, but it was the Capuchin Order of Spain, arriving at the dawn of the present century, who most profoundly altered the traditional culture of the Sibundoy Valley by implementing a systematic form of social engineering aimed at "improving" the native peoples.

As skeletal as taita Bautista's account may be, it still provides valuable insight into the Sibundoy scheme of things, and it is a useful device for organizing the extensive body of Sibundoy mythic narrative filling the pages of this collection. Taita Bautista tells of a series of successive cosmic moments, each one moving closer to the real world of modern experience. Cosmogonies based on successive stages in the creation process are widespread in the world's mythologies and, more particularly, in the mythologies of Native American peoples. The motif of a sequential layering of cosmic time is part of the Amerindian mythological bedrock, though this central concept takes radically different appearances in its different settings. The Kamsá case (as revealed by taita Bautista) parallels the Incan tradition as presented in Guaman Poma's *Nueva Corónica*, suspect in its capitulation to Catholic dogma but suggestive in its description of a substrate population of warlike heathens (the *aucas*), who closely resemble the *yembas* or savages inhabiting the earth at the time of the first dawning (see the Wangetsmuna cycle, this volume). Mesoamerica provides another analogue in the Mayan *Popol Vuh*, which presents a sequence of creations as the gods attempt to fashion people who can speak articulately and who can worship them in the proper fashion. More distant connections can readily be found for this prominent mythological archetype.

The Sibundoy scheme presents an image of cosmic evolution from more remote configurations to the world of contemporary experience. The time of darkness, *yibets tempo*, is hostile to life forms and yields to *binyea tempo*, the dawn time, after the first rising of the sun. The Kamsá word *binyea* is heavily freighted with meaning; it can mean "dawn," "light," "sight," "vision," and even "spirit." The dawn time is thus a dawning in the broadest sense of the term, an awakening to the spiritual destiny of the world. With the first dawning, the civilizing process is set into motion; the earth becomes inhabitable, and the rise of human society becomes inevitable. One is reminded of the description of the first rising of the sun in the Mayan *Popol Vuh* (Tedlock 1985).

However, the dawn time is still alien, because its creatures lacked fire. Taita Bautista is amused as he speaks of the raw time, a time when

all food had to be consumed uncooked. As in other mythologies, rawness is here an emblem of the distance between civilization and its antecedent social conditions. The Wangetsmuna cycle, to be explored in
detail (see m2, m3) depicts the heathens gulping only the steam from a
pot full of hens and turkeys and correlates this irregularity with irreg-
ularities in the arena of sex and reproduction. The dawn time, we learn
from the assembled corpus of Kamsá myth, is distinctive as the moment
when brute spiritual force, in the persons of the primordial people and
in the form of personified celestial deities, initiated the relentless chain
of events culminating in the establishment of our familiar reality.

Claude Lévi-Strauss titled the first volume in his study of South
American mythology *The Raw and the Cooked* in recognition of the cen-
trality of the acquisition of fire in Native American mythopoeisis. As
Roberta Segal (1989: 207) correctly notes, Lévi-Strauss "singled out the
mastery of fire as the key step in a transition from an animal-like state of
nature to a distinctively human state of culture. The chief symbol of that
transition was the shift described in North and especially South American Indian myths from eating food raw to eating it cooked." Taita Bautista invocation of the raw time as a counter to the way things are done
today captures the prominence of this same emphasis on the symbolic
importance of fire in the Kamsá account of the emergence of civilization.

Taita Bautista tells us that the raw time in turn yielded to its unnamed successor, which I would label the ancestral period, inaugurated
with the conquest of fire. In a mythic narrative recorded by Alberto
Juajibioy and reproduced in one of the few publications dedicated to
Kamsá language or culture (see Juajibioy and Wheeler 1973), taita Bautista tells how fire was procured by the weasel, who danced to make
Wangetsmuna laugh and took advantage of his carelessness to carry off
a live ember from his fire. There is at the end of this story a reference to
a Kamsá myth that has not yet been recorded in which the mouse in a
similar fashion steals a grain of corn and delivers it to the ancestors.
With fire and corn seed now in the possession of the ancestors, the advent of proper human civilization is close at hand. The great majority of
mythic narratives in this collection portray aspects and moments in this
progression from a chaotic, spiritually charged ancestral world to the
modern world with its muted and marginalized spirituality.

The time scheme elaborated in taita Bautista's account takes note of
one additional twist in cosmic evolution, the coming of the missionaries, specifically the ambitious Capuchin Order. Under the seventy-five-
year sway of these stern Catholic fathers, the valley's native peoples
experienced a devastating alteration of their traditional pattern of living:
the Indians were driven out of their settlements and resettled in
swampy land; the valley was invaded by "more desirable" mestizo settlers from the north who were given land previously occupied by the
Indians; with the use of Indian labor, a road was opened to connect the

Sibundoy Valley with the provincial capital city of San Juan de los Pastos (Pasto); the Capuchin Mission developed for its own exploitation large herds of cattle and sheep; and a rigorous campaign was instituted to eradicate the last remnants of indigenous culture in the valley.

The present plight of the Sibundoy Indians, impoverished strangers in their own land, dispossessed not only of land but also of customs, can be traced in large measure to the efforts of these energetic Capuchins, who operated, of course, with the encouragement of the national authorities (Bonilla 1972). It is a tribute to the vitality of oral tradition that somehow, in spite of all these measures, enough of the anterior belief system has persisted into the present to allow for a partial reconstruction of what must once have been a remarkable South American civilization. Taita Bautista's recollection of the raw time, when people ate everything uncooked, is a vital clue as we seek to recover what we can of its spiritual foundation.

4 The Wangetsmuna Cycle

Wangetsmuna is at once a deity and the principal culture hero of the Kamsá Indians, in many respects cognate to figures like Viracocha of the central and southern Andes (Demarest 1981) and Juan Tama, Bochica, and Guequiau of the Chibchan nations to the north (Castillo y Orozco 1877; Triana 1951; Simon 1953; Rappaport 1980–1981). The mythology indicates that once he was held in awe by his people, but his very name is falling into oblivion as the modern age washes over the Sibundoy Valley, breaking the ancient hold of tradition. There is no evidence of Wangetsmuna outside of the mythic narrative corpus; even his name remains obscure. The root *wangets* is close to Kamsá for "beak"; it is probable that Wangetsmuna was conceived of as a bird-like deity, perhaps the spiritual master of the many bird-people that populate Kamsá mythology.

Kamsá myths portray a powerful figure closely associated with the celestial deities: the thunder god is described as Wangetsmuna's grandfather, the sun as his brother's father-in-law, and the moon as his brother's wife. A narrative cycle has accumulated around this seminal figure whose exploits occupy a formative period in cosmic time and entail a remarkable displacement through various levels of cosmic space. The deeds and destiny of Wangetsmuna define a sacred geography and chronology of the Kamsá. I have in my possession seven mythic narratives, from four narrators, featuring this Kamsá demigod. Two of them, m2 and m3 in this collection, are complete tellings of the Wangetsmuna cycle in Kamsá; a third is a complete telling in the Spanish language by a Kamsá narrator. In addition, there is one fragment that I have titled, "The Death of Wangetsmuna," since it emerged in response to a narrator's claim that there was another ending to the cycle. Other mythic fragments portray Wangetsmuna as the keeper of fire and corn seed (see Juajibioy and Wheeler 1973) and as the hero who gathers all the winds of the Sibundoy Valley into a tube (see m10). A final text of considerable interest is an Inga version by José Chasoy Sijindioy titled, *Calusterinda Yaya*, "Owner of the Carnival," published by Editorial Townsend in 1983. This last text shares many of the episodes present in the Kamsá cycle but evokes the militaristic setting of the conquest rather than the mythopoeic times of the ancestors. Interestingly, this variant features a Wangetsmuna-like figure as the owner or sponsor of the yearly carnival, a linkage that is not actively present in current observance of that great occasion.

These texts constitute a mythology of major scope; they must be viewed as the foundation myths of Sibundoy civilization and cognate with the other great mythologies of the Amerindian peoples. The Wangetsmuna cycle is an account of the emergence of human society from the embryonic Raw Time. These myths incorporate themes and motifs that are common to the general body of Amerindian mythology; they compose, if you wish, the Sibundoy rendering of this cosmological bedrock. Episodes like the rolling or knocking head, the heathen savages without an anus, and many others, appear in mythologies throughout the native Americas and beyond (see Niles 1981; Lévi-Strauss 1969, 1973, 1978; McDowell 1989).

The Wangetsmuna cycle charts the evolution of human civilization in the Sibundoy Valley. It spans a continuum of cosmic time from the earliest ancestral period when the first humans interact directly with celestial deities, through a transitional period marked by the removal of savage heathen precursors, to the last flicker of the ancestral period when the configuration of the land and the customs of its inhabitants settle into patterns that are familiar to us today. There is a comparable process of displacement and linkage in terms of spatial alignment: the story begins in a largely undefined space, a celestial dominion with only a river running through it; it moves downward into the lowlands, the domain of the mule-like heathens; and it concludes with action in and around the Sibundoy Valley itself. This movement from celestial heights to lowland margins and back again to the intermountain highlands charts the significant topological consciousness of the Kamsá people, whose fertile domain lies nestled between the *páramo* (drizzly wasteland) of the high Andes and the Amazonian basin.

The story is fraught with transformations: from one gender to the other, from person to head and then to tender infant, from a savage condition to a civilized one. The relentless thrust of these transformations is toward a channeling of spiritual power into manageable conduits, and toward a hardening of ontological reality into the discrete categories that make civilization a viable enterprise. In this march through cosmic time and space, almost every action or encounter is weighted with the aura of sacred precedent. The narrators adopt a prophetic voice, shifting tenses easily as they depict eternal verities.

I have selected two versions of the cycle, both collected by me from Kamsá narrators, to present in this collection. There is some overlap between them, but each supplies important details that are missing in the other. They allow for the following reconstruction of the life and deeds of Wangetsmuna:

Phase 1: Wangetsmuna as a Primordial Human Being
  (a) Wangetsmuna begins as one of the first ancestors, a younger brother to a miner who goes about searching for gold and turning it into objects such as chains, mallets, and balls. (It is worth re-

calling that the casting of gold into ritual and decorative objects was a valued and elevated precolombian craft in the Andes of Colombia).

(b) The miner encounters a young woman who turns out to be the moon, daughter of the sun.

(c) They agree to marry and travel to the home of the sun, who makes a brief appearance but does not discover the miner.

(d) The miner's younger brother becomes foolishly curious and as a result finds himself transformed into a woman.

(e) The only means for returning to his previous identity is to lie at the side of a river and suffer all the animals to come by, each one taking a lick.

(f) The last animal to come by is a prickly one; when the younger brother throws it off, all the animals return, this time each one taking a bite.

(g) At last nothing remains but a head; this head bothers the older brother until an arrangement is made: the head is to be stuffed into a drum, the drum in turn is to be cast into the river.

Phase 2: Wangetsmuna among the Heathens

(a) The heathens find the drum spinning about in the foam; one of them takes it home and opens it, only to discover a beautiful babe.

(b) The heathen raises this child, who grows rapidly into an adventurous youth.

(c) The youth uses medicine and surgery to provide the heathens with an anus, which they had previously lacked, so they can now eat properly.

(d) The young man sets a trap and it crushes the tip of a collective male organ.

(e) He runs to his grandfather, the thunder, for protection. The grandfather has him hide under his chair.

(f) The heathens arrive and demand the "wicked" young man. The thunder first denies his presence; when the heathens insist, he pulls out his sling and utterly destroys them with thunderbolts.

Phase 3: Wangetsmuna Visits the World

(a) The thunder sends the youth out to visit the world with instructions to come back and report in a year's time.

(b) The thunder gives Wangetsmuna his name and provides him with a horn and a staff, and a special incantation, for protection.

(c) Wangetsmuna visits the place of the monkeys. The animal-people there have prepared an amusement for him—they will swing out on vines. He is not amused and, as a punishment, turns them forever into monkeys.

(d) Wangetsmuna gives various animals their voices and habits based on tendencies he observes in them.

(e) Wangetsmuna sounds his trumpet and thereby creates a line of demarcation between animals and people.

(f) Wangetsmuna visits various people working in the fields: those who politely answer his inquiries prosper; those who do not find only rocks and reeds in their gardens.

(g) Wangetsmuna arrives where a girl has lost her family. He calls them back to life with the sounding of his trumpet, but when the girl fails to remain silent as instructed, the family vanishes once again.

(h) Wangetsmuna arrives where an old woman is poor and without sight. She is kind to him, killing her only hen to provide him with food. He returns her sight and leaves her rich with corn and hens.

(i) At last Wangetsmuna returns to the sky to remain there with his grandfather, the thunder.

Myths outside this cycle add other details: they portray Wangetsmuna as the possessor of knowledge in the vicinity of the Sibundoy Valley. It is from Wangetsmuna that the animal-people acquire (through stealth) fire and corn seed; it is Wangetsmuna who goes about stuffing the harmful winds of the Sibundoy Valley into a gourd tube (see m10, this collection).

As suggested in the above parsing of motifs, Wangetsmuna's trajectory can be divided into three epochs. The first portrays his celestial origins and his kinship with celestial deities. The myths present a complex linking the thunder deity, the first human beings, and the pursuit of gold. The miner goes out searching for gold in order to fashion the mallets requested by his grandfather, the thunder deity. This deity, in turn, produces gold in the form of his droppings. The first humans exist in the rarified atmosphere of celestial figures such as the sun and the moon. Wangetsmuna enters this scenario as a disruptive element, a catalyst. His misbehavior precipitates the disintegration of the primordial scheme of things, as he crosses the gender boundary, then becomes a disembodied head. This initial segment can be read as a mythopoeic account of placer mining, a major economic function of the Sibundoy people within the prehistorical Quillasinga federation.

The second epoch in the Wangetsmuna cycle depicts the vanquishing of a substrate population and the establishment of appropriate norms for human social life. We follow Wangetsmuna to a lowland setting, where he is recast as a human infant. This locale is described as underneath the surface of the earth or beneath a river; its inhabitants are said to be mule-like. It would appear that we have entered a kind of Kamsá anti-world where the heathen savages do things backwards. They cook but do not eat; they copulate through a collective male organ. It is possible that these allegations represent an ethnocentric highland perspective on the customs of peoples in the adjacent Amazonian lowlands. In any case, Wangetsmuna enters the picture once again as a transformative element. It is through his initiatives that the heathen savages are destroyed, leaving the world safe for human civilization.

The final epoch finds Wangetsmuna wandering about in a world very much like the one we know today. The last vestiges of the ancestral period recede as Wangetsmuna sounds his horn and separates human and animal identities. From that juncture on, the primary elements in this epoch are moral rather than cosmogonic. Wangetsmuna travels from place to place rewarding the good and punishing the wicked. Once again, Wangetsmuna plays a pivotal role in furthering the prospects for human civilization, this time by exemplifying attitudes of mercy and justice that are appropriate to the conduct of human society.

If these phases mark a fateful displacement in cosmic time and space, they also contain a few constant narrative strands that assert themselves from one phase to another and thereby provide a measure of thematic unity. The miner's handiwork with gold in phase 1 supplies the thunder with the armament he will need to vanquish the heathens in phase 2. The miner sets a trap and snares the moon in phase 1; Wangetsmuna sets a trap and squashes the meandering male organ in phase 2. The miner hides from the sun in a large earthen jar in phase 1; Wangetsmuna likewise finds refuge from the enraged heathens in phase 2; and in phase 3 the orphan girl hides in a large jar while Wangetsmuna calls her family back from the grave. All three phases feature an interdiction-violation sequence, identified by Russian folklorist Vladimir Propp (1968) as one of several key structural patterns in traditional narrative. These recurring motifs endow the cycle with an aura of ritual inevitability, as significant actions repeat in the unfolding cosmogony. They anticipate the Kamsá postulate that all contemporary events are pale reflections of their ancestral counterparts, that history is destined to recapitulate its formative moments.

These mythic narratives portray a culture hero with celestial connections but intimately associated with human destiny. Wangetsmuna, whose name is largely forgotten in the Sibundoy Valley, lives on in the syncretic figure Our Lord, a composite of Christ, the sun, and Wangetsmuna. He is a vital component in the ancestral model that is cited in daily and seasonal encounters as the source of correct social mores (McDowell 1983, 1990). Wangetsmuna and his deeds apparently lie behind the feathered crowns and fervent dancing of the Kamsá carnival. But his identity is fading as the new generations replace the old, and as the old stories are less often performed. It may be, ironically, that he obtains his immortality through the pages of this book, where his pivotal role in the unfolding of human civilization is dutifully recorded in the voices of two Kamsá narrators.

The Wangetsmuna cycle draws together prominent strands in Native American mythology, evident throughout the first two phases of his career; the third phase builds in a decidedly European, and Christian, dimension. American Indian mythologies abound in parallels to the episodes set in the primordial world of the first phase and the lowland setting of the second. The motif of the sun arriving to dry a large body of water, revealing valuables on the floor, is present in Mesoamerica (Laughlin 1988, 233). The pivotal event in phase one, the dismemberment of Wangetsmuna in his female form, leads to a widely distributed motif that is often referred to as "The Rolling Skull" or "The Flying Head," which occurs all the way across the South American continent and widely in the plains region of North America as well (Lowie 1940; Morote Best 1958; Lévi-Strauss 1969, 54). The motif of the food-inhaling heathens has analogues throughout much of indigenous South America, with a concentration in the northwestern quarter of the continent (Bierhorst 1988, 193).

The third phase features some indigenous elements but moves toward a Judeo-Christian framework. A deity who transforms certain men into monkeys is a prominent theme in Mesoamerica (Laughlin 1988, 204) and occurs in the *Popol Vuh* (Tedlock 1985, 121). The episode at the home of the young orphan, in which Wangetsmuna calls her deceased family members back to life only to be thwarted by the untimely breaking of silence, is to be distinguished from the widespread Orpheus myth, since in this instance there is no visit to the underworld. Nonetheless, the revival of the dead is a prominent motif in Native American mythology, for example, on the North American plains (see Gayton 1934).

The remaining episodes in this final phase of the story invoke a moral universe in which kindness to the wandering deity is rewarded and its opposite is punished. These episodes have numerous parallels in the Americas and in European tradition. The motif of questions put to farmers resounds widely in the oral tradition of Christianity. It appears frequently along the Andean corridor in South America (Bierhorst 1988, 253; Rasnake 1988, 144-45). Robert Laughlin (1988, 274) notes that this motif, with Christ as the wandering deity, is "surely the favorite throughout southern Mexico and Guatemala." It occurs as well in New Mexico (Rael 1939). These European accretions register the assimilation of Wangetsmuna to the Christian paradigm, a process that comes full circle in "The Death of Wangetsmuna," which has the culture hero sacrificed to the "beasts" of this world.

(m2) wangetsmunabiama
About Wangetsmuna

As performed by Mariano Chicunque, in Kamsá, November 1978.

We had taken our places on the low wooden stools, and taita Mariano
was collecting his thoughts; Justo came around with a bowl of freshly-
brewed chicha for taita Mariano: *"nye kanyetema,"* "just a little drop,"
says Justo, as he leans gently in Mariano's direction; Mariano responds,
"as le pay, des pa gracho," "thank you kindly, God reward you," as he receives the gourd with its refreshing contents. It is mid-afternoon, the
sun outside is hot, but we are comfortable in the parlor in Justo's adobe
house. Taita Mariano has intimated that we are to hear a very special
narration; "This is a very old story," he tells us. He drinks deeply of the
chicha, places the half-emptied gourd at his feet, and begins his
performance.

Taita Mariano's version contains several episodes and numerous details that are absent in other performances of the cycle. For example, his
performance alone displays the generative power of dreaming, as the
miner dreams of the quarry (first a bird, then a woman) that he will
catch in his trap. Likewise, only this version explores the alliance of the
miner and the moon through the agency of spiritually charged cotton,
and the younger brother's transgression of this alliance. Taita Mariano
dwells on the arrival of the sun, his hefty meal, and his suspicion of an
alien presence: "Why does it smell so much of moss?" (line 66).

bweno
Fine.

anteona ana inamna bjakayaká
So in the old days there was a miner.

bjakaya wabochenaye wabentsana katxata ibonoiyena
The miner, an older brother, with a younger brother, the two lived
    together.

i chatena bjakayana ana ndoka remidio wabentsana wabwayana
And those two, the miner and indeed, the younger brother, a cook.

aray chana bjakayana nye chká chká jtsobjakañana   5
Damn! The miner just like that, like that, went off to work the mine.

kabana benache yojatenyena inawabana
Still he found a trail, he followed it.

morna ch intsoyungabiamka benache inamna[1]
Now that was the path of the coatis.

---

[1]line 7: *intsoyunga*, in local Spanish, *kusumbe*. The coati, most likely the South
American coati, *Nasua nasua*, a coon-like carnivore (Emmons and Feer 1990, 138-39).

i chorna ibojato antoja jwabochmayama²
And then he became curious to set a trap:

ndayá ch janbewabanaka
"What was it that used that path?"

bweno   10
Fine.

yojwachmayisa chorkokaye ch binyetamaka³
He set a trap, then surely on that eve of the full moon.

i yojtsabochmana orna ibsana ibojoftsenay
And when he set the trap, the next day he spoke to him,

u ch katxata wabentsa ch waibwayana ibojoftsiana
To that younger brother, that cook, he spoke:

xkwá xkwiyá mntena koisabwanayeka
"I will go, I will go again today, you stay and cook."

bweno   15
Fine.

**chorna yojá orna ch wachmanentxena yojtsetsebwana wabwangana
    plumubjwaka⁴**
Then when he went, then a red feather was caught in that trap.

wabwanganabjwa yojtsetsebwanaka
A small red one was caught.

ya chorna chana ibojatetnekwentá wachmanaya ch bjakayana
And then they spoke again, that trapper, that miner.

pero bweno
So, fine.

yojtatachmayika i ntxamo yojotjena⁵   20
He set the trap again and what did he dream?

i konforma yojotjena shema chentxe yojtsatsana
And he dreamed just like that, a woman was standing there.

---

²line 8: *jwabochmayama*, "to set a trap." This is a trap that catches its victim with a vine around the ankle.

³line 11: *binyetamaka*, "the eve of the full moon." Sibundoy Indians coordinate their activities, especially agricultural and spiritual, to the phases of the moon. The eve of the full moon is considered a benign moment, well suited to planting corn or communing with the ancestors (McDowell 1989).

⁴line 16: *wabwangana plumubjwaka*, "red feather." Very likely the feather of the *huacamaya* bird, one of several birds prominent in Sibundoy mythology.

⁵line 20: *yojotjena*, "he dreamed." Dreaming is taken as a primary channel of communication with the spirit realm.

i sertoka ibsana yojiya orna ch wachmanentxe shema yentxa shema
And truly the next day when he went, there was a woman, a female, in the trap.

ch wachmanentxe batatema xubjajeñe[6]
In the trap a little aunt tied around the ankles.

serto batatema chentxe yojtsenana ch biajaka
Truly a little aunt was caught there in the rope.

yojabokna orna ibojoyana ibojachuwayika   25
When he appeared they spoke to one another, they greeted one another:

bas deka
"Good day."

ndeka[7]
"Same to you."

chorna ndomoyeka
Then: "Where are you going?"

ralatema jongwangwama bejayoye
"I am looking for gold by the river."

chkaka ndayama mntxá biajaka xkjenaka wabaniñe   30
"Is that so? Why have you tied me like this with rope in the path?"

tjinyentsebonyi kausna tijoboma
Then he realized what he had done.

xmutsejabjoná ibojtsejabjonaka
"Untie me." He untied her.

ibojtsejabjona orna serto chorna ah ibojoyana
When he untied her, truly then, ah, she spoke to him:

asna kekatjañemwa atxebioy janaka
"Now would you like to come with me?"

i ch boyá ch bjakayana aiñeka ibojojwaka[8]   35
And that young man, that miner: "Yes," he answered.

ase kwayeka ibojwanats
"Then let's go." She took him with her.

---

[6]line 23: *batatema*, "little aunt." This is an affectionate label for a young Kamsá woman.

[7]lines 26-27: *bas deka, ndeka*, "good day." These are the conventional greeting terms for informal greetings among familiars. Their use at this juncture in the narrative indicates a routine quality to this remarkable encounter. But the two protagonists are about to become husband and wife.

[8]line 35: *boyá*, "young man, husband." Here the matrimonial intentions of this couple are made evident.

kausna bngabe taitá bngabe taitaka shinye este sol[9]
It happened that Our Father, Our Father, the sun, this sun,

bngabe taitá bngabe taitá shinyebe bembe inetsomiñe
Our Father, Our Father, she was the sun's daughter.

ibojaushjangoka
They arrived there together.

a la warda rato tsetebemana orna chorna ndeǫlpe nyetx̱á
    marisebiaka[10]   40
Heaven forbid, when they sat down for a while, suddenly, there by
    a large body of water,

more ch karusunga betsaibaika inabayushubwenana marioy[11]
like these trucks come nowadays, he came roaring to that water.

u ch i mari impase inabojojwiñe
And that body of water dried up completely.

eso sí ch chinyañena ana chakirmesha[12]
Yes indeed, that beach was pure beads,

kemsoye chakirmeshe chakirmeshe inetsomiñe ch chinyañc
these things, beads, beads, that beach was made of them.

bweno   45 `
Fine.

chore ibojtseitume ch shembasana ch boyá jaboknᇙ[13]
Then they went to hide, that young woman and her husband-to-be,

ch jobwamayama trata yojtsemna
they had agreed to marry.

ibojtseitume ṃallajkta btse mateba inajajonaye
They hid, a very large jar was kept there,

---

[9]line 37: *bngabe taitaka shinye*, "Our Father, the Sun." The sun is still referred to as Our Father or Our Lord, and sometimes identified with Jesus Christ.

[10]line 40: *ndeǫlpe nyetxá*, "suddenly, very." Here the narrator warms to the dramatic moment, prolonging each of the underlined vowels to a span of almost three seconds.

[11]line 41: *karusunga*, "trucks." The narrator uses a deliberate anachronism here to convey a sense of the large motor that powers the sun's cart. The national road from Pasto to Mocoa passes along the northern fringe of the Sibundoy Valley and the rumble of large trucks can often be heard across the valley.

[12]line 43: *chakirmesha*, "colored beads." Bulky necklaces of colored beads, most often red, white, or blue, are a sign of wealth and respectability for adult men and women. Kamsá adults often prefer to be photographed with their beads in place around their necks. This moment in the story indicates the mythical source of these colorful beads.

[13]line 46: *boyá jaboknᇙ*, "husband-to-be." The protagonists have agreed to marry, inaugurating a system of trial marriage that is still practiced in the Sibundoy Valley.

i ch i shoye ibojtsetebema jopodiak
and inside there they were able to sit down.

i chorna twambabe tjamenká inatebonsantsana choy   50
And then hen droppings were scattered about there,

shinyebe tjamena chká inatebonsantsana choyna[14]
the sun's droppings like that were scattered all about there.

choy yojtseitumena nyetxá
There they completely hid themselves.

choy yojtsetemena orna la warda shinye yojtashjango
As they were hiding there, heaven forbid, the sun arrived.

jasama yojtachnungun shkwanana
He stopped to eat as he went on his rounds.

ch i choy nyetxá ibojtsentxeniñana   55
And there it getting very hot for those two,

ch i xuboye santo dios nyetxá ibojtsentxeniñana[15]
inside there, saintly God, it was getting very hot for those two.

a chora jasana saná kada xnena arobaka
And then when it came to eating, each serving an arobe,

kada saná arobaka ana unga arobaka jaftsesanaka[16]
each serving an arobe, so three arobes he would eat.

unga arobe yojaftsesaye i a unga aroba yojasaye
Three arobes he came to eat, three arobes he ate.

i chor chora yojayana ndayeka ndayeka   60
And then, then he spoke: "Why, why,

ntxamo mwentxe ndayeka ibojatangtxana barbachanaka ndaye-
kaka[17]
what, here, why does it smell so much of moss, why?"

chora ch bembe ibojojwaka
Then that daughter responded:

---

[14]line 51: *shinyebe tjamena*, "the sun's droppings." These are identified by Kamsá elders as the source of gold.

[15]line 56: *santo dios*, "saintly God." Note the use of this Spanish invocation to heighten the impact of this narrative moment.

[16]line 58: *unga arobaka*, "three arobes." Each arobe is a bushel of twenty-five pounds, lending a sense of the immense scale of the sun and his effects.

[17]line 61: *ndayeka ibojatangtxana barbachanaka*, "Why does it smell of moss?." This detail suggests the widely-distributed European folktale motif of the suspicious giant whose nose alerts him to the hero's presence.

atxe tijebana ch tjoye babarchniña binyenoye niña tijokiñe
"I went to the woods where there was moss, I went to gather firewood."

chká ibojtsangetxana kwedadoka[18]
Like that they were giving off an odor, watch out!

a choye jtsatsukama ndoñika 65
He came there to take the lid off, but no,

ajá chorkokayé yojtisotebema i ch máquina ch yojtetenana
aha, right then he sat down and that machine roared.

i̱ chora marina mari ko nye impase ibojojwiñe
And then that water, that water completely dried up,

i chká yojtenatjumbañe ch marie impase
and like that the water completely disappeared.

i shinye ndmwá lware ora ch bejayina yojtatenabngo i impas
And when the sun took off to another place, the river completely came together again.

chkaka ajá 70
That's how it was, aha.

bweno
Fine.

chorna chorna ch shema ibojoyana boyan bndata jobwamayamasna
Then, then that woman spoke to the young man so they could marry:

asna bojajna metsekaka yibeta atxe chtashjango[19]
"Now take this wad of cotton, in the evening I will come to you."

yojaka tongentsesh yojenobojajo
She took the cotton, she rubbed it on herself.

shemna ibojantregaka 75
The woman gave it to him.

i ch anteona ch karilyesha ch karielo o ch karilyesha
And in the old days they had that sack, that bag, or that sack,

i ch mora mundetsabobwatemiñe morala
what we nowadays know as a pack,

---

[18]line 64. *ibojtsangetxana*, "they were giving off an odor." There is a hint here of sexual activity.

[19]line 73: *bojajna*, "spiritual cotton." In this episode cotton serves as a medium for containing and conveying a spiritual presence. It continues in use among the native doctors as a spiritual medium in healing and other spiritual actions such as locating lost or stolen items.

kachká chkatema inatxebwana choye yojtsabotswamina bojajnaka
like that he slung it over his shoulder, he had it stuffed with cotton.

bweno
Fine.

i sertoka yojtsojajwa kanyentxe ch wabochena   80
And truly she remained there inside with the older brother.

i ch wabentsana tsabjoka yojtsejajonaka
And that younger brother remained in the kitchen.

i chorna yibetna bejatenatstsenayika bejatenatstsenayika
And then in the evening there was talk among two people, there
    was talk among two.

i ache binyanoye ch wabentsana ndoñe borla yojtsebxena
And so at dawn that younger brother, no fooling, he awoke:

ndayeka chká bejtsenatsutsunaye
"Why was there talk among two people like that?"

i asna anteona opunga imanamna[20]   85
And then in the old days they were wicked,

yojtsemalisiay ndayá shemaka
he became suspicious: "What was it, a woman?"

i serta ndoká yojtsetsebanañe kanyay yojtsetsebanañe
And truly there was nothing, he awoke, alone he awoke.

i ch karieltema yojtantxubwaye yojiyitsoñika kusabwanaye
And he placed that sack over his shoulder and left: "Do the
    cooking."

bweno
Fine.

i chorna cha yojatobatsaye ch tanentxe   90
And then he laid out that bedding.

yojatontxá bonyanana bonyanana
He began to look through it, to look through it.

i ch espiritualkwentana nye ndoñe ibonjinyen[21]
And he just didn't find that spirit-like presence.

a cha ch ch bjayokna yojobwambaye
And there at the mine she told him,

[20]line 85: *opunga*, "wicked, foolish." Cognate with a Quechua root, *opa*, meaning
"foolish, timid, dumb"; literally, "someone who cannot speak."

[21]line 92: *espiritualkwentana*, "spirit-like thing." The narrator produces a hybrid Spanish and Kamsá word here to identify the spiritual presence contained in
the cotton.

ch shema ibojtsebwache ch bjakayoka
that woman came to visit him at the mine:

akabe wabentsana xondengwa casi xtajtsinyena   95
"Your younger brother was looking for me, he almost found me."

i chorna yojayana ar kochjebebokna ar ntxamo chakomojama
And then he said: "So, you will appear to him, then what will become of him?"

ajá inye ibsana chká yojiyema i chteko serta ibojebebokna
Aha. The next day he did it again and that day truly she appeared to him.

i ch tongentsesha yojinyena
And he found that wad of cotton.

i serta ch anteongna moknunga imanamna
And truly how were the old ones?

ch tongentsesha yojaka jntsaka yojenenutjo   100
He took that wad of cotton, he rubbed his ankles with it.

ch tongentseshe jwebiaka yojatenenututjo koshkeloka
With that cotton he rubbed all around his face, his underarms,

i kata koshkeliñe yojenuntutjo
and he rubbed both of his underarms.

i jayenana serta ch batasoye yojenanamba ch tongentseshna
And so to speak, truly he lowered that cotton to his crotch.

ajá chore cheshena ibojtsetotona ch shanyana[22]
Aha. Then that stuff stuck to that caretaker.

a chorna bngabe xukunatemana impase   105
And then there was nothing left of our penis,

nye shema yojtsebokna ch wabentsana shema
he turned into a woman, that younger brother a woman.

karay yojajetana ora yojontxe jwabwan[23]
Damn! As it was getting late, she began to cook.

kabá chor yojtsabwowana yojtsabwowana ora inatay ch katxata
Finally then the water boiled, as it boiled the brother arrived.

---

[22]line 104: *shanyana*, "caretaker." The word used to designate a person who stays behind to look after the house when other members of the family have left for town or for a distant field.

[23]line 107: "she." Kamsá pronouns do not mark gender, so there is no indication in the text as to whether the younger brother should now be characterized as a man or as a woman. I have elected to use the feminine pronoun during his tenure as a woman.

orna a chora tempo shembasaka ibojebionana
Then, right away he realized that he was a woman.

**ah tempo ch kuftsayebiá yojtsenakaye tempo
   yojwasundamana[24]**   110
Ah, right away she took off her poncho, right away she wrapped it
   around her waist.

chká bejtsetsana tukenana bejtsetsana
Like that she walked about, her legs open, she walked about.

ndayakama ibojauyana nye ndokaka
"What happened?" he asked her. No reply.

ndayakama ndayekse chkaka lempe kbondojo jebwenyá
"What happened? Why do I find you so sad like this?"

chore tempo yojtsetatxumbo yojtsayanay
Then right away he knew, he scolded her.

chorna nye kach shema o ch jajnayá ibojoyana   115
"Now you are surely a woman," he told that guilty one:

bwenosna atxebe cha xkojtsaboyinjasna
"Well, now, as for me, I no longer respect you,

ntxá xkojtsaboyunja mntxá jtsananasna
I have lost all respect for you, going about like that."

chká tanentxa tijareparay i tijenyena tijenobojajoye
"Like that I looked through the bedding, and I found it, and I
   rubbed it all over myself.

i chká tijtsepasá
And that's what happened to me."

i kubunduwatsa bngwana jutseshanyana   120
"And I told you: 'Take it easy, keep an eye on the house.'

ndayám chká tkjama mórnaka
Now what can you do?

i morna kache ntxamo masena ch bejayentxe
And now there is nothing else but to go to the river."

nye bayenga imojtsachnujna ch bejayoka
All the beasts were passing by that river,

mejtumbonga tojowanga ko che sundibayanka
wasps, bees, all those I mention here,

---

[24]line 110: *kuftsayebiá*, "poncho." Kamsá men dress in a characteristic poncho distinguished by vertical stripes alternating either red or blue with white. Women do not wear ponchos but rather wear a colorful blouse around their waists.

ch mongojo tigre todo animal[25]   125
that monkey, jaguar, all the animals,

ana nye jabjonanaka jabjonana ch uwatja jtsepochokama
but only to lick, to lick that vagina in order to destroy it.

chnga chká imojontxá chujwana chujwana
Like that they began passing by, passing by.

ultimokna ch ismanaka u ch maxuja[26]
At last that *isman*, that prickly one,

ntxamo ch kastellanoka yojtsabaiñe ch ch ichman
what is it in Spanish, I can't recall, that, that *ichman*?

chuj isman morka manuja choja   130
That *isman*, now, he has claws, like this,

i chuja stonoka i mntxá yojtojonyana
and that one came behind and like that he grabbed hold.

achka lempe yojtetsejabjo
Like that he really licked it,

ko serta ch uwatja salapo ibojtsejabjo
then truly, that vagina, cunt, he licked.

ay yay karajo ibojtsetjajo ibojtsabentaka[27]
"Ay ay." Damn, he grabbed it, he threw it off him.

ooh chora nyetska bayunga limpe imojishekona[28]   135
Oh, then all the beasts came back,

chora jabjonana ndoñese
now not to take a lick,

jwentsanán jwentsanán jwentsanaye[29]
to take a bite, take a bite, take a bite.

imojtsepochoka bestxabé ko ndoñeka
They finished him off, leaving only his head.

[25]line 125: *tigre*, "tiger (jaguar)." In Kamsá the Spanish word for tiger refers to the South American jaguar, a powerful figure in reality and in myth.

[26]line 128: *ismanaka*, translation uncertain. Nobody could positively identify this animal, other than to say it is small and has very sharp claws. I was told that a small bear was formerly found in the valley and adjacent lowlands; could this be the animal known as *isman* or *ishman*?

[27]line 134: *ay yay* = ouch!

[28]line 135. *ooh chora nyetska bayunga*, "Oh, then all the beasts." The narrator expresses the intensity of this moment in the narrative by extending the three underlined vowels; the *ooh* lasts approximately three seconds, and incorporates a striking rise-fall intonational movement.

[29]line 137: *jwentsanan jwentsanan jwentsanaye*, "to take a lick, to take a lick, to take a lick." The narrator makes use of an iconic device here, reproducing the sequence of licks through a sequence of verbal references to it.

moy lempe imojtsepochoka bestxabé ko ndoñeka[30]
Here they completely finished him off, leaving only his head.

i ch kabeká yojtatamashingo tsotxe tsotxe[31]   140
And even so he entered again: "Take me back, take me back."

i morna kache ntxamo masna ch bejayentxe xmetsashbwetxeka
"And now what else can I do but throw you in the river?"

ibojetsashbwetxe i nada ooh nye nye yojtuxena
He threw him away but to no avail, oh, he just came back.

bweno
Fine.

tempo chorna yojtsebiya tsotxe tsotxe tsotxe
Right away then he called: "Take me back, take me back, take me
    back."

yojtsostonaka chana jtsebetxama chká yojtsechama   145
He followed behind him to be taken back, he spoke like that.

chora ch wabochena ibojetena
Then that older brother became angry.

chor ibojauyana atxebe chaka akabe bonshana
Then he spoke to him: "You no longer respect me.

tamboñerbé majta iye chbeñe xmotsatsawamá[32]
Take down the drum and stuff me inside.

bien kuisatobobatseka xkochetseshebwetxena
Tie it well, then throw me into the river."

asni impasika obligada chbé yojtsajkaye   150
Then quite thankful he took down the drum,

i choye ibojwatswama bestxabé
and he stuffed the head inside.

yobojtsatjojo yobojtsatjojoye
He took it with him to the river, he took it with him.

ya mallajkta la marokna ch bestxabena xexona yojtetobema
Later far out in the waters that head turned into a child,

[30]line 139: *bestxabé*, "head." The rolling or knocking head is a familiar motif
in South American Indian mythologies (cf. Lowie 1940; Morote Best 1953; Lévi-
Strauss 1978).

[31]line 140: *tsotxe tsotxe*, "Take me back, take me back." The head becomes vexa-
tious, repeating this plaintive demand, and in other versions, knocking rudely
against the calf of the older brother, or even biting him.

[32]line 148: *tamboñerbé majta*, "take down the drum." Most Kamsá houses have a
drum suspended on a wall, to be taken down and played during carnival or when
chicha is being served to a work crew.

xexona yojtetobema
it became a child.

i chokna washabiyayunga shemanga imenawashabiyayunga   155
And there the washerwomen were out washing clothes.

chkabe yojtawabokna imojoshache
Like that it appeared, they caught it.

imojatsuká orna xexonika
When they opened it, a child.

i xexone cha imojontxa wamanana wamanana
And they began to raise, to raise that child.

ooh boyabasa nyetxá mobun yojobocha mobun
Oh, the boy grew very, very quickly.

i cha asna ch lware ch imba shemanga ina shemanga[33]   160
And he, then in that place the heathen women, only women,

ase chngana ndasatebjunga tonday satabjuxe ndbomnunga del todo[34]
then they had no anus, they were completely without the anus.

ntxamo jasan ndoñe imundobena
How to eat, they weren't able to.

i jenana chumbunga nyetxá imenaftsejena
And they had turkeys, they had lots of them.

jashbwana chumbo botamana jashbushtsana i jwexniyana
They would kill a fine turkey, pluck it and place it in the pan.

i chunga jasanema mntxena ana nye ch vapor ch tajwetsa jutseb-mwanayana   165
And to eat the meat they would just gulp the vapor, the steam.

nye chká chngana bida imnabomen
And just like that they found nourishment.

bweno
Fine.

i ch yentxá imojoshubjka cha ch basana bobonsetemna
And those people gave food to that child, that little fellow.

kokaye yojtsesaye ch mntxena txabá yotsesaye
He ate that meat, he ate it fine.

---

[33]line 160: *imba*, "heathen." This is the Kamsá word for "savage" lowlanders, perhaps referencing the tropical forest peoples of the adjacent Amazonian basin.

[34]line 161: *ndasatebjunga*, "they had no anus." This motif appears widely in the north-central Andes and adjacent lowland areas (Bierhorst 1988; Rasnake 1988; Kane 1987).

serta joyebontxayeka yojtsekalay txabá 170
Truly, to put it bluntly, he shat well.

chkana chana tsasañe tsasañe mntxenaka
Like that he was eating, he was eating meat.

asa chore ch mamanga imojuyan karay
Then after a while those mothers were saying: "Damn."

i asna bnga chkana satebjuñe tonday siñalanana inetsosenñalañika
And then they had no anus, only a mark, they were marked.

chorna a vera mas que chayobana xmatabjoka
Then: "Please, even if it kills me, make me a hole there."

i chká yojovalentia ch jovalentiakaye 175
And so they made up their minds, they decided on it.

i ch señalanentxena kochilloka jisatobjwanaye³⁵
And on that mark, with a knife he opened them.

i shnana nday shnana betiyish jatungentsana jtsanatwanaye
And a medicine, which medicine? he chewed some bark and
    rubbed it on them.

iye serta nyengna ndoká i txabá yojtatekja
And truly some of them had no trouble and healed well.

chnga imojontxa ch sayana txabá imojtsetjanmiyanse serta
They began to eat well, truly they could shit.

ajá imojtsobanaka 180
Aha, others died.

bweno
Fine.

chana yojubwashjache mobuna ch bobonse
He quickly came of age, that young man.

inyengna ch imbanga shemashunga chká satabjunga imojtsemna
Some of those heathen women like that were with the anus,

chká podeska i txabá
like that either poorly or well.

ajá i kachiñe bestxabé yojtetinyena benache³⁶ 185
Aha. And again the head found a trail,

kachinga wabaniñe yojtaitinyenaka
again he found a place where something was passing by.

---

³⁵line 176: *kochilloka jisatobjwanaye*, "with a knife he opened them." Here
Wangetsmuna serves as the first Kamsá native doctor.
³⁶line 185: *bestxabé*, "head." Note that the narrator continues to refer to him as
"the head," even though now he has taken the form of a young man.

a chore i chentxe chentxe yojatachumaye ch btsana ijwachmaye[37]
And then there, there, he set a trap, that man set a trap.

i ch biajakna ndoñesna wantxenesha wantxenesha yojatantxa
And he didn't use rope, but made a trap that crushes its prey.

i ch wantxeneshanena an de la warda bejaye mallájta inamna
And by that crushing trap, heaven forbid, there was a great water.

i ch ntsekotema ch bosheko imenaboremediana   190
And that long or short thing, that penis they had there.

chorna boyá imbangana shemangana imnakjanaye[38]
Then the heathen husband, the women were lying there,

i chká serse baká joyebontxayka jensemillama
and like that truly, to speak in vulgar terms, they would copulate.

chká yojtsántxaka as cuando chorna chká yojtsenchenjwana che
    shemangabiama
Like that it was crushed in the trap as it was passing to visit those
    women.

ch busheko chká yojtsenchenjwana iye ch wangesanujena yojtse-
    shaje
That penis like that passed by and it tripped that support.

iya ibojtsenutxe busheko wantxenabek   195
And a heavy log came down on that penis.

ah chora nyetxá yojateshenduntjaye moikna i choikna
Ah, then there was quite a scream on all sides.

chora ch shemanga ch bobonse imojachembo
Then those women called for that young man:

ndayakama taitiko mala tkjapasa
"Why did you do this? Lord, you will be in trouble now,

btse taitabioye kbotsechá
to your grandfather's you must run."

i btse taitabioye imojtsechak   200
And he ran to his grandfather's.

karay serta choka imojarwa ch btsetaitaka
Damn, truly they went to ask for help from that grandfather,

---

[37]line 187: *yojatachumaye*, "he set a trap." This is a different kind of trap from the
one encountered earlier. This trap involves a heavy log hoisted on a support; when
the support is removed, the log falls and crushes its victim.

[38]line 191: *boyá imbangana*, "the heathen husband." The narrator describes here
a collective male organ, long enough to stretch across a wide body of water.

btsetaitana wajwesaiya inamna wajwesaiya[39]
the grandfather was the thunder, the thunder.

i chorna yojobwambaye mntxá
And then he advised him like this:

bweno asna mwentxa kbotseitume
"Like this, fine, now here I will hide you."

lo mismo mallajta btse matabutxe inajajona   205
Right nearby was an enormous earthen jar.

choye ibojtseitume choye yojtsetbemana orna
There he hid, and then he sat down inside there.

**tempo ch boyá iyembangena bobachetstxeka jtsebesjwako
  alambrejká**
Right away those heathen men coiled that penis, they rolled it on a
  pole like wire.

besjwakuyema sersa ch bushekwiyema imnetsenebkutsniye
Coiled truly that penis had to be carried by two men.

chana inochnaye chká pasanan imojashajna
They wanted him, after suffering like that,

tempo cha jtsobama ch wachmanayá jtsobama   210
right away they came to kill that trapper, they came to kill him.

**imojanotisia mwentxa ndwamanya mwentxe tkmonjabwache nd-
  wamanye sobrenaka**
They inquired: "Who came here? Did that bad nephew come to
  visit?"

o ndoknaka
"Nobody came."

i derado mwentxa kmontjabwache ndwamanye sobrenaka[40]
"Most likely he arrived here, that bad nephew."

ndoknaka
"Nobody came."

**nay nye permiso xmatxetá armo ndayeka mwentxa chajtseitemena
  nya ch mataba chentxeka**   215
"Well, just give us permission to look about, he might be hiding in
  that jar over there."

ntijayana ndokenaka ndokenasa
"I already said there is nobody, nobody.

---

[39]line 202: *wajwesaiya*, "the thunder." The young man's grandfather is in fact the
thunder deity, part of a trinity of Andean deities that includes the sun and the culture hero as well (see Demerest 1981).

[40]line 213: *sobrenaka*, "nephew." A general term of reference for a younger man.

nye ndoñe xkochanjakortisia
But you are not going to take my word for it.

chkasa taixmojtatxumboka
Like this maybe you will understand."

shinyaka yojtsatjajo tsinjnujaka[41]
By the fire he picked up a sling.

tempo mntxá yojabwertataye ch beka iyojatekunyaye   220
Right away like that he swung it about, he really let it fly.

i tempo yojajwesika
And right away it thundered:

armas motsemolestanika yojtsejwesa uta
"Yes, keep on making trouble." He thundered a second time.

pobre imbanga yojtsapochoka
The poor heathens were completely finished off.

wajosayá ibojobouweyana impas
The thunder surely defended him.

chora cha yojteta yojobocha choye i imbangoye jtetana
    ndoñe   225
Then he left, he grew up there, and never returned to the heathens.

chora ch btse taitá ibojouyana
Then that grandfather said to him:

bwenoka ndoñe kamwentxe cha kmetsejetana
"Fine, now don't return there, stay here for a while.

ibsa kokaye kochjá nyetsmundo rodiaká kekoshkona[42]
Tomorrow surely you will leave to wander the world.

iye xkochtabwenaye chora ndayamanda kbochjatatxetaya
And you will come and tell me, then I will give you some errands."

bweno   230
Fine.

a de la warda serta ibsana ibojamanda
Heaven forbid, truly at dawn he sent him.

---

[41]line 219: *tsinjnujaka*, "sling." Ordinarily denotes a small woven pocket used to hurl rocks to scare off the parrots that feed on corn. In this and the following lines, the thunder deity is depicted in much the same fashion as his sixteenth-century Incan counterpart (see Cobo 1956), as an awesome figure who wields a sling to produce bolts of lightning and peals of thunder.

[42]line 228: *nyetsmundo rodiaka*, "to wander the world." This is a variant of the familiar theme: the deity commands a junior partner to wander among human beings and report back.

ibojwantxame jatonuxeka i beko barbujate ibojantrega[43]
He lent him a horn, and he gave him a fine short staff,

joshkonama nyetsamundo jarodiamaka
so that he could wander about in the world, so he could walk about
in it.

bweno
Fine.

iye jasama ndayentxe jatema ndayentxe tbojoshuntsena   235
And as for food, wherever the dawn might find him, wherever he
was hungry,

sanama ndoñe palta sanama ndoñe palta
food would not be absent, food would not be absent.

jomena nye ch niñebetema sanana lempi jabomwanamana lempe
All he had to do was raise his staff and there would be food to
swallow.

i jatema ndayentxe fshantsentxe jatema jajatetanika
And wherever on the earth dawn might find him, at dawn he just
had to blow the horn.

tsbananoka asna tsbananok i fshantsokasna fshantsoka
As above, then, above, the same on earth, on earth.

i chká inaye inaye   240
And so on and on he went.

i serto i chká yojajateto
And truly like that he blew the horn again.

**tsbananoka imojontxe ena bayungentxeka iye fshantsokasna
   ndokaka**
From above all kinds of fowl started to appear on earth, like
nothing.

i chká inaye kabana yojabokna wajchonjema inoyenentxeka
And like that he wandered until at last he appeared where a poor
orphan lived,

wajchona shembasaka shembasa wajchona inamnaka
an orphan girl, an orphan girl, it was.

chore ibojauyana   245
Then he said to her:

---

[43]line 232: *jatonuxeka*, "horn." Horns fashioned from cattle horns, sugar-cane
stalks, and conch shells are still sounded during the Kamsá carnival. *barbujate*,
"staff." Throughout much of the Andes, indigenous political office is marked by the
possession of a ceremonial staff.

i kanyaka an chaka taitá mama
"And all alone? Your father, mother?"

atxebe changa wabtxanga lempe bayá tojtsañika lempe impas
"My brothers and sisters were eaten by a beast, completely, forever.

nye atxe tstsajamnika
Only I remain."

apayka
"What a pity!

bweno mwentxe posada kwaxkwantxame mwentxa
    xjuftseteyekna   250
Well, here you gave me lodging, here I awoke this morning.

mora kochjawantasa
Now you must be strong.

asna tsemioka matebaña kbochjawotsjatseya
Now you must go and hide inside that jar in the attic.

chká akabe taitá mama akabe wabtxunga lempe ch jiseshjango
Like that your father, mother, your brothers and sisters will surely
    arrive.

kbochjesentregay i koisatsjatsana
I will return them to you but you must remain covered."

iye txenuxe ch jtskjaye⁴⁴   255
And he arranged the benches for them.

kmochjabochwaye iye atxe chjojwa
"They will arrive greeting and I will answer.

i atxe ketsjaordena ora kbochtustjango
And when I tell you to, you will come down.

akabe taitá lempe ainungaka
Your father completely alive,

bweno chká konforme inetsiñe konformaka
fine, just as he was in life, just like that.

pero kochjawantaka   260
But you must be strong."

sertoka ch shjokana yojajatutoka yojajatutoye
Truly from that patio he blew the horn, he blew it.

ndoñe ratoye tempo imnatababana basenga imnanatsana
Before long, right away they arrived, the little ones came ahead.

⁴⁴line 255: *txenuxe*, "bench." In addition to small wooden stools, Kamsá living
quarters often contain long plank benches that are placed against the walls of public
rooms.

ch wabochena ch menor ntxam primero ch ntxamo ch bayá ibojasa
That sister, the younger one, first, the beast had eaten her.

i chká lempe imojtashjajna
And like that they all arrived.

aray kaba tsatsuntsaka   265
Damn! finally they came to the middle of the room.

imojtsataye orna ah taitá mama taitá mamaka
As they arrived: "Ah Father, Mother, Father, Mother."

orna tsbananokana ch matebusheka yojtsotsetsatxe
Then from above that jar fell with her inside it.

de contenta xachenaka yojtsotsetsatxe
From happiness, in tears, she fell:

taitá mama taitá mama kwaxmuntashjajnakaye
"Father, Mother, Father, Mother, you have really come back to me!"

impas imojtsosaisobokañe i chnga tsnunakwanga kem
    lware[45]   270
Forever they vanished, and they became parrots in this world,

impasna tsunakwanga imojtsaisongwebubjoñe
forever as parrots they flew off.

i chore ch wangetsmuna wabainana ndayama chkaka[46]
And then that Wangetsmuna, as he is known: "Why did you do
    that?

chká ch kubunjawiyana
Like that I told you."

impas chká kausa ch tsunakwanga kamjena chká disobediente
    kausaka[47]
Forever because of that the parrots exist, thus because of her
    disobedience.

ajá i chentxana yojataka yojatabokna inyoka inetsieña   275
Aha, and from there he left, he arrived where others lived.

---

[45]line 270: *tsnunakwanga*, "parrots." A species of parrot visits the Sibundoy Valley to feed on its corn. The Kamsá view parrots and other animals who share our appetites with special regard. They maintain that parrots were formerly people; that's why they are so fond of corn.

[46]line 272: For the first time the narrator refers to this transforming character as Wangetsmuna.

[47]line 274: *chká kausa*, "because of that. . ." The narrator sees this episode as explaining the origin of parrots in the world; it could also be taken as an explanation for the relentless fact of death.

ana ch poblangoka yojabokanaka[48]
He arrived in Santiago.

komenderungaka chnga chora imojwajwatxiye
The monkeys then threw him a feast.

tswambiana yojtsasayika chká
Like that he ate chicken.

chor kwatstatxumbona taita bakona ndomokañe[49]
Then they inquired of him: "Father Uncle, where are you coming
from?

i kwabo keketsetatxumbo serta mora taiwabó wangetsmuna wa-
baina kemaboka   280
And maybe you know if truly he comes now, the one called
Wangetsmuna?"

chana kachay inamna chká imojayana kausna
He was the very same one, so he told them so.

ajá chteskana cha jebiajwamna
Aha, from that day in order to please him:

atxena mntxaka biaja imnabwajonyana jochebonjama[50]
"Like this I will swing on this hanging rope.

mwentxe jotebemana
You sit down here."

i betsko jojwantsuntxanaye asta ndomoka jaftsechebunjana   285
And quickly he pushed off to swing far over there,

i jitisebayana kamtxoye i jabwastotañe
and he returned to the same place, he scraped his bottom.

mntxá wangetsmuna jebiajwama tsobatmanaka
Like that they hoped to please Wangetsmuna.

i chká kausa teskana ni masa chngana yentxana ndoñe
And for that reason from that day they were no longer people.

imontjobenaye jtobeman impase komendero
They became and have remained forever monkeys.

---

[48]line 276: *poblangoka*, "Santiago." The Kamsá term for Santiago, the home of the
Ingano Indians of the Sibundoy Valley, comes from the Spanish word, *pueblo*,
"town." A certain bias against the Inganos can be detected in references to them in
Kamsá mythic narrative.

[49]line 279: *taita bakona*, "Father Uncle." The respectful form of address to an older
man. (The *-na* is a narrative morpheme).

[50]line 283: *imnabwajonyana jochebonjama*, "I will swing on this hanging rope." A
similar episode is recounted in the *Popol Vuh* to explain the origin of the monkeys.

ch komenderunga ch betiyiñe chká imenoyena ch biajaka   290
Those monkeys like that live in the trees on those vines.

i ko serta nye biajeñe mochandebetsjenunga
Those vines, and so truly they travel hanging on those vines.

chká kasteo yojtsatxataye wangetsmunaka
That's the punishment Wangetsmuna gave them.

ibañe chká inaye nye wangetsmuna asta watetay
He walked to several places, Wangetsmuna, until the year was
    finished.

yotaisashjango ch wajosayabioye
He arrived to the place of the thunder:

i more cha bndata boisatenuta nyets utata   295
"And now let's stay together, the two of us."

chieka uta wajosayata kabunamuna[51]
So there are two thunders.

chká tijaparla ch wangetsmunabiama
Like that I have told of Wangetsmuna.

(m3) wangetsmunabiana
About Wangetsmuna

As performed by Estanislao Chicunque, in Kamsá, December 1978

We visited Estanislao Chicunque, taita Mariano's nephew, at his home
on a sunny December day. All was quiet around the house as the other
members of the household were out working in the fields. Estanislao
received Justo with a gesture of courtesy and we sat down to hear tales
of the old days.

   This performance of the Wangetsmuna cycle conforms in broad out-
line to the three-phased trajectory of Wangetsmuna's life as presented in
taita Mariano's version (m2). But there are important differences as
well, attesting to the flexibility of narrative tradition even when the
storytellers are members of the same extended family. Estanislao's telling omits some episodes that are present in his uncle's, provides alternative renderings of others, and includes some episodes that are
missing altogether from his uncle's performance. If the two men received this story from the same source, as seems likely, these differences
reflect the personal relationship forged by each raconteur with his materials. One episode or detail caught the fancy of one man, another re-

---

[51]line 296: *uta wajosayata kabunamuna*, "there are two thunders." Kamsá elders
explain that one often hears two thunder claps, and this proves that Wangetsmuna
returned to stay with his grandfather.

mains salient in the mind of the other. Myths are open narrative structures, susceptible to voluntary and involuntary modification as they persist in individual performance repertories.

Juxtaposing the two performances of the Wangetsmuna cycle illuminates additional dimensions of the underlying story. Estanislao's version starts with three orphans, two brothers and a sister; the sister spins thread, thereby serving as a primordial model for the women who maintain the weaving tradition today in the valley. This version dispenses with the episode involving the miner and the moon; instead, the younger brother's curiosity is aroused when he hears his brother conversing with the *chiwako*, a large black bird with yellow feet and beak (line 7). The younger brother is transformed into a woman after sitting on his sister's stool and receiving a bite from a large earthworm (line 21). Estanislao provides additional details concerning the work of the older brother, the miner: we learn that he forges golden objects at the behest of the thunder (line 30). Later we will observe the thunder making use of these objects in his wrath against the heathens (line 158). Estanislao tells us that the last animal to come by the river, the prickly one, is known in Spanish as *cajero*, "the drummer" (line 48).

In Estanislao's version, the lowland heathens are characterized as mule-like; some of them are said to live "under the earth, under the river" (line 84). The drum comes to rest in the swirling foam at the edge of the river, and a heathen takes it home, opens it, and decides to raise the "beautiful" child inside it (line 92). In this version Wangetsmuna is first forgiven for trapping the heathen penis; only when he repeats this travesty is he rushed off for protection at the dwelling of his grandfather, the thunder. Estanislao also gives us useful information about the third phase of Wangetsmuna's trajectory, his visiting of the world. The thunder endows him with his name: "You will be called Wangetsmuna" (line 166) and provides him with extensive instructions regarding the voices and habits he must confer on the animals. This version of the myth contains the remarkable moment of ontological demarcation (lines 180-83):

> At the next dawn he had to sound the trumpet
> Whatever day it was, we humans in God's world,
> we humans became people for all time,
> the animals remained animal from that time on.

This seminal event is implied but not fully stated in the other versions of this story. It is Estanislao who interpolates into the Wangetsmuna cycle the well-traveled episode of questions put to the farmers (see the notes to m12 in this collection). Finally, Estanislao makes clear the identity of the protagonist of the cycle (line 215), saying, "He, Wangetsmuna, he was Our Lord."

wangetsmuna wabainana ana mntxá chabe barina
Wangetsmuna, as he is called, goes like this, for his part.

mntxá unga wajchunga imoftsokedá melwar[52]
Thus three orphans remained in this world.

kanyana ana waben ana wabena inamna[53]
One of them a sister, a sister she was.

i utatena kanyana bjakayá yanyana waubwayá
And the other two, one a miner, the other a cook.

ch wangetsmuna jutsenana ndayá bjakayabe wabentsá bjakayabe wabentsá[54]   5
That Wangetsmuna would be the miner's younger brother, the miner's younger brother.

cha chabkwaloftaka yebunenakwentaye tjoka bjakayoka[55]
He was conversing with the chiwako in the mountains by the mine.

i chana mntxá jutsenabestxakwatjonan
And he lay there like that with his head propped up,

jutsetsuntxiñana kukwatxeka jutsobestxatsebanañanaka
using his hand as a pillow, he lay there with his head propped up.

i chorna ch wabentsana jutsewenanaka
And then that younger brother heard them talking:

ntxamo jutsemana ndayaftaksa ibwenokwenta   10
"What's that? Who was he speaking to?

ndasa ndmwana nemunaka[56]
Who could it be?"

a vera biena ndayasa yochtachnungo tondayana yendomunaka
He wondered who might have come, nobody was there.

iye ch wabenena jutsoshabiamunañanika jutsoshabiamunañana[57]
And that sister was spinning thread, she was spinning thread.

---

[52]line 2: *melwar*, from the Spanish "lugar" with an aborted Kamsá prefix, *kem*, meaning "this." A cosmology-laden word indicating the world inhabited by human beings and under the watch of *taita dios*, Our Lord.

[53]line 3: *waben*, "sister." Estanislao's version includes a primordial sister, but she is given little to do other than spin thread.

[54]line 5: Wangetsmuna is named at the outset of this telling. In Mariano's version the name is withheld at the outset.

[55]line 6: *chabkwaloftaka*, "with the chiwako." The *chiwako*, according to Justo, is a black bird with yellow beak and feet; it "says its prayers" at five in the morning.

[56]line 11: *ndasa ndmwana nemunaka*, "Who could it be?" This line is whispered, just as the protagonist might have whispered it to himself at this suspenseful moment.

[57]lines 12, 13: These lines are spoken in a subdued tone of voice.

la warda trabajo taiteko iye ch opatswaubjoná⁵⁸
Heaven forbid, what a thing, my lord, that crazy brother,

a chana yojoftsetsebana ch wabenena 15
now she had gotten up, that sister,

a asna txenexoikna inatobjona
and then there was a hole in the stool.

**chorna cha yojatotebema txenuxe chuwabena tebemana txenuxe ch
    wabena**
Then he went to sit on the stool where she would sit, on the sister's
stool.

chorna ch jwaxoikna chujna inawaxaja
Then his bottom was bare.

yojtojayé orna ch jwaxatubjoikana ibojatsasjochumomunaye
When he sat there with his rear over that hole, he felt something
prick him.

ah yojtswatjana mntxá yojaisobwatsjexiye orna 20
Ah, he was frightened. Thus when he began to look around,

ah fchekoyemaka ibojoftsabinyna
ah, he saw a large earthworm.

impaseka yojtacha ay impasa yojtachajema bnoka
Right there he took off, ay, right there he took off into the distance,

chká loco ch wabtxejema wabentsanaka
crazy like that, that poor brother, that younger brother.

i wabochenana jitsoñana bjakayoye
And the older brother would go to the mine.

bweno 25
Well.

chana kadenojwa wapormayá ch kastellanujwa⁵⁹
He forged a chain of gold,

ya cha yojwaporma ch kastellanojwa botamán
already he forged a beautiful golden chain.

morkokayé ntxamo mases
"Now what else?"

---

⁵⁸line 14: *la warda*, "Heaven forbid." This is a Kamsá exclamation apparently derived from the Spanish, *dios le guarde*, "God protect you."

⁵⁹line 26: *kadenojwa wapormayá ch kastellanujwa*, "He forged a chain of gold." Here
the miner's work is presented as a crafting of gold objects. Lines 29 and 30 make it
clear that the miner is working for the thunder deity.

morna mntxaka unga masebé kochjapormaka
"Now thus you will make three mallets."

iye mntxá koisemandana wajusayana unga jutsemañana   30
And like that he commanded, the thunder, there must be three.

iye ch inyebena ana jatsebwetxanaka
And that other fellow, he will just have to discard him.

ch bestxabé yojtsechjangwa cha ch despedido wabentsá
That head, he acted badly, he, that younger brother,

chana yojtsechjangwa mala yojtsechjangwa
he acted badly, he misbehaved.

shembasa obiamnaykausa ch wabochená rondankausna
He turned into a woman for spying on that older brother, for going
    around like that.

shembasa yojtsebokna shembasa yojtsebokunakausna   35
He became a woman, for that he became a woman.

ibojabwayena mntxá shnana kutsemna
He explained it to him like this: "There is a cure.

ndayama chká tkjobwachjangwa
But why did you behave like that?

ndayama chká kaftsengwaye
Why do you spy on me like that?

mora tondaye mase shnana kwatjinyina
Now you will surely find no other remedy.

nyetskana bayungabe benachentxna butachjakna   40
In the path of all the beasts, on the trail,

joshnana inamntjaja kochjojajwa
to be cured you must lie down, face-up and naked.

bayunga kochjontxa jachinajnan
The beasts will start to pass by,

kanye jabjon kanye jabjon kanye jabjon[60]
each one taking a lick, taking a lick, taking a lick.

nyetskana bayunga jinero cha kmochjachnujna batesajana
All the beasts will pass over your legs,

asa libre koisokedá[61]   45
then you will be free.

[60]line 43: *kanye jabjon kanye jabjon kanye jabjon*, "each one taking a lick, taking a
lick, taking a lick." The storyteller makes this sequence iconic by repeating his verbal
account of the repetitive action.

[61]lines 37-45: These lines in which the older brother counsels and instructs his
younger brother are spoken in an allegro pacing.

ultimamentna kwabaina ana ichimasheka[62]
The last one is called the *ichimashe.*

ichimashena ochmaxushe chushe stonoka kochjabayobonjnaye[63]
The *ichimashe,* a prickly one, that one, you will come moving behind
   the others.

kajeroka kwabainaka
The drummer he is surely called.

chikjowenajemaka ibojatjayika aiñeka
Do you hear me?" He answered: "Yes."

chana ochmaxeshe komena chakjwenochjexpega   50
"That one is prickly, he is about to strike you,

impasa cha kanye jantsana cha kmochanjisatutjo[64]
quite a bite he will take from you,

kanye ora kmochanjisetabe kochjishekwanaka
then you will throw him aside, you will make him run."

chora chjemna ntxamo jutsemanana
Then that poor fellow, what can he do?

iya chexe lisianjema yojalimpia orna
And that prickly one left him wounded then.

i ch ichmaxe yojaye yojachjexabajto   55
And that prickly one came, he scratched him.

yojtsenochjexshebjwajema
He came to strike him.

ibojtsawatjana ndoñe yenjawanta ibojtsechamoye
He feared him, he couldn't stand it, he ran off.

chora chentxana kanye ibojoftsejantsay
Then from there he came to take a bite,

iye nyctskan bayunga imojisachnujana
And all the beasts passed by again,

kanye jantsan kanye jantsan kanye jantsan kanye jantsan[65] 60
taking a bite, taking a bite, taking a bite, taking a bite.

[62]line 46: *ichimasheka.* This is the name Estanislao provides for the mysterious
animal with the sharp claws. In line 48 he refers to this critter as the *kajero,* from the
Spanish for "drummer."

[63]line 47: *kochjabayobonjnaye,* "you will come moving." The narrator has the
miner address this animal directly, lending the passage a distinctly prophetic tone.

[64]line 51: *kmochanjisatutjo,* "he will take a bite from you." Again (as in line 47) the
storyteller adopts an unusual point of view, addressing the protagonist in the second
person. Perhaps this passage is simply a continuation of the older brother's advice or
prescription to his younger brother.

[65]line 60: *kanye jantsan kanye jantsan kanye jantsan kanye jantsan.* As in the licking
episode (line 43), this biting is made iconic in the repeated phrases.

bweno
Well.

chorna ntxamo remidio chjemna lempe impase imojtsoshañe
Then without remedy they completely devoured that poor fellow,

jabjonan jantsanan jantsanan jantsanan[66]
licking him, biting him, biting him, biting him.

chorkokayé nye bestxatema imojisajan
And right then they left only the little head intact.

chora bjakayokana inataye ch wabochena   65
Then that older brother arrived from the mine.

chorna ch bestxabé yojabato juntsentxutje
Then that head came knocking against his calf:

xmeisokeñe xmeisokeñe xmeisokeñe xmeisokiñeka[67]
"Take me with you, take me with you, take me with you, take me
   with you."

i achká ibonatostona
And like that he followed behind.

chana jaisetjajwana jisabentana o jaisajshabentana
The other one grabs him, he throws him, he throws him away,

ndomoyka podeska jshemanashoye jutisajshengwebjana   70
where, to the ugliest place, he sent him flying.

i choikana jtabatsbokenajemanaka i chká ibonatastona
And from there the poor thing came out again, and he followed
   behind.

la finalna trato ibojenabema
At last he offered him a deal:

biena mntxataye pabor xkwatjabemaka
"Well, perhaps you will do me this favor."

bwenoka tonday mase ch ungamenanasa
"Fine." "To put an end to this bother,

ch tsuma xunjanabé choye xkoisatwamajema   75
inside that drum, there you must place me."

ch bestxabé ibojwatswama ch xunjanabioy
That head he surely placed inside the drum.

---

[66]line 63: *jantsanan*, "licking him." This is surely a mistake on the narrator's part,
who meant to say *jabjonan*, "biting him."

[67]line 67: *xmeisokeñe xmeisokeñe xmeisokeñe xmeisokiñeka*. The narrator captures the
head's persistence by stating four times its request, "Take me with you."

iye jaotsubutxenana bejayoye
And he threw it into the river.

i ch bejayokna bejaiñe inobwaye
And in that river, in the river the water flowed.

i choka yojaotsebwajwa ch xunjanabé ch bestxabeka
And there he placed that drum, with the head.

iye cha yojatujo imbanga imenawaserñiaye[68] 80
And it carried him to where the heathens were sifting sand.

ch mulangaka ch bejaye jashenoye ndosatubjunga tonday[69]
Those mules live under the river, they have no anus, nothing.

i melwarna satubjunga imenámena
And in this world they were without the anus.

imenoyena juboye mntxá fshantsoye
Some of them lived like that on top of the earth.

i anyengna fshantsa jashenoye bejaye jashenoye
And the others lived under the earth, under the river.

chorerentxe yojotsalxeka ch xunjanatema imenawaserñiaye 85
The current deposited that little drum where they were sifting sand.

chokna mntxá yojtsotsobobwertana
There like that it spun about,

bweno yojtsotsobobwertana shashiyiñe chbé
well, it spun about in the foam, that round thing.

ch imbana betsko yojokuñe ch xunjanabeka
The heathen quickly picked up that drum.

yojabonye yojoftsokiñe ch xunjanabeka
He saw it, he went to pick up that drum.

yojtay ch bobonaye yojwamba ch oyenoye 90
He went along beating the drum, he took it home.

a chora chana kwaotsekaka ch xunjanatema
And then he surely removed the top of that drum.

a chorna xexonatema betsoixajoñeka nyetxá shabotamanatxeka[70]
And then a little boy appeared, a very pretty fellow.

[68]line 80: *imenawaserñiaye*, "they were sifting sand." I have no explanation for this curious detail.

[69]line 81: *mulangaka*, "mules." The narrator characterizes the heathens as "mules," a generic term for (lowly) non-humans. *bejaye jashenoye*, "they live under the river." This motif is reminiscent of "the world upside down," and in fact, the heathens do many things contrary to accepted custom.

[70]line 92: *nyetxá shabotamanatxeka*, "a very pretty fellow." The Inga variant, *Calusterinda Yaya*, describes this baby as fair-skinned and blond, thus possibly Spanish. But the Kamsá variants make no such move.

ah ndoñe mase jaftsenaboshjonakaka xexona nyetxá shabotamana-tema
Ah, he couldn't just abandon that beautiful little babe.

ibojokuñetema ibojontxá jabobochan
He took the little fellow in, he began to raise him.

iye mobuna cha yojontxá jotsebanana   95
And rapidly he began to grow.

yongentxe yojtsemenatema
It was in the hot lands.

patronangna jwabwana fshenduxe blandutxa jashebwana
His hosts would cook yucca, plantains, they would slaughter animals.

chngna ana ndayá ch waixneneshoye nyemtxaka huhká huhká
They would, what, approach the pot to eat (gulps twice).

chká jasamenaka nye ch shachenaka shachenaka
Like that they would feed themselves, only on the steam, only on the steam.

kachká kukwatxeka jasamna ndoñe   100
Like that, they wouldn't eat with their hands.

nye ch waixnenushoye nye chká shachinaka bida imenabomna
Only the pot they would approach, only like that with the steam, they nourished themselves.

ya btsatema yojtsemna orna ch shabiamanubjaka yojobongumuchá yerubjaka
Then when he was grown he filed a spinning needle like iron.

chká imenaseñalán chká yojtsabonyana
Like that they were marked, like that he saw them.

chana kanyana ibojarwaka
One of them came to ask him:

i kondosaka malaye atxe stjutsesayika   105
"And as you eat, please, so I would like to eat."

ñemosna kabatjasatubjwaka
"If you are brave I will make an opening for you."

ibojasatubjwa i serto ibojobenaye jasatubjwana cha
He made an opening and truly he was able to shit, that one.

i chore chana ibojontxá parejo jasana
And then he began just like the other to eat.

ya sayá yojabokuna ch yimbana ch imbá
Then they ate together, that heathen, that heathen.

i ya inya inya ch patronanga chká yojtsshnañeka 110
And then others, others of those hosts, like that he cured them.

yojasatubjoye iye ya saynga imojabokna
He made them an opening and they became eaters.

i chana ya btsá
And he was already grown up,

chorna chana jwabna ibojushebé
then he made a mistake of judgment.

benache inawambana ya bobonsetema yojtsemenana
There was a path, he was now a young man.

benache inawamban[71] 115
There was a path.

chana yojtsejwabenaye ndayá bayá mojana i kwabana ching-
wanoikana
He wondered: "What beast is this that passes back and forth?"

ch bayá yemba mntxá ch bayuja a chntsko lotxuja inabomna
That heathen beast, like that the beast, he had a long penis.

chká jutsambañan inyek shemangaka inyek boyangaka chká im-
namnaka
Like that they would do it, the women on one side, the men on the
other side, like that they were.

jwantxas ch mntxasa wantxeniñe mntxá ibojtsashngutsewenuntxe
A trap, like that in the trap, the tip was crushed in the trap.

tsuntseto ora cha konduntjaka[72] 120
At midnight he howled with pain.

chorna ibojaweyana ch ndweñe
Then they said to him, those hosts:

de la warda ntxamo mexexona impasaka
"God save us, what have you done, child?

taiteko ch bayunga mala toktsakedaka[73]
Lord, those beasts have been damaged.

i morna ndomoye mwatjechumwajemaka
And now, where are we going to send you?

[71]lines 114-15: These lines are spoken in a stage whisper.
[72]line 120: *tsuntseto ora*, "at midnight." The Kamsá pay special attention to the
phases of the day; some are thought to be spiritually auspicious, others not. Midnight is seen as a spiritually difficult time, just as twelve noon, at the apex of the sun,
is thought to be beneficial.
[73]line 123: *bayunga*, "beasts." Here the narrator has the heathens refer to themselves as "beasts."

ko kochjaboye chora ch ndweñangena[74]   125
They will come here looking for you now, those owners."

imojtsobweitume imojtsenengañe
They hid him, they denied having him:

ndokená mwentxe kenatsmuna tokutsoñajema
"He is not here, he went away."

ne nya mwentxe kutsomiñeka
"No, he must be here."

chana batxa rebajoñeyekna imojtseperdonaka
But they insisted only a while, they let him be.

i ndoñeka ibsana imojabwayenatemaka   130
And no, the next day they advised him:

ndoñe chká batamajemanasna mwanjutseshbwajemaka[75]
"Don't be doing like this, they could come and kill you."

iye ch xexona ndoñe ibonjutswenana
And that boy did not listen to them.

inyoye yojatuchumo i choka chká inetsatajtsañetema
He went off and there, like that, he walked in the mountains.

inyoka kachká yojatantxa benache yojatinyena
In another place like that he set a trap, he found a path.

tsuntseto orna serta yojatsetushendontjaye   135
At midnight truly there came a great shout.

mo kem mundo babonjo nyetxá yojoteshioyeka
This entire earth trembled.

chorna ndweñangena imojaweyanaka morna ndoñe mwatjobenaye
Then his hosts said to him: "Now we cannot help you."

ibojowiyana morna btse taitabioye koisachajema
They told him: "Now you must go to your grandfather's.

btse taitá kochjetserua cha kmotsobweitumaka
You must ask your grandfather to hide you."

chngena imojwanatsa btse taitabioy btse taitabioy
   imojarua   140
They took him to grandfather's, they begged his grandfather:

xmutsebwetumajema
"Hide him for us."

---

[74]line 125: *ndweñangena*, "owners." A key word in Kamsá thought; owners are masters or those who maintain spiritual power over a domain.
[75]line 131: Whispered in awe.

ntjutseyamiknanasna moye motseboñetemaka xexona
"If it doesn't repulse you, come here child.

moye kema tajtsoye mosha kem silletushaka
Come under here, come under this chair."

inetsojakeñe ch wajosayá
He was seated there, the thunder.

tajtsoye yebojtsobochekwa choyina 145
He crawled underneath where he was sitting.

tjamana uftsotbontsañikamaniñe ntxamo katjutsoyamiyeka
There the turds were scattered all about: "I hope you can stand it."

bweno choye yojtseitumena orna
Well. There when he hid himself,

chora ch biajasha imenabayene bkutsnaka palankashiñeka ch bayunga
then they came along carrying it among several on a long pole, those beasts.

ch btse taitana imojauyana derado okasiona[76]
They said to that grandfather: "Verily we have a complaint.

mntxena ch obxexona diosa kbuntjabolisensia 150
Look what that wicked child has done. Please hand him over."

ndokenaka yojtsengañe yojtsobwetamiñe
"He isn't here." He lied to them, he turned them down.

ndokena mwentxe omena ndokena
"He isn't here, he isn't here.

tonday mwentxe notisia kenatsemuna
We have no word of him here."

neborla nya mwentxe kutsemenaka
"Don't fool with us, he is certainly here.

ndoñe mondetayinjana kmochjapalankaka 155
If you don't give him to us, we will lift you off your chair."

imojotxatjayiná ch imbanga
They were angry, those heathens.

a ver xmopalankaka
"Fine, let's see you lift me."

chorna ch tsenjnuja yojwakaka yojantsenja
Then he picked up that sling, he swung it about.

---

[76]line 149: *derado okasiona* "verily a complaint." This is the ritual language formula for pressing a grievance.

iye lempe chjemunga ch tkunyujaka yojobaye lempe impase
And those poor creatures were completely wiped out with those
   thunderbolts.

ch ora ch ndetxebe kastellanuxe kastellanubeka
   yojawarakia[77]   160
At that time that rock of gold, that ball of gold, he spun about.

lempe yojtsobaye ndoñe imonjobenaye ch yembanga
He completely destroyed them, those heathens couldn't stand it.

ch mayora jaftsebonjwan jobana
They couldn't move that elder to kill the young man.

ndoñe ni japalankan ndoñe ibojtsobolibra xexona
They couldn't even lift him, no, he saved that boy.

chora ch btse taitana ibojamanda kema trompetubjwa[78]
Then the grandfather sent him into the world with a trumpet:

kbantxabwaché nyets lware kochjapasia   165
"You will visit the world, to all places you will travel.

kochantsabaina wangetsmunaka[79]
You will be called Wangetsmuna.

chká bayinga kochjiyatena chká kochjiyenoyebaye[80]
Like this you will go among the beasts, like this you will defend
   yourself with an incantation.

i mntxasa kmochjibobinynaka bayunga
And like that you will survive among the beasts.

kochjoprontaye chká kochjayajemaka
Prepare yourself, like this you must travel.

mamaxna mntxaka kochanjebiajwa wangetsmunaka[81]   170
The weasel like this you must make her laugh, Wangetsmuna,

iyendona mntxaka mntxá chanjebiajwaka monona
the squirrel like this, like this you will make the monkey laugh,

---

[77]line 160: *kastellanubeka*, "ball of gold." Here we see a use for the gold objects
crafted by the miner.

[78]line 164: *trompetubjwa*, "trumpet." In former days the Kamsá made use of an
indigenous trumpet that consisted of a horn placed at the end of a long blowing
tube. This instrument has recently disappeared from the valley.

[79]line 166: *kochantsabaina wangetsmunaka*, "you will be called Wangetsmuna."
Here the narrator portrays the thunder as name giver to the culture hero.

[80]line 167: *kochjiyenoyebaye*, "you will utter an incantation." Unfortunately, we
have no record of the content of this charm.

[81]line 170: *mamaxna mntxaka kochanjebiajwa*, "like that you must make the weasel
laugh." Through lines 177, Wangetsmuna is portrayed as a giver of habits and voices
to the animals.

mntxaka osungatxiyeka chkurobjwa nyetxaka chubjna ko che twamba jashbwanaka
like that the weasel, the weasel surely, that one kills the hen there,

iye ch wasasha jetsasubjusasanika
and that rump is eaten first.

chuja chorna ibojayabojwaka
That one then squealed.

mamaxna kachkaka ana jashbwana ch twamba 175
The weasel like that she kills the hen,

ibojatsyabojwa choka yojabokna dañino ch osungutxiye
she squealed at her, there she turned out harmful, that weasel.

kach maldision txetaná
You must lay a curse on her.

monona ndoñe ana ch shekenajeñe biajuñe joftsubtxiyana
The monkey, no, he must hang on that rope, on that vine,

jotajsbinyianana chká jotajseitunjanana
he must fly, like that he must fly."

ntxamo jiyebinyentena trompetubjwana jiwajatulanaka jiyana 180
At the next dawn he had to sound the trumpet.

ndaité kejutsemntena iye bnga naturala melware diosa[82]
Whatever day it was, we humans in God's world,

ibojuftsabashejwankana bnga naturala yentxanga
we humans became people for all time,

bayingena yojaisakedá chentxena ya
the animals remained animal from that time on.

chorna ch yentxangoye yojtabokna
Then he appeared where those people lived.

chokna ibojtatjaye ndayá kjenaka 185
There he asked them: "What are you planting?"

ndtxebeka impas ena peñutxe inye ibsana
"Rocks." The next day, nothing but rocks.

inyoikaka ndayá kjenaka xbwachanatema
At another place: "What are you planting?" "Little corn plants."

---

[82]line 181: *bnga naturala yentxanga*, "we people of the valley, people." A fateful line of demarcation separates humans from the animals. "We people of the valley" captures the connotations of *bnga naturala*, a term that is used by the Kamsá with some irony to refer to themselves. Since colonial days the Indians of the Andes have been dismissed as *naturales*, "natural people."

achalay ibsana jabinynana lempe[83]
Wow, the next day on waking, plenty of it.

inyokna de ombre bomotema tsjenaka
At another place: "Upon my word, I plant potatoes."

**i txabá jonanjana ch wangetsmuna jaftsalkansana posado jibema-
naka**   190
And well he treated them, that Wangetsmuna, where they gave him
food and lodging.

i txabaka inyokna koibokna inye ibsana
And safely he came to another place the next day:

ndayam mwentxe kjenaka inyuwashaka
"What are you planting here?" "Reeds."

nye chká jibinynana inyuwasha tonday bien ena inyuwashaka
Only like that to awake, reeds, nothing good, pure reeds.

ndtxebeka ibojojwa chentxena ena peñuntxe
They answered "rocks," there nothing but rocks,

tonday jasama injabinyna   195
they awoke to nothing to eat.

i chká imenajna chká bida inayobomiñe maldisionaka[84]
And like that they were, like that he lived pronouncing judgments.

**ultimamentena katoika jtanajema welajemabioka wangetsmuna
yojashjango**[85]
At last Wangetsmuna arrived at the home of an old lady blind in
both eyes.

posada xmuntsantxame btse mamaka ibojawiyanaka
"Let me stay with you, Grandmother," he said to her.

apayajemaka amo taitasa i kotsomiñe
"By Our Lord. And wouldn't you be Our Father?"

ch jtanajemena ibojaboshtseñe ch twamba despedida[86]   200
That poor blind woman plucked her last hen.

kanyetema ibonawamenajemnaka
Only one little hen remained to her.

---

[83]line 188: *achalay*, exclamation for something good.
[84]line 196: *inayobomiñe maldisionaka*, "giving judgments." It is stated clearly that
Wangetsmuna went about establishing precedents.
[85]line 197: *welajemabioka*, "place of the old hag." Here we encounter the word
welaj in its benevolent meaning; it can also signify a "witch" in the sense of "an evil
old woman."
[86]line 200: *twamben despedida*, "last hen." The Spanish word, *despedida*, takes on
the meaning "last, final" as an adjective in Kamsá constructions.

ibojoboshtse ibojontxa jajabiana
She plucked it, she began to wash it.

moknoye jwambana chjema nye ndoñe yenjotstatxumbo
That poor woman hardly knew where to wash it.

owenanana ibojtsanbayika
She followed her ear.

pero ch plumeshamuna ibojawiyana biakotemiñe biakotemiñe 205
"But those feathers," he said to her, "in a small basket, in a small
    basket.

moboshtsajema koisabwatsjatseka
Pluck the hen, cover the basket.

ibse bominye kochajajwaka
Tomorrow you will see with your eyes."

i serta ibojawiyana
And truly he said to her:

ch ndereche chorerotema konswenan
"Right there, that little stream you are hearing.

ndereche motsá i choka kochjajabiaka 					210
Go straight there and wash your face in the water.

chora primero kochjeshetsobuchjabiajemaka
Then first go and wash your face in that water."

yojtsobochjabiaye ibojwabinyna
She washed her face, she could see.

ch twamba boshtsena serto iye ibojoisobojabia ibojawaixniye
Those hen feathers, truly she washed the hen, she put it on to cook.

chore ch wangetsmuna yojtsetcbemana
Then that Wangetsmuna sat down.

chana wangetsmuna bngage taitá inamna[87] 					215
He, Wangetsmuna, he was Our Father.

chore ultimo dia milagro ibjatsebema chentxe[88]
Then on the last day he performed there again a miracle,

ch btse mamajementxe
at the grandmother's place.

ibsana ibojabobinyentena
The next day she arose to recover her vision.

---

[87]line 215: *chana wangetsmuna bngage taitá inamena*, "He, Wangetsmuna, he was
Our Father." The narrator connects Wangetsmuna with the sun (also known as
bngabe taita, Our Lord) and with the Christian God.

[88]line 216: *milagro*, the Spanish word for "miracle." Here the narrator uses the
language associated with Jesus Christ of the Christian Bible.

ana twabunga plumetemunga ketsabinyañeka
The feathers turned into hens,

bashetemasna basetema i btsashasna btsa   220
the little feathers, small ones, the big feathers, big ones.

lempe de todo plumusha inawamenká chká boletotemunga
Just as the feathers were, like that the chicks.

ibojoremediá xbwachanatema ibojoremediá yojtsusana
She found corn, she found it, it was standing.

mnteskana chká kochjoftsebinyana mntskoñina
"From this day on you will have vision, from this day on.

ndoka remidio tsachnujwanaka mamajema
So be it I have been walking about, Little Mother.

chká xmopasentsiaka[89]   225
Like this, please forgive me."

chká ibojoftsiana ch mamajemnaka jtananana
Like that he spoke to her, that poor mother, the blind one.

ya wabinyna ibojoftseboshjonaka
He left her with her sight.

nyetxá ndoka remidio tstatxumbo
So be it I know the story only so far,

ndoka remidio sobrino xmopasentsia
without remedy, Nephew, please forgive me.

---

[89]line 225: *chká xmopasentsiaka*, "thus forgive me." Even Wangetsmuna uses the ritual language formula for closing formal greetings and leave-takings, symbolizing perhaps a movement into the conventions of civil society.

5 Tales of the Ancestors

The ancestors in Kamsá thinking are an ill-defined collectivity including demigods, assorted personages, and animal-people, whose common destiny is the founding of Sibundoy civilization. At the dawn of the ancestral period the very first ancestors appear on the cosmic stage, the primordial miner, his younger brother Wangetsmuna, their sister who spins thread. These people interact directly with celestial deities: the moon, who marries the miner; her father, the sun, who almost catches them *in flagrante*; the thunder god, who rallies to save his grandchild from the wrath of the heathen men. As the ancestral period continues and the world evolves toward civilization, the ancestors emerge as a general class of protagonists inhabiting a spiritually charged world and moving easily between human and animal states. By the close of this period the ancestors take the form of adventurous people in a world rather like the present one who make contact with spiritual forces and profit from these encounters.

What marks all of these actors as ancestral is the exemplary character of their actions; they are at all times setting precedents for the future generations of people. As the world matures in its progress from brute to contained spiritual potency, the scale of the precedents diminishes but does not altogether vanish. Celestial bodies give way to ambitious mortals and rambunctious animal-people, but the events recorded in this portion of the mythology retain their instructive quality as a guide to the origins of customs and to proper (and improper) modes of behavior. These tales of the ancestors return to the cosmogony where the Wangetsmuna cycle leaves off, in the formative period of human society as the boundaries of human experience are taking shape. They traverse a cosmological arena initially formed of indigenous matter, as in the removal of substrate populations in "About the Red Dwarfs" (m4), but one that becomes increasingly hospitable to Christian overlay, as in m13, "The Judgment." This last myth places us at the verge of historical time in the Sibundoy Valley since the great earthquake it refers to probably occurred in the early decades of the nineteenth century.

Several myths in this group take us to *shatjoy*, the forest, and place us among the *shatjanga*, the forest people living at the eastern edge of the Andean *cordillera*. Two of these, "The Tale of the River Master" (m5) and "About the Hunters" (m6), mention a primordial hunting ground along the shores of the Tamboriako, most likely the Putumayo River as it descends to the perimeter of the Amazonian basin. These forest hunters are portrayed as an ancestral branch of the Sibundoy peoples, and the River Tamboriako emerges as a kind of ancestral home. "The Tale of the River Master" and "About the Wild Pigs" (m7) depict the powerful masters of the elements that figure prominently in this lowland antecedent of the modern-day highland Kamsá population.

A series in this set of mythic narratives deals with the origins of prominent natural phenomena. "About the Poor Scabby One" (m8) accounts for the fertility of "our little mother" (the earth) in terms of the festering scabs of an itinerant woman. "About the Wind" (m9) describes the source of the winds that blow across the valley as the stirring of ponchos worn by three tall brothers in the mountains. Another take on this topic, "About the Wind" (m10), tells how the culture hero stuffed the unruly wind into an empty gourd, only to have it released again by a curious child. This cluster of myths exhibits the classic mythopoeic quest for a humanistic understanding of the forces of nature.

"The Tale of the Two Little Children" (m11) exists as a mythic cycle, but reduced in scale from the grand dimensions of the Wangetsmuna cycle. Here the young protagonists team up with the rainbow to bring about the removal of the pernicious *antewelaj,* the witch of the forest, but later perish at the hands of the scheming Santiagueños. The presence of a discrete human community signals a comparatively delimited world, though remarkable transformations are still possible within this setting. The metamorphosis of these protagonists at the end of the narrative projects an indigenous rather than a Christian impulse.

The link to Wangetsmuna is prominent in "The Tale of Our Father" (m12) in which the synthetic deity *bngabe taitá* walks about dispensing alternately mercy and justice. This figure, a blending of traditional and imported elements, evokes that final phase in the Wangetsmuna cycle when Christian piety rather than celestial lineage determines the fate of story protagonists. Our Lord, at once the traditional deity and the Catholic Christ, activates the principle that rewards attach to virtue whereas punishments attend vice. "The Judgment" features a dramatic appearance of the Christian deity, who puts an end to the boisterous festivity during a celebration of Corpus Christi, but this Christian element is presented within an Andean framework of salvation obtained through the intervention of conversing animals.

Taken as whole, these mythic narratives lend voice and body to the Kamsá precursors who set about purging the cosmos of inappropriate life forms and channeling the rampant spiritual potency of the raw time into conduits friendly to the establishment of human society. Ellen Basso (1985, 71) observes that the Kalapalo of Brazil describe a similar paradigm, in which "the human beings who existed in the Dawn Time were different from those of the present because . . . they were capable of 'approaching powerful beings.' " The Sibundoy ancestors depicted in this chapter can interact profitably with primordial mythical personages, though, as we saw in m2 and m3, the miner is anxious to avoid the direct presence of *bngabe taitá*, Our Father the Sun, and perhaps not only because he has become intimate with the sun's daughter. Later in the account of Sibundoy ethnogenesis, people will lack the resilience of these ancestors and encounters with powerful beings will be far less auspicious.

(m4) shatxemungabiana
About the Red Dwarfs

As performed by Mariano Chicunque in Kamsá, December 1978

What were the *shatxemunga*, an obscure Kamsá word that I have translated, somewhat arbitrarily, as "red dwarfs"? We can join taita Mariano, the storyteller, in wondering about the true identity of these mysterious characters, who were small and reddish in coloration. From the myth we know that they were a kind of spiritual substrate in ancestral times, that they inhabited caves, that they called human beings through hand gestures and verbal invitations only to destroy them with their "electricity." The red dwarfs apparently were a malignant spiritual protrusion into the later ancestral period whose removal is entrusted to the elders of that time.

This narrative is among the more conversational in the corpus. In the opening utterances, taita Mariano identifies the source of this story, Benito Muchjavisoy, a remarkable elder, blind in both eyes but knowledgeable of the old days. The next portion of the story describes the red dwarfs—their appearance, speech, and harmful actions. The final section narrates the work of the elders in ridding the valley of this nuisance. Taita Mariano sprinkles in a number of personal recollections, as the content of the story reminds him of places he saw as a child. He also digresses on some of the customs and conditions marking these earlier times. We see in his performance that mythic narrative can be permeable to the deflections and distractions of conversation.

Taita Mariano stresses the capability of the elders, the Kamsá progenitors. Even though they lacked instruction in the Catholic faith, they possessed traditional knowledge that enabled them to vanquish the red dwarfs. There is an implicit claim for the superiority (or at least the parity) of the old ways here; as taita Mariano says, "So wise were our elders . . . they understood even though they weren't baptized." The Sibundoy Valley was isolated then but the elders knew how to take care of themselves.

The red dwarfs signify the presence of a spiritual underground that constantly threatens the security of human arrangements. They possess or carry *binyea*, a form of spiritual power that is extremely harmful, even fatal, to those humans who come into contact with them. Such contact produces spirit sickness and leads to rapid physical decline. One supposes, although it is not stated in this account, that the elders had recourse to the visionary substances, *yagé* and *borrachera*, in designing the proper remedy. Other mythic narratives (see for example m29) make clear the diagnostic procedures of the elders: the native doctors among them would ingest the visionary remedies and gain access to the true cause of their problems as well as the indicated remedial measures.

The area that housed the red dwarfs is located as a specific place in traditional Sibundoy topology and called *bayiñe*, an evil spot, a spiritually dangerous crucis. Not only must the substrate population be eliminated, but their former abode must be spiritually cleansed. This narrative describes a well-known process in the Andes, the imposition of a Christian shrine (in this case, a statue of the Virgin of Fátema) on a locale previously recognized as spiritually potent.

shatxemungabiana mntxá
The story about the red dwarfs goes like this.

bueno ntxamosa inetsomañanuna
Well, just what were they?

ana mwentxna atxebe barina nye koftsekwentanga nye nyetxá[1]
So here for my part they have only told about it just like this.

serto taita kompadre tekwanabwatemana benito muchjavisoy kata-toy jtanjema btska waxebwaná[2]
Truly, Father Compadre, did you know Benito Muchjavisoy, blind in both eyes, with a large swollen throat?

tateko jinye o ndoñe bndinye ko tangwakna   5
Lord, have you seen or haven't you seen that old man?

katatoika jtana benito muchjavisoy wabaina
Blind in both eyes, Benito Muchjavisoy he is called.

ch xjuftseparla ana ana shatxemiungaka shatxemienga imenamna
He told me about, about the red dwarfs, red dwarfs they were.

anteona mwentxe imnotajtsayenaka shatxumiengaka
In the old days here they lived under the hills, the red dwarfs.

bueno ana mntxá orasiona tojitsemena i basenga chnga shatxe-mingena[3]
Well, so like that at prayer time they would come out, and they were small those red dwarfs,

---

[1]line 3: *koftsekwentanga*, "they have told me." The narrator denies personal accountability for this tale; he is only passing on what he has heard from others.

[2]line 4: *taitá kompadre*, "Father Compadre." Taita Mariano addresses Justo Jacanamijoy, his principal audience, through this respectful term; Justo and Mariano are related to one another through ritual co-parenthood. *benito muchjavisoy*. This remarkable elder is the source of the story.

[3]line 9: *orasiona*, "prayer time," around five in the evening. The missionaries established a religious daily routine marked by the hours of the cross.

btsetsanga basese tangwagenga base welabenga[4]   10
the adults were small, little old men, small old witches.

chká jaboknana a chbe chká jutsobjajanán jutsobjajanán
Like that they would appear, those ones, like that they would ges-
    ture, they would gesture.

nye tkjobekona choye nakanye tkjwinye chbé
Just go near them there, just look at them,

nye kacha ntxam txa txa txa txa ch kukwatxaka mntxá[5]
just with that "txa txa txa txa," their hands like this,

i con electricidad ndayujungase imenamna[6]
and with electricity, just what were they?

choye jobekonana iye ajá kwevushe ntxamse inamenana   15
There they would come around, and aha, in caves, what were they?

choye imenoyenunga chngana chjungena imenoyena
There they lived, those guys, those creatures lived.

iye choye mabo mabo ko biyajungesa imenamna chbenga ch
    shatxemunga[7]
And there: "Come here, come here," they were able to speak, those
    guys, the red dwarfs.

iye ch tkjobekona nye mo che jutsefchanan
And if you approached, they would just laugh there.

nye batxa bekontskoñe iye anye jatsshajayana ko nye obanaka
But if they came a little closer they fell dead there.

chká inobanaye nyetxá binyea bomenunga[8]   20
Like that they had a very evil wind.

chnga ch shatxemiunga imenamna chkajunga imenamna
They, those red dwarfs they were, that's how they were,

a nye chká nye chká ajá
just like that, just like that, aha.

---

[4]line 10: *welabenga*, "old witches." The narrator is casting about for a characterization of these creatures; he views them as witch-like, as odd creatures on the fringe
of civilized society.

[5]line 13: *ch kukwatxaka mntxá*, "their hands like this." The narrator demonstrates
a beckoning hand movement. *txa txa txa txa*, the voice of the Red Dwarfs, a series of
staccato, rhythmic affricates.

[6]line 14: *electricidad*, "electricity." The narrator's attempt to convey the power of
the Red Dwarfs through reference to a facet of modern technology.

[7]line 17: *mabo mabo*, "come here, come here." The Red Dwarfs can also speak
Kamsá, though to a limited degree.

[8]line 20: *binyea*, "wind, spirit." The Red Dwarfs killed by delivering spiritual
sickness to their victims.

bweno ana shatjoye ndoñe benache yendemuna[9]
Well, so there was no trail to Mocoa in those days,

del todo ndoknoye benache yendemuna
there were no trails anywhere at all.

nye mwentxa chká chká nderado yentxangena ana kwakjonaye
                                                              25

Only here like that, like that, truly people went by way of
    Kwakjonaye,

chjansa kwenachenungwana
over there was the passage.

ch mora ch herradura ndayá ch chiñe atxena tijuftsinye
Now there is that stone road, that one I have seen myself.

**serta ooh ena ngutsiangusha nye ena ngutsiangusha betiyebjunja
chuxe kwanamana**
Truly, oh, pure reeds, nothing but reeds, some trees, those are
    over there.

**atxe basajema orna tijoftserepara ch ena limpia i mas chkoyina
matseyeká**
When I was a child I saw that whole place and further along to
    Matseye,

kwanabaina matseyoka ch batsjaka   **30**
it is called Matseye, a stream with high banks on each side.

more ch mameta ch fátema indokolokando choka[10]
Now a Virgin, the Virgin of Fátema, is located there.

chiñe bayiñe ana bayiñe inamna[11]
By there an evil point, so, an evil point, it was.

ana ch shatxemunga chenache chká imenamna imenoyiyena
And those red dwarfs, there like that they were, they lived.

ana chká ch orasiona ana nye chká ana lo mismo
So like that at the prayer hour, just the same thing.

yana tangwanga imojatstudia a ver ndayeka chjunga nyetxá[12]
                                                              35

So the old ones thought about it: "Let's see, what can we do about
    these guys?

[9]line 23: *shatjoye*, literally "place of the forest"; the traditional name for the area
that now houses Mocoa, the lowland capital of Putumayo Territory.

[10]line 31: *mameta ch fátema*, "the Virgin of Fátema." A Catholic shrine has been
erected in this spiritually dangerous space.

[11]line 32: *bayiñe*, "evil point." Certain points on the land's surface are regarded
as spiritually dangerous, places with special topographical features, or where fatal-
ities have occurred.

[12]line 35: *tangwanga*, "the elders," the ones entrusted with the spiritual protection of the community, a council of native doctors.

i chká chunga a vera ntxamo montjaobrana
So like that, let's see, what should we do about it?"

ana shatjoya ndoñe imondajna
So they couldn't go to Mocoa.

ana tondaye mase remedio kamwentxe atxena tijoftsinyena
So there is no other remedy, right here I have seen it.

kekabwatama ch entsentsisyexeka wabaina niñuxe[13]
Do you know it? The incense-tree it is called, a tree.

i bweno yojatabaná btska chká jatatsetxana jatatsetxana 40
And fine, they gathered a lot of it, they cut some and they cut some more.

i chiñe ch tstxiyana tstxiyana
And that one brings tears, it brings tears to the eyes.

i chana yojatobaná iye i chana jwakoñe joyambana
And they gathered it and placed it in a large cauldron.

i ana chubjungena por ejemplo ch kwevoye chká oyenunga
And those guys thus lived in those caves like that.

yibeta jana i chentxa jetsajajwañe che entsentsiyuxe
At dusk they went and there they placed that incense-wood by the door,

i btsetsá ena jomaxe nyetemaka jetsajajwana 45
and the elders placed a lot of carbon and some small kindling by the door.

i ch tojtsungetxana impase i chnga katamunjana
And they smelled that and sure enough they were dying.

yojontxá jtsayetanana entsentsiyuxeka jtsayetanana
They began to kill them with that incense-wood, they killed them.

i chiñc bwetaña katunjanopodia jayetanana achká kulta ch bnga tangwanga[14]
And they killed as many as they could with it, so wise were our elders.

krischanga chká are bngana anteona ndwabainungasa ch tangwanga
Like that our ancestors were not Christians, those elders were not baptized,

---

[13]line 39: *entsentisyexeka*, "incense tree." One of many substances burned in ritual curing sessions whose smoke is regarded as beneficial.

[14]line 48: *achka kulta ch bnga tangwanga*, "so wise were our elders." Note the general vote of confidence in the elders and their traditional knowledge carried in the Spanish loan, "culta," civilized, learned, wise.

yojowenana ndwabainungaka[15]   50
they understood even though they weren't baptized.

**ana serta nye ch jajoka nombre tatanga ch tatanga chká podeska
konyebenabayana imenamna**[16]
So truly those garden names like Tatanga, Tatanga, like that they
would give each other nicknames.

iye pero chká imojajastudiana ana ch katamunjanenobowiyana
But like that they thought about it and they were able to defend
themselves.

**pero ch kwakjonaye choye chká katumunjoftseobra ch ana chiñe ch
katuntsanayetananga**
But by Kwakjonaye, there like that they worked it and so they finished them off.

ah chinsa baiñe wabainiñe
Ah, that evil point as we call it.

i chana chana komena   55
And that, that is the story.

pero ya tijatsekwentana komo koftsekwentanga
But now I have told it to you as they told it to me.

bueno allí no mas es corto
Well, that's all there is, it is a short one.

ese es del shatxume
That's the one about the red dwarf.

(m5) buyesh ndweñobe parlo
The Tale of the River Master

As performed by Mariano Chicunque in Kamsá, October 1978

"The Tale of the River Master" takes us back to a moment in Kamsá ethnohistory when the ancestors hunted game animals by staking out salt
licks at the proper phases of the moon. The actors in this mythic narrative are referred to as *shbwayunga*, hunters, and also as *shatjanga*, forest

[15]line 50: *yojowenana ndwabainungaka*, "they understood even though they
weren't baptized." Another affirmation of the elders, who were clever in spite of the
fact that they lacked Catholic instruction. The verbal root here is *-wena-*, "to hear,"
used in this passage in the sense of "hearing and knowing the truth."

[16]line 51: *jajoka nombre*, "garden name." A kind of nickname given to the infant,
usually by its maternal grandmother (see McDowell 1981). The notion of masters,
owners, or bosses of the natural elements is probably a very ancient mythological
conceit. It is prominent in Native American mythology on both the North American
and South American continents. Schultes and Hofman (1979) identify these nature
guardians as components of a paleolithic hunting complex.

people or Mocoans. These events are located at a prominent junction in Kamsá mythology, the river Tamboriako (from *tambor*, Spanish for "drum," and *yako*, Quechua for "river," hence "Drum River"). I was never able to pinpoint this important spot. Even taita Mariano, who had traveled to Pasto by foot as a boy and knew most of the places named in the mythic narratives, could not locate the Tamboriako for me. The mythic narratives describe a large, cascading river, which leads me to speculate that Tamboriako might identify the places where the Putumayo River plunges to the northwestern edge of the Amazonian basin. If so, this spot would lie at a point of contact between highland and lowland Putumayo Territory. The Tamboriako emerges as a kind of spiritual homeland of the Kamsá people. The mythological evidence suggests that these lowland hunters, known today as *amigos*, were either the source of the Kamsá population or a closely allied people.

"The Tale of the River Master" is remarkable for its gripping portrayal of a powerful spirit, the "owner," "lord," or "master" of the river, one of several spiritual masters overseeing a particular natural domain, and for its juxtaposition of Christian and indigenous spiritual forces. Kamsá mythic narrative recognizes as well the master of the wild pigs (m7), and other mythologies of the region display elaborate networks of resource exchange governed by guardian spirits of the natural elements. Among the people of lowland Ecuador, for example, the cosmos is governed by a hierarchy of spiritual masters, ultimate authority resting with Sungui, master of water spirits, and Amasanga, forest soul master (Whitten 1976; Brown 1985). The river master brought to life in the present mythic narrative is most likely of spiritual kin to Sungui and cognate figures throughout the mythologies of the northwest Amazon (Reichel-Dolmatoff 1971). The notion of masters, owners, or bosses of the natural elements is probably a very ancient mythological conceit. It is prominent in Native American mythology on both the North American and South American continents. Schultes and Hofman (1979) identify these nature guardians as components of a paleolithic hunting complex.

The Kamsá master of the river, like the master of the wild pigs, is a formidable presence, but, unlike the latter, the river master is intensely hostile to human welfare, reflecting a fundamental ambivalence toward the river in Kamsá thought. Undeniably, its waters contribute to the well-being of the people; beyond the realms of food preparation and hygiene, river waters figure in many Kamsá spiritual remedies (Seijas 1969). However, the river appears in another aspect, as a serious threat to human welfare. This mythic narrative pits the river master, portrayed in diabolical terms and actually labelled *bayá*, or beast, against a prominent symbol of the Catholic faith, the blessed medallion.

Rivers and brooks crisscross the valley floor, which literally bubbles with moving water. The Quinchoa River (its name translates as "bar-

rier") flows down out of the foothills to the west of the valley and runs
between the towns of Santiago and San Andres; before the construction
of the new bridge, this river formed an impassable chasm during times
of high water. A smaller river, Huarmi Yaku, runs right through the
town of Santiago: a few years back it gorged with flood water and
heaved rocks and boulders through houses, roads, and fields along its
course. The Putumayo River originates in the mountains to the north of
the Sibundoy Valley and descends near the town of San Francisco to
course across the valley and tumble several thousand feet to the Amazonian basin where it becomes a major tributary to the Amazon. In the
valley this river can surge to create dangerous floods along its course.
The potent Sibundoy hydraulics have been the object of a protracted and
as yet largely unsuccessful (at least from the point of view of the natives)
INCORA (the Colombian agrarian reform program) project aimed at flood
control and land reclamation.

The river, in Kamsá thought as in Kamsá life, is both a source and a
nemesis, a blessing and a curse. This ambivalence is expressed in a
number of formats. Consider the following fable-like narration of taita
Bautista Juajibioy, depicting and animating the destructive potential of
the river:

> *jachinya bayá*, the beast of the forest, the beast of the forest.
> Imagine, from time to time it says:
> "When I am passing by, don't provoke me;
> you have intelligence, eyes to see with;
> on the other hand, I don't have these things.
> But if you provoke me, I will carry you off."
>
> In winter weather, you know,
> when there is thunder and the floods come down.
> One is on the other side and wants to get home,
> or else one is travelling and wants to cross the river.
>
> One is thinking:
> "Maybe I can get across. Who knows?"
> Look first, think first, or just take a chance.
> The other one says:
> "Since you have provoked me,
> I don't have eyes to see with or anything,
> I am going to carry you off."
> And it drowns him.

A set of traditional sayings associates the dream of fording a river with
legal problems in the court or *cabildo* (the community council); if (in the
dream) one is able to ford the river successfully, one should experience
success in the legal dispute; if, on the other hand, the dreamed river
refuses to allow passage, one is destined to suffer at the hands of the

authorities. As an Ingano consultant stated (see McDowell 1989): "When you are made to dream that a river prevents you from crossing, you are thinking that you will just have to go to the cabildo, but you can't go; you just leave the complaint pending. In the meanwhile, the others will prevail over you. Your case remains forgotten." This nexus of Sibundoy tradition evokes the presence of the pan-Andean thunder deity (see m2, m3), for it is the action of thunderstorms in the adjacent mountains that causes the rivers to crest as they move across the valley. Although the connection is not explicit in the commentaries I have collected, it is plausible that this stern celestial judge stands behind the dream proverbs centered on fording a flood-swollen river; it is likewise plausible that the river master portrayed in this myth operates under the authority of the thunder deity. Andean thought gives prominence to rivers as avenues linking the different segments of the cosmos (Bastien 1978), and there is evidence for this pattern in the Wangetsmuna cycle, where a river connects the celestial and the lowland narrative settings.

Whatever the lineage of the river master, the story at hand sketches for us in elaborate detail a truly frightening creature, an imaginary composite of normally discrete elements, a figure adequately captured by Victor Turner's discussion of "betwixt and between" as a cultural locus (Turner 1967). This story draws us into its web of suspense by dramatizing the solitary hunter's anxiety as the master of the river first shouts from a distance, then approaches and comes into view, and finally recedes upstream, shouting as before. At the climactic moment, the river master appears as an eerie, watery presence:

> He appeared in that large river,
> on top of those rolling boulders.
> And there, yes sir!
> With the face of a bird, something like a beak, it was,
> the body just like a monk's habit,
> dressed in black he was,
> with a head like a bird's, with a white beak.

It is the blessed medallion of the hunter that staves off the advance of this watery demon, establishing a radical opposition between the spirit forces of nature and those of the Catholic faith. The medallion previously blessed by the priest creates a sanctuary, a sphere of spiritual safety, that repels the master of the river. But the hunter is so overcome with fright that he ages prematurely and remains sickened by this close encounter with a malevolent natural spirit. The Christian overlay surely contributes to the negative portrait of the river master in this mythic narrative. Christian interpretation consistently transformed native spirits and deities into demons and devils throughout the Andes (Marzal 1985). In the syncretic worldview proposed by this narrative, powerful Christian artifacts enter into the eternal struggle for spiritual health, within a largely non-Christian spiritual environment. It is, after all, *binyea*, evil wind or spirit sickness, that the stranded hunter fears the most, and that causes his misfortune.

bweno anteo shbwayunga imenamna shatjangaka[17]
Well. In the old days there were some hunters, forest people.

i anteo inotatxumbo ch tamboriakoka wabainoy inamna
And in the old days they knew of that Tamboriako, as it was called.

i choka bejay btse bejay inobujna
And there a river, a large river flowed.

i tsachañe tsachañe wabaina tjayema btse tjatxe inamna
And by the edge, by the edge, as we say, a cliff, a high cliff there was.

i chentxe inamna saladoka ana salado inamna   5
And by that place there was a salt lick, thus a salt lick there was.

i chentxena kada binyetna kada jwashkona jwashkonama[18]
And so there every full moon, every new moon, for the new moon,

jashjajnana chentxe nyetska bayingaka
many would arrive there, all kinds of animals.

i chamna shatjangana chentxe pasel joshebwañamna
And because of that the forest people there could easily hunt them.

achkaté ch binyeteté shebojweté o ch jwashkonté
On those days, the eve of the full moon or dawn after the full moon,

jangana joshbwanama anya mata ch saladoy janganaka   10
they would go to hunt them at that place, to the salt lick they would go.

bweno chentxena jashangwana kokwanga torkasunga lorunga[19]
Well. There would arrive pheasants, ducks, parrots,

nyetská wongwebjunga i ya ch mongojo ch btsayá
all kinds of fowl as well as the deer, the tapir,

[17]line 1: *shbwayunga*, "hunters." The myths suggest that the Kamsá people trace their origin back to these hunters, who inhabit a lowland area; they may preserve a recollection of the community's existence before it ascended into the Sibundoy Valley. Alternatively, this body of myth may have been acquired from lowland friends, with whom the Sibundoy natives retain important material and spiritual exchanges.

[18]line 6: *binyeta, jwashkona*, "full moon," "new moon." The Kamsá time many of their subsistence activities to the phases of the moon. They generally view the moon as a powerful influence over human destinies.

[19]line 11: *kokwanga torkasunga lorunga*. These are three edible birds: *lorunga* are parrots, *torkasunga* are described as "silver with dark spots, about the size of a dove." At present I have no description for *kokwanga*, which I have arbitrarily translated as "pheasants."

lempe jashjakjnan
all of these would arrive.

i chentxe shatjangana ana jwesanxaka i flechubjwak
And there the forest people thus with blow gun and arrows,

chentxe jobojwesana iye inye pasela   15
there they could shoot them easily,

chentxe anya ndata takjsanka
there, without having to track them through the mountains.

bweno inyenga chká imojoftshebwañe inyets txabaye
Well, the others were hunting just fine,

i kanya kodisia yojatajsamingo mas bnoyeka kanye yojtsokeda[20]
and one more ambitious fellow wandered further off, he remained
    alone.

i kwando cha jatusetama yojajwaboye yojatejana ora yibetata
And when he thought to catch up with the others, night had fallen.

impas yojtsetajtselxe impas yojsotxeye   20
He was quite lost in the mountains, he was completely lost.

i chorna ne borla ndoñe jetsebokniñe
And then, no fooling, he couldn't find his way out.

i chorna peñuxe inamna kweva
And then, a cliff, there was a cave,

peñuxe chentxe inenebengwana mntxá inamna[21]
a cliff, there between two rock faces, like this it was.

**i chentxe la fwersa choye yojtsamashingo ase chentxe yojtsetbe-
    mana**
And there by necessity, there he entered, then there he sat down.

i ch jwesanxaka i anteo ndayá   25
And that blow gun, and in the old days, what was it,

slebonashá fosforeshakwente inowabomna
a flint stone, instead of matches, he had with him.

i chká yojtsetbemana chentxe
And so he took a seat there,

tonday mas defensa nye jwesanxá base kuchillotema inawambaya
with no other defense than the blow gun and a small knife he
    carried.

---

[20]line 18: *kodisia*, "ambitious." From the Spanish root for "greedy."
[21]line 23: like this*. The narrator gestured a tight spot by holding the two palms
of his hands close together.

nyetxá i ya na medallaka
That was all, except of course that medallion,

medalla inetsontxubwañe shatjas   30
a medallion hung around the neck of that forest man,

pero sempre wabaintem medallika[22]
but naturally a blessed medallion,

i ch medalla chká inetsontxebwañe orna
and so that medallion was hanging then around his neck.

primera ndoñe intsejwabenaye bayabiamas
At first he didn't think of the wild beasts.

yojtsawatja mtxkwaybiamaka tigrebiam yojtsawatjaka
He feared the snake, the jaguar he feared.

elay binyiam yojtsawatjaka[23]   35
Surely he feared that evil wind.

i yojtsetbemanaka
And so he sat there.

ndeolpe nyetxá bjabinyenushe shbojweta ora[24]
Suddenly, it was a clear night, the day after the full moon,

ndeolpe nyetxá yojoboyoyeka
suddenly it came shouting,

txa yojashawanan ch bejayeka nye ndoñe bna
how it roared in that river, and not far off,

i timpo bekoñe yojaboyoyeka   40
and right away from nearby it shouted.

chor choykan txa yojtsabejungwá yojtsereparana
Then he stuck his head out from there, he looked around.

asna yojabobokna ch bejayiñe
Then, then it appeared on that river,

btsetsa ndetstxiyemunga wakolmanayema
on top of those rolling boulders.

i choka eso se
And there, yes sir!

choka ana jubiana nye shloftxeka wangutsakwenta inamna   45
There, with the face of a bird, with something like a beak, it was,

[22]line 31: *wabaintem*, "blessed." The same word is used to refer to a baptized person; it thus means "blessed by the Holy Sacrament of the Catholic church."
[23]line 35: *binyiam*, "evil wind." This term translates also as "spirit presence capable of producing spirit sickness."
[24]line 37: *shbojweta*, "the day after the full moon." The period when the moon is waning is thought to be spiritually disadvantageous.

kwerpna abito konforma ermankamana waftsengejwa maná inamna
its body like that of a monk's habit, dressed in black it was,

bestxaxna shloftskwenta bestxexubjantse wangetsá maná inamna
its head like a bird's, a white head, with a beak, it was.

i cha chká inachnungo iyoye
And like that it passed by shouting,

i ch bejaye santo diosa jabshawenanán
and that river, saintly God, how it roared!

i chor yojachnunga   50
And there it passed by,

i antigena inawachwana buyesh ndweñoka[25]
and the old ones knew it, the master of the river.

i chká yojenojwaboye a ver btse
And so he came to himself, let's see, that fellow:

ntxam i tsepasaye
"What will become of me?"

ndoñe injomana ch shatjajemaka choy yojtsechekjwanaka
He didn't sleep a wink, that poor forest man, there he remained
   hidden.

**de la warda ah chorna ndayá mallajkta bna ora
   yojtabatoyoyika**   55
God forbid, ah, then, after some time it came shouting again,

ah iye tempo ibejtaboyoyika
ah, right away, it came to shout nearby.

i ch tamboy tempo yojababoyika[26]
And it appeared right away at that refuge,

ermankaka ch ermano maristaka chká manaka[27]
like a monk, like a Marist brother, that's how it was.

aray chorna ndoka remidio ndoka ndayentxe yojtsemna
Damn, then, without remedy, there was nowhere he could be,

shatjajemna yojtsaitmena ch peñuxoye   60
that poor forest man hid himself in that cliff,

---

[25]line 51: *buyesh ndweñoka*, "the master (or owner, or lord) of the river." Kamsá
thought locates in every natural domain a controlling deity or spirit, a master, lord,
or owner of that element.
   [26]line 57: *tambo*, "rough camp, shelter, refuge."
   [27]line 58: *ermano maristaka*, "Marist brother." The Marist lay order has had a mis-
sionary effort in the Sibundoy Valley for some time now.

ch tetchetxoye yojtsaitmena
by the foot of that cliff he was hiding.

yojabobokna chentxe
It came to appear there again.

yojtsajonyaye medelley yojtsajonyanayekna
He hung the medallion, and because he hung it there,

ndoñe choy yonjobenaye
it couldn't enter there.

ch medalle wamantemna ndoñe pronto yonjobenaye ch bayá chan
    jajatskamaka[28]   65
That blessed medallion would not allow that beast to carry him off.

ah yekna nye nyetxá chana ndoka mases
Therefore, since there was nothing else it could do,

kachká ibojesonyayika i bejayoye yojtaisotsatxe
just like that it left him there and fell back into the river.

i ch ndetxiyemunga yojtaisoyoye yojtsatotswañe
And among those rocks it shouted and drifted back upstream.

i ya impas i shatja ana ch medallaka yojenueyana
And so that medallion completely protected the forest man.

i chká inaitemnaka   70
And there he hid,

i ya bojoftsebobinyenaka tbemanana
and there he remained sitting until dawn.

ibsana tamboyamna yojtotontxa jenashekwastonan shekwatxe
The next day he began following his footsteps from the refuge.

i nye tram yojtsepasanan
And that's how it went with him.

ah ibsana chana bekwentxiye tamboye yojtatabokiñe txabase
Ah, the next day he came out nearby that refuge with ease.

i ibsana shatjangana imojesanga   75
And the next day the forest people returned:

ndayek ndokna i ch nye enuta ndoknaka
"Why is there nothing, just nothing of our companion?"

imojetsengwango i pronto imojetsenyena
They went to look for him and soon they found him,

---

[28]line 65: *wamantema*, "the sacred earth." The narrator uses a key word in Kamsá religious thought, *waman*, and appends the diminutive ending *-tema*. The root implies sacred ground, ground that can nourish. A similar root means "hawk" in Quechua. Compare the *wamani* in Peru, a high mountain deity (Isbell 1978, 59–60).

del todo impas anteo xokaka impas beshajantsajem
completely aged, sickly, very pale, the poor fellow.

i yojtsatajsan kabá i cha yojobwambaye
And still he walked in the forest, and he told them:

mntxá tijapasaka   80
"This is what happened to me."

chor imojisebetxe imojtanatse shatjoye
Then they called him, they took him along to Mocoa.

tmojtanushjango impase xokaka
He arrived there completely sick.

chkase ch antewan
That's how that old myth goes.

(m6) **shbwayungabiama**
About the Hunters

As performed by taita Mariano Chicunque in Kamsá, November 1978

"About the Hunters," like m5, "The Tale of the River Master," takes us
to a primordial scene of Kamsá ethnohistory, the Tamboriako, the Drum
River, possibly along the course of the Putumayo River's long tumble
from highlands to lowlands. Stories come in storytelling sessions, and
this mythic narrative was performed just after "The Tale of the River
Master." This fact explains Mariano Chicunque's first statement:

bweno ah an el mismo shbwayungabiana
Well, ah, concerning those same hunters.

These two myths, imbued as they are with the lore of the jungle, could
be read as evidence of a lowland origin for the Kamsá people. But it is
equally probable that they index the intimate relationship between
highlanders at the eastern edge of the Andes and lowlanders at their
western slopes, an intimacy that persists into the present and is captured in the Sibundoy term of reference for these lowlanders, *amigos*
(friends). Near the end of the story the narrator refers to the hunters as
shatjanga, the forest people, and *shatjá* is the contemporary Kamsá name
for the town and people of Mocoa, at the eastern margins of the Andes
just over the rim and down from the Sibundoy Valley. Ethnohistorical
sources indicate the Mocoans were a fierce lowland tribe just beyond the
fringe of the Quillasinga federation. Whatever the historical anteced-
ents, the vertical movement of material goods and the spiritual exchanges between lowland and highland native doctors preserve a
significant relationship between these Putumayo communities.

"About the Hunters" introduces us to the *volcan kexebjunga*, the dogs
of the volcano, who emerge from the very rock of the mountain wall to

aid the hunters in their quest for game. Andean cosmologies present numerous parallels to the animate rock presented in this mythic narrative. In the central and southern Andes, mountain deities known as *apus* and *wamanis* play a critical role in shaping the destinies of the people who live along their slopes (Bastien 1978; Isbell 1978; Urton 1981). In Chuschi, a central Peruvian town, the mountain deities are viewed as "owners of all plants and animals" (Isbell 1978, 59). The literature features inumerable accounts of mythological figures emerging from the substance of the mountains and returning to this substance. One of the most remarkable prototypes for the animacy of mountain rock can be found in the *huarochirí* manuscript, dating perhaps to sixteenth century Peru, with its portrayal of the mountains as active mythical protagonists and featuring a spiritual plasticity that allows for continuous transformations of rock into animate beings and animate beings into rock (Salomon and Urioste 1991).

Mariano Chicunque does not merely describe these remarkable dogs of the volcano, he impersonates them. On three different occasions in the narrative he recreates their voice. We hear them as the primordial hunters heard them, barking in the distance: "*kwe kwe, kwe kwe, kwe kwe.*" The barking comes in paired ideophones, each sustained for a full second or more on the pitch of a pure tone, the first pitch at the interval of a minor third above the second pitch. The barking is an early warning; soon the dogs come into view and drive their prey, the *btsayá* (a tapir), to within reach of the hunters. An interplay between the mountain deity as keeper of the game and the hunters is suggested in the statement:

> **i ordene inamna chubjunga ch kexebjunga**
> And there was an order, those little ones, those dogs,
>
> **volkan kexebjemungana lempe chingashan lempe jesabwakjayanaka**
> those dogs of the volcano, all the entrails, they were to leave them.

"There was an order," a principle of cosmic reciprocity, a "natural" law, requiring that the hunters leave behind the entrails as a consideration for the help rendered by the dogs of the volcano. This mythic narrative, like many others, advocates through exemplification a harmony between humans and their natural environment to be achieved through the conscious designs of reciprocity. Reciprocal arrangements between different social entities, between human beings and the natural world and between humans and the supernatural powers, is a cornerstone of Andean cosmology (Harrison 1989; Dover 1992).

> **bweno ah an el mismo shbwayungabiana**
> Well, ah, concerning those same hunters.
>
> **ana kach bejay monbetseparlay ndoñe kitsatabwatema**
> And that river they speak of, I have never been there,

bejay nye tamboriako
just the Tamboriako River.

bweno chokna utatena txabá imnashbwaye
Well, there for a couple of days they hunted very well.

ya i anye kutisa ana ndoka shloftxungabiamana imojtsenunga
   menaye 5
And then another time they heard nothing of fowl.

ndayak tonday shloftstxunga tonday
"Why is there nothing of fowl, nothing?"

kwatwena imojatwena bnoka kwe kwe kwe kwe kwe kweka[29]
Surely they hear, they were hearing: "kwe kwe, kwe kwe,
   kwe kwe."

ana volkan kexebjunga mn chechubjunga[30]
The dogs of the volcano, only so large,

volkan kexebjunga ana chebjunga
the dogs of the volcano, only so large,

chká imnawakmena btseyaka[31] 10
thus they pursued the tapir,

i chngana chká imojtsakmena ch btsayá
and they like this pursued the tapir.

i ya inyebjunga bejengoka imojtsaiwangonjna
And then some of them were gripping the animal's neck,

jayitsosañan itsosañe itsosañe
eating as they went, as they went.

ch btseyana nye jetschaye i jetsachayamnaya
That tapir would just run and keep on running.

i choka a chor i chká ch kwe kwe kwe kweka 15
And there, then, like that: "kwe kwe, kwe kwe."

imojatawenan orna achká imojabowabokna btsayaka
When they heard that again, they came upon the tapir.

i chor ch btse bejay inamna ch tamboriako inamna
And then there was that large river, the Tamboriako it was,

---

[29]line 7: *kwe kwe kwe kwe kwe kweka*. The distant barking of the dogs is conveyed
in three pairs of phones, in each pair, the first one is sounded at a pitch a minor third
above the pitch of the second one.

[30]line 8: *mn chechubjunga*, "only so large." The narrator gestures with his hand
above the floor to indicate a height of approximately two feet.

[31]line 10: *btsayá*, "tapir," probably *Tapirus terrestris*, referred to as *danta* or "wild
burro" by Kamsá elders.

i choye imojabashebwetxunga
and there they would bring it down,

i ch btseyá chentxe imojobekonanga
and that tapir there they would approach.

anteona kuchillo rebaja inamna ana lantsoxá jajwesan   20
In the old days there was no knife, only lances to throw.

ndoñe ch btsayana lantsaxaka imnetsotatxumbwanungna
No, they knew how to handle that tapir with lances.

ch btsayá de todo ndoñe iyendototo ch bobache
The tapir in any case does not have a tough skin,

nye kelabastemkwenta
just something like a squash.

ana chentxe chká imojtsejantsantsan
So there they were barking like that,

i chentxe ch bejayentxe chentxe shbwayungana lantsejwaka   25
and there by that river, there the hunters with their lances,

imojetsenktjo ch btseyá i chentxe katamunjanshbwanga
they nailed that tapir and there they brought him down.

i ordene inamna chubjunga ch kexebjunga[32]
And there was an order, those little ones, those dogs,

volkan kexebjemungana lempe chingaxan lempe jesabwakja-
yanaka
those dogs of the volcano, all the entrails, they were to leave them,

i lempe imojesosañunga imojtsatoñe
and they ate them all up, they left.

i ch kexebjemunga ndomoy   30
And those little dogs, where did they go to?

ch volkan volkanbe inamna[33]
That volcano, they were of the volcano.

choy imojtetoñe ch volkanoye oyen kexunga
There they returned to the volcano where they lived, those dogs.

kexetemunga nye ch kwe kwe kwe kweka oyanayungna imnet-
somiñe
Those little dogs, just, "kwe kwe, kwe kwe," they were barking.

---

[32]line 27: *ordene*, "order." License to move within a certain segment of the cosmic design.
[33]line 31: *volkanbe*, "of the volcano." The narrator is at pains to get across the idea that the dogs were animate pieces of the actual volcano, animated chunks of its rock. Compare *paria qaqa* in ancient Peru (Salomon and Urioste 1991).

i ch chingabeyeka pasel mntxena imojoftsonyena ch shatjanga anteona
And because of them, easily those forest people found meat in the old days.

chan i ch conversa del casador hasta allí no mas   35
That's the story about the hunters, that's all there is to it.

ese es corto
That is a short one.

ese es de los perros que hay esos chiquitos
That's about those dogs that exist, those little ones.

esos perros ya son de dicen que son de roca
Those dogs are of, they say that they are of rock.

una cosa así pues del volcán sabemos decir
Something like that, well from the volcano as we say.

de las rocas de las piedras sí de esos   40
From the rocks, from the stones, yes, from those.

(m7) saina kotxebiana
About the Wild Pigs

As performed by Mariano Chicunque in Kamsá, November 1978

This myth takes us into the spiritual dominion of the masters or owners of the natural elements. We journey with two ambitious hunters to a special hollow trunk; when they pound on this trunk, the wild pigs are summoned; the hunters are able to kill them easily there. But lurking behind the others is the master of the wild pigs, a powerful elder, awesome in appearance with his crossed tusks. As the wild pigs enter a cave they are transformed into humans, and the elder warns the hunters not to take so many lives. He provides them with a small vial of *shnana*, a greenish liquid, presumably a *yagé* concoction. This drink affords the hunters a powerful vision; when they return to society they are remarkable doctors, knowledgeable about the hunt and able even to bring the dead back to life.

The story is composed of four units. The hunters (a) hunt the wild pigs; (b) enter the cave of the wild pigs; (c) take a visionary medicine trip; and (d) return as powerful doctors. This tale can be seen as a narrative of the acquisition of spiritual knowledge and power: the two hunters leave society, sustain an encounter with a spiritual being, and return to society possessing valuable spiritual vision.

As noted for m5, the nature guardian is an ancient mythological projection with analogues throughout the Americas and beyond. Good descriptions of South American parallels can be found in Reichel-

Dolmatoff (1971) and Whitten (1976). Américo Paredes (1970, 198) presents a close equivalent from the Zoque Indians of Chiapas: "They become angry at men if one is greedy and kills too many deer." The notion of a vision quest or the acquisition of spiritual power through contact with supernaturals is another prominent pan-Indian theme. In Kamsá thinking, it is through encounters with the ancestors and other spiritual sources that the native doctors acquire their knowledge. A central component in this process is the visionary medicine, *yagé*, which allows people to see beyond the misleading surface of experience.

Taita Mariano Chicunque performs this narrative with evident zeal. He dwells on the physical appearance and comportment of the master of the wild pigs, whom he characterizes as follows: *ch tangwayema tatxumbwan ndayase inamna*, "That powerful old man, what a doctor he was!" In line 21, he receives the appellation *verakoyema*, based on the Spanish word for "feisty male." Each verbal portrait employs the Kamsá suffix *-yema*, which marks something gigantic or grotesque. The master of the wild pigs, it would appear, is one supervisory node in a well-regulated natural system. We know from other sources dispersed throughout native America and beyond that his job is to negotiate with the native doctors for the exchange of human souls. The master of the animals controls access to the game and regulates human consumption of his species. Hunting societies throughout the Americas project this association between visionary experience, natural guardians, and the pursuit of game (Schultes and Hoffman 1979).

saina kotxebiama antewana mntxá[34]
The story about the wild pigs, in the old days, goes like this.

saina kotxena ana ongabnutsana utabnutsana imnenuta tajañe kotxenga
The wild pigs, as many as thirty or twenty, travelled together in the forest.

y chnga waskwatxana tondayika nye koñishkwenta sain kotxenga
The pigs, they had nothing of a tail, only like the rabbit, the wild pigs.

i chunga joshbwañamina ana kanya inamna anteona btse tronkuyema
And they went to hunt them, so in the old days there was one large hollow trunk,

tajwashena tabjusheka niñuntxe tronkutxe   5
the hollow trunk of a large tree.

chentxana nye inetsojajoñe shbwayungabe utsajanganjana niñuxe
Just to that place the hunters went, to knock on that trunk.

---

[34]line 1: *saina kotxena*, "wild pigs," most likely the collared peccary, *Tayassu tajaca*.

ndanatekwa iye nye jautsjanganjan ch niñuxe
Whoever went by would just knock on that trunk.

i tempo ch kotxengana imnowena
And right away those wild pigs heard it,

i chká jtajnana ch choye ch niñuxe chká tajwashina tbjushoye
   jtangan
and like that they went there, to that hollow trunk they went.

i ache shbwayungna jaxungwana niñuxuñe   10
And so the hunters would climb that trunk,

i choka tsbananokana ch jajwesamna chokana tsbananokana[35]
and there from above they would shoot them, there from above.

fshansiñam imwatsesa ana chungena wabowanunga
They would be eating nervously on the ground.

serto chkaka yojautsjanganja i tempo biatababanunga
Truly like that they went to beat on that trunk and right away they
   came along.

i chokana ibojajwesa ndoñe ordene yindemena[36]
And from there they would shoot them without having any
   permission.

btsa ch mayor stonoye cha jajwesan ndoñe   15
The large one, that elder, stayed behind, they didn't shoot him.

cha inetsotatxumbuñiyekna ana nye unga yojtsajosá del viaje
They didn't understand that they should only take a few each time,

chunga imojobana
they killed them.

bweno
Fine.

chorna kachká imojisonyaye
Then like that they took off.

chorna mejor kachká yojisenyayena kotxenga imojatoñe   20
Then like that they left the place, the wild pigs went away.

i ch verakoyema stonoye chká imojtá imojtá
And that fierce one moved along, moved along, behind the others.

i chutata ibojisastjango ibojá
And those two climbed down and followed them.

[35]line 11: *jajwesamna*, "they would shoot them." With arrows, most likely
through a blow gun.
   [36]line 14: *ndoñe ordene yindemena*, "without having permission." The word *ordene*,
from the Spanish, implies a systematic comsos with each component regulated and
coordinated with the others.

i ko chorna ndoñe bnoka peñexuye inamna
And then not far off there was a cliff.

i ch peñuxentxe chngana chentxe imojetsatemejiñe
And beside that cliff there they entered a cave.

**choyna ch sain kotxengana yentxangaká ana yentxangaká ch sain
    kotxena   25**
There those wild pigs were like people, like people those wild
    pigs.

i choka ch patrón patrón wabayina dweña sain kotxengaben[37]
And there that master, master as he is called, owner of the
    wild pigs,

dweiñina ana moyen enobtuxkrosena inamna
the owner here [indicates fangs], they were crossed.

ch tangwayema tatxumbwan ndayase inamna[38]
That powerful old man, what a doctor he was!

ina chungabe patron choka de la warda choka yojtabokna
And their master, there, heaven help us, there he appeared.

chata yojanye yojobwajaja ibojobekoná   30
He saw those two, he called them over, they approached him.

choka yojawinyana
There he spoke to them:

tonday ordena jaxokayana
"You have no permission to hurt so many,

nye tbojtsajabota nyetxana kanyetema o utatema
only what you need, just one or two,

nye utatematna txamna koshachiñe nyetxana unga ndoñe
only two poor ones will you take, but never three.

ana morna kbochjaperdoná i anyna ndoñe perdón watjamna   35
So this time I will pardon you, and the next time there will be
    no pardon.

choye xmochenakwenta ndoñe chkana masna
There we will tell you: never again so many.'"

---

[37]line 26: *patrón, dweña.* The Spanish words are used to denote the powerful
"owners" or "masters" of the natural elements.

[38]line 28: *tangwayema,* "remarkable old man." The narrator uses the affix *yema*
here, which marks something unusually large, ugly, or intimidating. His admiration
for the scale of this figure is further signalled by the expressive elongation of the penultimate vowel. *tatxumbwan,* "doctor." From the root for "to know," this is the standard Kamsá term for "native doctor."

yojaukakán saká de usto txamo bnga
He scolded them: "Beware of mistreating us."

ibtsepasana shnana inamna kokorxebeñe ngobshniye[39]
The next day there was a medicine in a small gourd cup, a greenish liquid.

ibojwabwiyiye yebojonanjaka
He handed it to them, he offered it to them.

iye chiye ibojabmwana ase chiñe yojanye ntxamo mnashu-bwayana[40]   40
And they drank it, then they saw clearly the hunt.

ana nye ch ngobshniyetemaka impasa yojatamena impase[41]
So with only a small drop of that green liquid they became entirely drunk.

intseko ora kwatobxenana ndoñe yentsotatxumbo ch lware
When they came around from drinking that stuff they didn't know the place.

i asna ch mayor inamna yojtanatse yojtenyanyiye chentxe
And then that elder appeared, there he showed them the way.

nye yibsana ibojtashjango
Just the next day they arrived.

i chata ndoñe borla tatxumbwata tbjetsanabokna   45
And those two, no fooling, had become powerful doctors,

chor i ch sain kotxe usetonatna
then those two who followed the wild pigs.

ana manté tojtsobanana ibsana chata tubwañe pronto jatayenana
So if today someone died, tomorrow those two would go quickly to revive him.

nyetxá tatxumbwata chutata choye
Powerful doctors there those two.

chkasa ch antewana
So that's how that myth goes.

---

[39]line 38: *shnana*, "medicine." The generic term for botanical remedies, but more specifically a term used to refer to the visionary substances, *yagé* and *borrachera* (see McDowell 1989).

[40]line 40: *yojanye ntxamo mnashubwayana*, "they saw clearly the hunt." The idea is that the hunters saw the spiritual interior that controls the ephemeral world of experience.

[41]line 41: *yojatamena*, "they were drunk." Intoxication is denoted here, akin to the sloppy condition of one who has consumed alcohol, but implying also a state of visionary transcendence.

(m8) ngwayejemabiana
About the Poor Scabby One

As performed by Estanislao Chicunque in Kamsá, May 1979

"About the Poor Scabby One" is a morality tale with very high stakes indeed, for it associates the earth's fertility with the festering scabs of an itinerant young woman; where she is received graciously, the earth becomes fertile and people are able to find a living. The story has a happy ending for the Sibundoy peoples who at first sent her away to Aponte, where the rocky soil began to produce corn, but later brought her back to the valley where she has remained ever since. The Sibundoy Valley and its peoples have been renowned for agricultural output since the moment of European contact and probably before, and this story accounts, in mythical terms, for the magnificent productivity of the valley's soil.

The story envisions a time before the cultivation of corn, when the ancestors struggled to obtain a living. The scabby young woman appears and barren rock gives way to productive soil. She is identified as *mamatema*, "our little mother," and it turns out that the very scabs that make her unwelcome are the source of her productivity. Those who "know God," who exhibit the proper values of (Christian) piety, will be the ones to benefit from the earth's fertility. Since she has found a home in the Sibundoy Valley, both the *señoranga* (white people) and the Indians (*bnga naturala*) have prospered.

Although the setting of this tale is autocthonous, the notion that prosperity depends on kindness implicates Christian rather than traditional Sibundoy thinking. This myth, though it works with indigenous elements such as mother earth and the ancestors, invokes a decidedly Christian orientation to success in life. It must be construed as a hybrid, a confluence of Native American and Catholic elements, richly symptomatic of the historical currents that have brought these two systems into prolonged contact with one another.

mwentxe anteujemunga mwentxena bida imenabomina[42]
Here the ancestors, here they were able to survive,

lastemendentxe bida imenobomiñe
in hardship they were able to survive.

granotema induwabaña tondaye yondewaba
Corn and other crops were completely lacking.

ndeolpna shembasajema yojtsobokiñe lempe ngwayejema[43]
Suddenly a poor girl appeared, completely covered with scabs.

[42]line 1: *anteujemunga*, "ancestors." The presence of the empathy marker, *jemu*, indicates the recent ancestral period, when subsistence has become a struggle.

[43]line 4: *ngwayejema*, "poor scabby one." In Spanish, *Chandosa; Chanda* is a Columbian term for standard Spanish *sarna*, meaning approximately "mange" or "psoriasis."

ch ngwayejema wabá inamamna[44]   5
That poor scabby girl was the earth's fertility.

i mwentxena inyana diosa bewabwatema inyana ndoñe[45]
And here some of us know God, others don't.

posado imondewantxam posado imojwantxamientxena
They wouldn't offer her lodging, others did offer her lodging.

yojoftsochwaye bwetinache yojoftsepasiantskonuña
She proved to be grateful in those places where they received her.

chenachna wabaña ntxamo ketsemantena
In those places the earth became fertile, whatever they planted.

**ana imojabwetsetxe ch shembasajema xokajemama
    ngwayejemama**   10
But they rejected that poor scabby girl, because of her sickness, because of her scabs.

chorna chjemna yojtsenchnungwañe tambilloye
Then that poor one decided to move on to Aponte.

choye ch tambilloyena ndoñe ndwaba ena peñuxe
There in Aponte the earth was not fertile, nothing but rock.

i chká jistutjoña ena peñuntxe induwabañe
Like that it's in the mountains, pure rock, the earth was not fertile.

choye yojtsenchnungwañe choka wabañe
There she moved, there the earth became fertile.

**i choye chká lwar keisomiñekana chkoye
    teijtaftsotjumbambaye**   15
And there in that place she stayed, there she went to live.

**chorna mwentxena pwerte imojtsatenungumenaye ch tobiaxbiama
    ch ngwayjemabiana**
Then here they were really missing that young woman, that
scabby one.

morna moknoisa kutsoñajema chjemna
"Now where has that poor girl gone?"

chora inye ndwayejabotena yojayana
Then one who wasn't supposed to speak spoke up:

tambilloka kantsomiñe mornaka
"She is in Aponte now."

---

[44]line 5: *wabá*, "fertility." This term refers to the earth's productive capacity and
more generally to all generative sources.
    [45]line 6: *diosa bewabwatema*, "we know God." A means of referring to those who
have been brought up with Christian instruction.

i mora ntxamo chjema kwantiyaka   20
"And now how are we going to call her back?

a mo ntxamoka kachabe pronto mntxoye teochtutabajemaka
Perhaps without saying a word she might decide to return.

pero ko mwentxena jwisio moisenobomiñe
But those of us from here must understand:

sempra ko kortisioka muchenjwá kortisio muchabomina
surely we must show her courtesy, we must treat her kindly."

ch shembasajema ch tobiaxajema chana wabá yojtsomiñe
That poor girl, that poor young woman, she was the earth's fertility.

i ch tambello lwarna yojatamantxeñe chjembiamna   25
And there in Aponte they grew tired of that poor one,

ana imojatsebotsetxe ch tobiaxe ch ngwayejemna
they sent her away, that young woman, that scabby one.

imojabotsetxentxanena yojtsataboñe kamwentxe yojabatokedá
After they sent her away, she returned here, she came to stay.

yojtokedentxana chentxana bngajemunga kriatura melware toshá
Since she came to stay, from that time on, we poor creatures of this
    place have prospered.

yoweisokedankana ya mamatemena ya wabañe[46]
After she came to stay, our little mother has been quite fertile.

ndaitemena komoboseora ndayeoranak ska   30
Whatever is planted, in whatever season,

bominye kochjajajwa ndaye matatemena txabá kochjojwa
you will see with your own eyes, whatever plant it is, it grows well.

chana mamatema ndoñe ch tobiaxe ngwayaka tobiax
She was our little mother, you see, that young woman, the scabby
    young woman.

chtemena fshantsa ch mama ch tobiaxna mama
From that day on, the earth, that mother, that young woman,
    mother,

ch tojtsetuchungwaye chana ana tojtsabanaka
those scabs she carried on her body, that is what makes the earth
    fertile,

chama chká ch ngwayaka   35
that's what those scabs are for.

---

[46]line 29: *mamatemena*, "little mother." The earth is thought of as a mother to all
creatures that live on her surface.

ana morna ch tobiaxe ch ngwayajema mwentxe yetsaisomiñe
So now this young woman, the scabby one, here she remained.

ndokenoye kandatsabonjon mwentxa del todo tojabatanokeda
She hasn't gone anywhere else, here alone she has come to stay.

chiyekna mwentxna bida o ngwayamena ni señoranga ni bnga naturala[47]
Because of that here we find our living, the whites as well as us natives.

o kedanujemungena nyetskanga mntxá mwentxe
We have remained, all of us, thus here,

bida imongwajemunga karidad ibwabamena   40
to make our living from what God has granted us,

mamjemena ch tobiaxe ngwayejemena
our mother, the young woman, the poor scabby one.

ndoka remidio nyetxana tstatxumbo
So be it that's all I know of it,

nyetxana tijenoyebwé i respeto tijenoperdey
I have told it all without losing respect.

(m9) binyeabiana
About the Wind

As performed by Estanislao Chicunque in Kamsá, May 1978

This myth situates us in the topography of the Sibundoy Valley; it describes the experience of a person who wanders deep into the adjacent mountains where he comes across the source of the wind. High in the mountains an old woman is weaving ponchos for her three sons. As she finishes them, she gives them to her sons who take up positions in three corners where they whirl the ponchos to create the winds that blow across the valley. One of the three sons is relatively tame, but the sons who blow from Aponte and Mocoa are angry ones; for a week or even two they leave the corn plants flattened on the valley floor.

This myth is one of two that deal with the wind; the other (m10) relates the efforts of Wangetsmuna to bottle up these winds and thereby remove them forever from the valley. The wind is a constant presence in

---

[47]line 38: *señoranga . . . bnga naturala*, "the whites . . . the Indians." The mestizo settlers, many of them first sponsored by the priests, are referred to as "whites" in Spanish and Kamsá; they are also designated with the Spanish roots, *señor*, meaning "gentleman" or "lord," and *colonos*, meaning "settlers." By way of contrast, the natives refer to themselves as "we natural people," which can carry the positive implication of "native" but can also imply "those lacking in refinement." For this reason, of late, this term is most often used by Indians with some irony.

the Sibundoy Valley, where houses are deliberately oriented to shield their residents from the dominant breeze originating at the northeast corner of the valley, sweeping down the hills above San Francisco (this town is known as *binyetjoy* in Kamsá, "the town of the mountain wind") and fanning across the valley. Periodically the Kamsá veredas experience a shift in the prevailing direction of the wind; especially notable is the stiff gale that sometimes blows down out of the mountains from Aponte, a wind that comes during the growing season in the cycle of corn cultivation.

The wind as a concept has special force in Sibundoy thought, acting as the medium of spiritual transfer and contamination. In fact, the Kamsá word for "wind," *binyea*, participates in a rich nexus of meaning that includes the following referents: wind, dawn, spirit, and spirit sickness. This word thus evokes the first dawn, the formative ancestral period, and the continuing presence of a pugnacious spirit realm. Throughout the Andes the wind is conceived as a spiritual agent, medium, or conductor, but in the Sibundoy Valley it emerges as the primary vehicle of spiritual process. These spiritual connotations are not directly addressed in this myth, although the other-worldly portrait of the sons (they are tall, their feet don't touch the ground, they survive without eating) conveys the experiential otherness of the wind.

The word *binyea* is abundant in this story because it serves as the root of a verbal complex, *jabinyianana*, incorporating the semantic units "to blow" and "to shake (and create a wind)." This word thus references each term of the cause-effect linkage, the shaking of the ponchos and the blowing of the wind. In the end, the narrator tells us that this story accounts for the existence of the valley's winds:

chiyekna chasa ch binyea
Because of that the wind is like that.

In this myth a prominent natural feature is explained through the invocation of a familiar domestic activity, a mother weaving ponchos for her sons, but the family is situated at the extreme margins of the civilized world and provided with a set of appropriately unusual attributes.

binyeabiana ana mntxá
The story about the wind goes like this.

btse mamajema bebma ibunabomina
A poor grandmother, a mother lived with her children,

kansomiñe mnteskoñe ch binyeana
they exist to this day as the wind.

ch btse mama wabiayana
The grandmother weaves.

chabioye jaboknamana ibotsoitume kanye bnganajema   5
To her place he arrived, he was lost, one of us poor mortals,

bna tjoka chjemena inaye inaye
far into the mountains this poor fellow went walking, he went
    walking,

jitena iye jibobinyana chká jutsoñana
all through the night until dawn came, like that he wandered.

ndeolpna onuna tambotementxna kutsobokuñe[48]
Suddenly he came upon an old sooty cottage.

ch btse mamajemna ibetsabiañika biyaka inetsabiañe[49]
That poor grandmother was weaving, she worked with her weaving
    stick.

chorna chentxe ibojakonbida   10
Then she invited him there:

xmetsetjumbambajemasna ndomoye kwatátanas
"Would you stay and keep us company? Where are you going?

kam mwentxeka ungayá ibsa chanjwapochoka moyanaka
Here I will finish three weavings tomorrow, over here."

iye jutseshuntsanana ndoñe ibonjuntseshuntsan ch bwachujemana
And he wasn't hungry, no, that visitor felt no hunger.

ndayá jasam nye tonday pero ch tambotementxe yojtsetebemana
As for food, there was none, but she sat there in that cottage,

chká inetsapormañe tsabiañe yojwapochoka   15
like that she was weaving, she finished one.

iye ibsana ibojwantrega ch wakiñá
And the next day she gave it to her son.

pero de la warda ch wakiñaka ana bendotatxumbo
But heaven forbid, that son, he didn't know what he was!

mokna btsá bemana bna yentxayema[50]
Over there very large he is, a very tall person.

ibojwantrega ch tsuma ponchiya
She gave him that new poncho.

iye chna bnoka jaxungwana lomutxe   20
And he climbed high on a hill.

[48]line 8: Delivered in a subdued tone of voice.
[49]line 9: *biyaka*, "weaving stick." Kamsá women use a thin, wedge-shaped stick
to select the threads that will move forward into the design of the belt, known as the
labor, the worked part.
[50]line 18: *yentxayema*, "large person." This word is based on the Kamsá root for
"person," but the suffix *-yema* indicates that this son is a very odd person.

chorkokayé chiyana jwabinyianan
Right away he shook it,

mntxá ch banderiya klistrinyité mo nye betsabinyianaika[51]
just like the banners on carnival day, here we just shake them.

jwabinyianan jwabinyianan
He was really shaking it, he was really shaking it.

i chana chká jawatsayan pero chana ndoñe fshantsuñe atsana
And like that he went to stand there, but his feet didn't touch
    the earth.

nye kachká binyea kache binyea chká jwabinyianaka   25
Just like the wind, like the wind, like that he stirred the air.

chorkokayé mallajkta jatushebinyiananaka
Right away a very strong wind came to blow.

chká ibojoftsinyika chká ch wakiñá
Like that he was watching, that's how the son was.

iye kotutontxe inyiya chngana
And she began another weaving.

unga wakiñunga kamenamenunga ch mamabe wakiñá
Three sons she had, the mother of those sons.

mwentxa mas rebajoka ya ch shatjoika cha kobinyiaya
    kanemuna   30
Here a more tame one, while the one from Mocoa blows hard,

btsewanaka ch shatjoika wakiñá
he's an angry one, that son from Mocoa.

kanye mama iye tambilloika wakiñá choya yanya ibunechumwa
One mother, and the son from Aponte, there she sent another,

ora chana txatjayaka chana granotema perdenaka
now he is an angry one, those corn plants are lost.

morna chana ana ndoka remidio tojtsabinyiana
Now he without remedy was blowing,

mntxá tojtsabinyianana korente jutsabinyiananaka   35
Like that he was blowing, very hard he would blow.

iye matatema lempe jutsejatombayana
And the little plants are thrown to the ground,

oh ndoñe mase matatema jisonyaykaka
oh, no more little plants are seen standing.

---

[51]line 22: *banderiya klistrinyité*, "the banners on carnival day." During the annual
carnival, people from the different veredas carry and wave large colorful banners.

semana hasta uta semana jabinyianana
A week, even two weeks he will blow.

elay cha ch btsewanaka
Lord, he is an angry one.

i chká jamase kochjisomiñe mwentxna kwenta dia ndoñe mas
And like that forever it must be here, but only from time to time.

pero eso sí cha kokayé btsewan palabraka
But really, he is quite an angry one, by my word.

pero mntxá oyená moika ch tjoka inayejema
But like that one who lives here, into the mountains he wandered.

i chká ch palabra ch tjoka yojaftsebana ch tambotementxe
And like this he brought word from the mountains, from that cottage.

chká ch btsemamá jutsapormañana
Like that the grandmother weaves.

iye chká ibojaftsantxinyi ch wakiñá jwantrega ch tsuma ponchiya pardiyaka   45
And like that he saw her deliver to her son that dark-colored poncho.

i chiyaka chká jtsebinyiayana
And with it like that he makes the wind.

jachnungwana pero ndoñe ch fshantsiñe ntjujtsatsanká
He passes by but his feet do not touch the ground,

ana tsbananoka chká bnujaka chuja chká kaonyebetsabinyiaye
just over it, like that, tall, just like that he goes about making the wind.

chiyekna chasa ch binyea
Because of that the wind is like that.

chkase atxena tstatxumbo   50
Just like that I know the story.

nyetxa xmopasentsia
Please forgive me.

(m10) binyeabiana
About the Wind

As performed by Mariano Chicunque in Kamsá, December 1979

Taita Mariano had alerted me that this story would be about Wangetsmuna, the Kamsá deity-culture hero, but when he sat down to perform it he attributed the action instead to "a hunter," an unnamed ancestor of the present people. It involves the intervention of a powerful figure who makes his way to Portachuelo, at the eastern edge of the Sibundoy Valley, the point of entry of its dominant wind. There he sets about capturing this harmful wind, which was interfering with the hunting, and stuffing it into a jar. The story makes it clear that if it hadn't been for the meddling of a curious child, we would not have to endure this wind today, and thus articulates a theme that is prominent in Kamsá mythical consciousness, the notion that the world could have been a gentler place if only people had known how to receive the benefits intended for them. It is not exactly a loss of paradise as in the Christian account but rather a forestalling of the establishment of paradise.

In spite of the cosmic importance of the theme, taita Mariano imbues this narrative with the texture and aroma of everyday life in the Kamsá hamlets. The experience of being called in to share in the drinking of chicha is a very common one, and the narrator reproduces the pleading of those who stand at the entrances of houses and call passersby in: *metsamashingo metsamashingo*, "Come in, come in." The visitor warns the father of the household to keep an eye on the children, but, sure enough, as the chicha draws the adults into its social embrace, the children tinker with the visitor's things deposited in the patio, and an especially bold little girl releases the wind collected in the gourd jar.

This was my second recording session with taita Mariano; it is clear that he is hitting his stride and enjoying the attention. In closing this performance, he states with evident glee: "Ooh, I have stories enough to tell for a month or two months. I can tell them, I know lots of them." Alas, our most agreeable storytelling sessions were cut short by taita Mariano's untimely death a month later.

> **anteona anteona nya desde anteo jwesanuxa imenawabomena[52]**
> In the old days, in the old days, from time past they had the blow gun.
>
> **ana anteo iye chká jutsatajsajnana ch shbwayana podeska**
> So in the old days like that they would walk through the mountains with difficulty.
>
> **iye ajá asena nyetxá ch nyetxá ko ch portachweloye**
> And aha, then right there, right there, by that Portachuelo,
>
> **choina jashañe komena nyetxá binyea nyetxá inetsebinyiaye binyeayana[53]**
> there it was wet highlands, nothing but wind, how the wind blew through there, how it blew.

[52]line 1: *jwesanuxa*, "blow gun." Middle-aged Kamsá friends recalled using blow guns when they hunted in the valley as youngsters. Today there is little game in the valley, and the rifle has replaced the blow gun, which is still used in the tropical forests of the Amazon drainage.

[53]line 4: *jashañe*, "in the wetlands," a special ecological zone marked by constant drizzle and cool temperatures found only in the high central Andes.

ch binyeaykausa joshbwañama ndoñe txabaka 5
Because of that wind, they could not hunt well.

a ver ch shbwayá ibojetana ah ch binyea a vera[54]
"What now," that hunter, it was getting dark, "ah, that wind, let's see.

atxe tstatxumbo a ver a ver a ver chaotsebinyeaka
I know what to do, go on, go on, go on, keep blowing."

bweno
Well.

ndeolpe cha btsá jasabé yojoftsobwatsebaye tsmabé
Suddenly that fellow fastened on a new jar.

iye yojá nyets tjañe ese lempia ch binyea lempia
    yojtsatswama 10
And he went deep into the mountains, he completely stuffed that wind, completely,

yojtsatswama ko ch jasabesa choye yojtsatswama lempe
he stuffed it there into that jar, he completely stuffed it.

yojtsawastona i yojajetana
He covered it as night was falling.

chora bwachoye yojaisaka pues choka metsamashingo metsama-
    shingo
Then he went on a visit, and there: "Come in, come in."

imojonanja saná bokoytema imojonanjaka[55]
They offered him food, a drop of chicha they offered him.

ah chora yojobxiye ora kwatayanaka 15
Ah, then he drank, then he warned them:

karamba shjoka bxaka taiteko moxexunga
"Damn, there in the corridor by the patio, those children,

taitá kwanjetsuyana ojala chamojtsebanaka
Father, keep an eye on them, I hope they won't be fooling around."

tempo chora cha ch basa ya ch binyea chká inawatswamina
Right then that little one like that uncovered the wind.

---

[54]line 6: *shbwayá*, "hunter." In conversation, taita Mariano indicated that the protagonist here was Wangetsmuna; yet in the story, he refers to him simply as "that hunter," and in line 9 as "that fellow."

[55]line 14: *bokoytema*, "a drop of chicha." The root for chicha, *bokoy*, is dressed here with the diminutive, *tema*, indicating affection for this welcome refreshment.

ch basenga klaro tempo chká imojtsawabana ch jwesanuxe i ch jasabé i yojtsabana
Those children, sure, right away like that were playing with the blow gun and the jar, they were handling them.

i inye lokna nye yejwana yojtsestoñe ch binyea   20
And another bold one, that wind was tightly covered,

i chentxe yojtsatsaka iye de la warda[56]
and there she uncovered it, and heaven forbid,

mediatamente kachá ibojtsabinyiana tsbananoye seloye
immediately like that it carried her high into the sky.

ibojtsebinyeana ndoknaka
The wind carried her away, there was nothing of her.

i chora ndayam i chkase taitá tkunjwawiyana ojala ch basenga
And then: "Why did this happen? Father, I warned you about the children.

ana ndwamanye baseshema tmuntsoperdeye   25
Now which little girl have we lost?"

iye ndoka remidio ch binyea mwentxa kokaye tonday remidio
And without remedy that wind, here surely without remedy.

mwatjabema chkase xmochetswantañe xmochetswantañe
What can we do? We must endure, we must endure.

despuesna xexonga ndmwanyingabiamana impasa chká ch binyea morko impasama toktokedaka
Since then for the children and all of us that wind forever has remained, forever.

ana binyea atxe tswiyambaka impasa jutsepochokana
"But I was taking the wind to be rid of it forever.

tswiyambasa ndayama chká tonjasweltaka   30
I was taking it away, why did she let it go?"

i ch basajema chká yojtsayanaye orna del todo yojabatobotá ch seloikana
And that poor child, as he was scolding, she fell from the sky,

yojabatoshjabotá limpia impasa ftsenga[57]
she fell onto the patio, completely black.

yojtsabatsjajona obanaka
She lay there, dead.

---

[56]line 21: This line and the two that follow it are spoken in a heightened tone with a rapid delivery.
[57]line 32: *ftsenga*, "black." This may be a sign that she passed close by the sun.

chjasabia wabaná chká yojtsepasa
For handling the jar, this is what happened to her.

ch binyea choye inawatswamana   35
That wind was stuffed inside there.

**ndoñe ch basa chká bndebonjnasna tondaye binyea jamenana mna
   lwarna**
If only that child had not fooled with it, there would be no wind in
   this place.

chkasa chabe rasona
That's the reason for it.

ch palabra xmunjoftseparlanga chká inamanaka
This story they have told me, this is how it was.

ana ndoka remidio komo atxena tatxumbwanana sertsa
So without remedy this is how I know it, truly.

ooh atxe sunjaftsayanaka shinye o utay shinye   40
Ooh, I have stories enough to tell for a month or two months.

atxena stutsokwentañe mallajkta tstatxumbo
I can tell them, I know lots of them.

(m11) uta xexonatemabe parlo
The Tale of the Two Little Children

As performed by Mariano Chicunque in Kamsá, November 1978

This story, describing the travail of two heroic orphans, is one of the
best-known myths in the Sibundoy Valley. Like the Wangetsmuna cycle,
it presents themes and motifs with cognates throughout the Andes and
the Americas, and it occurs in the form of an accumulation of mythic
strands that sometimes appear as independent units in the corpus,
sometimes in different clusters. This mythic narrative, unlike the
Wangetsmuna cycle, is clearly rooted in the familiar, contemporary
world; its episodes invoke a recent time after the establishment of Sibundoy civilization, when social actors and relations were much as we
know them today. "The Tale of the Two Little Children" can be seen as
a scaled-down excursion into cosmogony; here we encounter the rainbow, a lesser celestial deity, instead of the sun, moon, and thunder. Yet
elements of cosmos-building are evident even in this reduced cosmic
framework.

I have recorded several versions of this mythic cycle, from Kamsá
and Ingano narrators, adults and children, women and men. The essential plot structure is well represented in the version performed by
Mariano Chicunque, who relates some of the episodes in unusual detail

even as he omits some interesting nuances present in other tellings. In view of the complexity of plot, it may be worth outlining the sequence of episodes:

Phase 1: Two children are abandoned in the woods by their father at the behest of their stepmother.
- (a) The stepmother treats the children unkindly, insulting them and denying them food.
- (b) She persuades their father, who is a carpenter and travels into the woods, to take them along and leave them behind, where a witch or beast may devour them.
- (c) After some hesitation, he agrees to abandon them, but the youngsters have overheard this talk and marked the trail junctions with ashes.
- (d) The father abandons his children, but they find their way back, to the chagrin of the stepmother.
- (e) He abandons them once again, further in the woods, and this time they do not attempt to return.

Phase 2: The children at the home of the witch.
- (a) The boy climbs a tree and discovers an old cottage in the distance.
- (b) He finds a witch sleeping there and removes several cakes to share with his sister.
- (c) The children go to the cottage for more cakes, but the girl laughs, either at the sight of the sleeping witch or at the sight of her brother taking the cakes; the witch awakes and grabs them.
- (d) The witch keeps the children, feeding them and measuring their girth; the cakes they are eating are made from their father's flesh.
- (e) One day she orders them to fetch water and kindling so that she may bathe.
- (f) An ant warns the children that they are going to be eaten and devises for them a plan of escape.
- (g) When the witch tells them to blow on the embers, they ask her to show them how; as she bends down to show them, they turn the boiling water over on her and make their get-away.

Phase 3: The witch pursues the children
- (a) The witch grabs a gourd bowl to hold her guts from spilling out.
- (b) She runs after the children, entreating them to come back.
- (c) The children come to a large river; by the side is the rainbow, in the form of a handsome young man sharpening his ax.

(d) They beg him to make a bridge for them; he agrees on the condition that the young woman have sex with him.

(e) He arches his back and makes a bridge, and the children cross safely to the other side.

(f) The witch approaches and asks the same favor; he agrees under the same condition.

(g) This time he withdraws as the witch is crossing; she falls into the water but emerges and asks for a bridge once again.

(h) This time he withdraws at the half-way point; the witch falls into the water and they throw stones at her until she drowns.

Phase 4: The children are sent to Santiago.

(a) The rainbow gives each child a wad of cotton, and sends them to visit Santiago.

(b) Each wad of cotton transforms into a wonderful hunting dog.

(c) The children prosper among the Santiagueños; their dogs are able to hunt the wild pigs that inhabit the area.

(d) The Santiagueños become greedy and kill the two children one day when the dogs are out at the hunt.

(e) The dogs return and scratch at the door of the church where the children are buried.

(f) The children are disinterred and reburied, this time with their faces downward.

(g) The dogs and children transform into two pairs of doves who fly off into the sky.

It is evident that this narrative shares prominent features with European folktale, in particular with "Hansel and Gretel," Type 327 A, which appears to be a direct prototype. It would be an overstatement to call this mythic narrative a variant of Type 327 A, though that international tale type surely provides the armature for this story. Several motifs here coincide with the type: the cruel stepmother, the abandonment of the children, their return by the device of scattered ashes (R 135), the encounter with a witch who fattens them for eating (G 82), the warning from a friendly helper, the feigning of ignorance so that the witch can be foiled in this attempt (G 526). Boggs (1930, 48) reports that this tale is popular in Spain; Hansen (1957) reports variants from Chile, Peru, and the Dominican Republic; Paredes (1970) provides a parallel text from Mexico (#31, "The Little Guava"); and Robe (1973) makes note of some twenty variants in Mexico and Central America. The Latin American variants, usually from *mestizo* sources, sometimes include elements such as the children crossing a river or dogs who come to their aid. But an element that is foreign to the Sibundoy version is one that appears in several Latin American variants, the children acquiring the witch's wealth.

There is clearly a major locus for these accounts of the old hag in the Central Andean corridor. Variants that closely resemble m11 have been recorded in Northern Ecuador among the Quichua-speaking communities around Otavalo (Parsons 1945; Jara and Moya 1987) and Roswith Hartmann (1984) argues for an ancient Andean origin for this tale based on a set of variants found throughout Ecuador and into Northern Perú. The Kamsá version contains many of the common elements that identify this cycle, but more thoroughly assimilated to local patterns of mythical thought. Whereas the closest Ecuadorian parallels have the children inherit the wealth of the vanquished old hag, the Kamsá version has them charged by a deity to wander amond the Santiagueños and there engage in further mythical encounters.

Taggart (1986, 435–36) proposes that the variants he collected "from contemporary Spanish and Nahuat oral tradition probably evolved from an unknown prototype that existed in Spain at the time the European colonists immigrated to the New World." But this would be a hasty conclusion for "The Tale of the Two Little Children," in view of its resonance in some details with South American Indian mythological prototypes. Andean oral tradition contains examples of the adventures of twin heroes, and lowland parallels are also evident, for instance, with regard to the despised stepchildren who experience the same problems as the jaguar's son in Kayapo and Apinaye myths (Lévi-Strauss 1969, 67–69). Francisco Tandioy (1988) has published an excellent bilingual version of this myth, in Inga and Spanish.

There are also evocative analogues in what John Bierhorst (1988) calls the Twin Myth, found widely in tropical forest societies of South America. Nonetheless, the story remains firmly rooted in the ethos of the Kamsá Indians, suggesting that the ultimate origin of a narrative may be of less significance than its assimilation to an adoptive cultural setting. The Kamsá versions locate the impetus for the story in the stepmother's abhorrence of her new husband's children. The father, who is disloyal to the children, is made to pay the ultimate price: the witch kills him, taking his head as a trophy and preparing cakes, which the children unknowingly eat, from his flesh. The Kamsá versions thus originate in a moral imperative: that parents should care for their children and, moreover, that food should never be hoarded. Kamsá ceremonialism dramatizes the sharing of food and drink, and it is safe to say that such conviviality is a moral imperative in Sibundoy society.

The *antewa wela* or "ancestral witch" is a prominent figure in Kamsá mythology. Her portrait in this myth is rather European in flavor; she comes across very much like the old hag in so many European folktales. Other Kamsá myths present a far more alien creature: in m28 she appears as a luminous vagina staked out on the face of the earth, while in m29 she is a temporary hardening of mud into a pernicious humanoid figure. Kamsá children know many stories about this feminine spook who is most often conceived as a liminal creature, neither human nor animal but rather some terrible combination of the two. Taita Mariano's version presents an Inga-speaking witch, who displays apparent kindness to the children with the ulterior motive of fattening them for a feast. With the aid of the rainbow, she is vanquished in a river that the storyteller remembers from his travels as a youth. Like the heathens in the Wangetsmuna cycle, this pernicious feminine spirit must be destroyed to make the world safe for Sibundoy civilization.

The intervention of the rainbow in behalf of the youngsters and his command that they visit the Santiagueños also evokes the Wangetsmuna cycle. Like Wangetsmuna, they are provided by their benefactor with a powerful substance, in this instance the wads of cotton that take the form of superb hunting dogs. The Santiagueños turn out to be treacherous; historical and contemporary rivalry between these adjacent communities is reflected in such mythical nuances. (In the Wangetsmuna cycle, it will be recalled, the culture hero transforms the foolish Santiagueños into monkeys). "The Tale of the Two Little Children" comes to a tragic end, like one variant of the Wangetsmuna cycle, as the children perish and they and their dogs transform into pairs of doves and fly off into the sky. In this instance, a possible Christian interpretation is forestalled by the narrator's insistence that they flew off into the sky, "but not to heaven."

bwenosna xkwabobojatxe
And so, I will begin.

anteona tempo chká inopasana uta xexonata wajchonata
In the old days, so it happened once there were two orphan children,

kanye shemabasa kanye boyabasa ibonamena wajchonata[58]
one a little girl, one a little boy, they were orphans.

mama perdido ibonamena i taita bida inabomna
Their mother was lost, their father lived.

i ch taitase yojtobwamaye ya inye kompañeroftaka   5
And that father married again with another companion.

i ch uta basatana yojtsabwayunja ch mamamnana yojtsabwayunja
And she didn't care for those two little ones, that stepmother didn't care for them.

i ndoka remidio pwes kachká yojtsunyaye
And so it was that she abandoned them.

i ch propio taitana karpintero inamna
And their real father was a carpenter.

---

[58]line 3: *wajchonata*, "orphans." Note that they are considered orphans because they have lost their mother, even though their father lives.

ooh tjoy inetshukwañe inetshukwañe[59]
Oh, he walked far into the mountains, he walked.

aja baseshemata shuntseka chká mamamnana ndoñe korente yont-
    sabwabwanyishañe   10
Aha, the little girl was hungry but like that the stepmother didn't
    care for them at all,

nye kachka yojtsinyaye[60]
she just abandoned them.

kabana mas biena boyá inataye i bebte inataye
At last the husband came home, the father came home.

i chorna ibojoyana
And then she said to him:

mejor ch basatana mejora koisinachaye ch basebiata lwaroye
"You had better take these little ones, these little brats, to another
    place,

ch tjoye ndayentxe i kokarpinteria ch bachexe[61]   15
somewhere in the mountains where you make those wooden bowls.

i koporma choye koisinachaye ch basebiata
And take them there, those little brats.

koisenachaye mwentxa ndoñe cha xmundetsestorbana
Take them so they will not be bothering me here.

bayá ndayan chaotsañe
Some wild beast will eat them."

i deombre serto mntxá oboja bebta inamna
And by my word, truly that father was foolish like that.

aja nye basata yojauwiyana   20
Aha, he just told those two children,

ah ch basata sempra ibowena batxayekna
ah, those two children did overhear a little:

bweno basatana xmochjatjumbambaye ndayentxe ch karpinteria i
    tsebomena
"Well, children, you are going to accompany me to where I do my
    carpentry.

[59]line 9: *inetshukwañe inetshukwañe*, "he walked, he walked." The repetition here
emphasizes the distance that the man covers.
    [60]line 11: *nye kachka yojtsinyaye*, "she just abandoned them." An Inga variant is
more explicit on this point; it has the woman yelling at them, and deliberately spilling food on their chests so that the father will think they have eaten (Tandioy 1988).
    [61]line 15: *bachexe*, "wooden bowl." The carpenter makes the distinctive wooden
bowls to be found in Kamsá kitchens to this day, carved with a machete out of a single block of wood.

xmochjatjumbambaye ijouwiyana muchjaka
You will acompany me," he told them, "let's go."

bweno
Well.

ch baseshematna yojobliga ch bebta junatsama   25
That little woman forced that father to take them,

ndoñe jatjumbambaya mase choka kachká jisenyayama
so they wouldn't be around any more, there like that he should
    abandon them,

ch tamboka jisabashejonama[62]
he should leave them at his forest camp.

choka bayá jtsañama
There a beast might eat them,

wela antewa wela inamna yentxanga asayá[63]
a witch, an old hag there was, who feasts on people.

bweno   30
Fine.

i serta yojaonatse ch basatna
And truly he took those two along with him.

ch boyabasana ana jatinyushe yojotsoñobo[64]
That little boy grabbed a fist full of ashes.

ch ndayenache eskina inye benache joyenama
Wherever there was a turn or they came across another path,

yojtsementxna jaisebotebotana ch jatinyuxe jtsayoboseñalayana
they were tired, but they went along dropping some ash to mark
    the way.

chká ibojtsostona ch bejtisenatsana i chká imenajna   35
Like that they followed, he went ahead, and so they walked on.

i serta ch tjoye ibojaushjango tamboye
And truly they came to a camp in that forest.

i chokna yojoftseyana
And there he said:

[62]line 27: *tamboka*, "forest camp." These are clearings, sometimes provided with
a few amenities, where work is conducted over a period of time, usually distant from
the home.
[63]line 29: *antewa wela*, "old witch." A spiteful figure in the form of an old hag
thought to live in the mountains and to feed on people.
[64]line 32: *jatinyushe*, "ashes." This manner of marking the trail is repeated in
many folktale traditions. In the Aarne-Thompson motif index it is R 135 (Thompson
1955–1958).

mwentxe xoisetebemana a ver atxna choye xkwareparaika
"You can rest here, I will have a look over there."

i kwando chora ch bebtana yojtatoñe[65]
And so then that father went away,

kachká yojoftsenyaye ch basatna yojoftsabashejona   40
like that he left them, he abandoned those two children.

i chorna ch basatna ibojeniana
And then those children spoke to each other:

mwana ndayeka taitá mntskwana
"Why is father taking so long?

ndokená bwauftsatoñeka
There is no sign of him, let's go."

chora ch wabena ibojojwa i taibocheta
Then that sister said to him: "I hope we can find our way."

serta chorna ch boyabasa ch wabtxe yojayana   45
Truly then that little boy, that brother, said:

aiñe aiñe yojtá sertañe
"Yes, yes." Truly they left.

tijwinynaná jatinyesheka kada benachunga
"I left a trail of ashes at every crossing of paths,

chká jtsena batanan tijwinynaná
like that at every fork in the path, I left a mark."

i serta chká ibojtsatoñata orna
And truly like that they made their way then.

chore tsokna tempo twambiana yojwabwach mamamnana[66]   50
Then inside right away the stepmother cooked a hen,

ibojtsesaye kata chore ch twambiana
she cooked then a hen for the two of them.

chora ch basata ibojtsatsebokna bejatantjexana orna
Then those children returned, they were looking at it then.

chora ch mamana yojatschembo jwané akaja taitana bashejwana
Then that mother shouted: "Didn't your father leave you behind?

---

[65]line 39: *ch bebtana yojtatoñe*, "that father went away." In other versions the father makes use of a clever ploy: he ties two gourds on a rope and leaves them hanging in a tree; as the wind causes them to knock together, the children hear what sounds like their father at work.
[66]line 50: *twambiana yojwabwach mamamnana*, "the stepmother cooked a hen." Throughout the corpus the denial of food to a deserving person is a sign of

awa ch biata tojtabetsatobokiñe inye
Look at those brats, they've come back again."

ntxamo mas inye kutamashingo ubwayinjentxe   55
What else could they do but come inside, even though she didn't
   want them.

chorna serta nye batatema karidad yojabiama yojaujwatxiye
Then truly she cooked only a little food, and gave it to them.

i kachká baté kachká
And she let them be for a while.

chorna ibojtisemandaye pronta motsenachabiata
Then she ordered him: "Take those brats away right now!"

ay de ombra serta yojtisenatseka
Ay, by my word, truly he took them away,

a chore serta yojtisenatsa kache tamboka yojtaisabashejona   60
then truly he took the two of them, he abandoned them in the
   camp.

iye chorna ch bebtena lo mismo
And then that father did the same thing again.

xkwá ratose stetaboye xochjaftsabwaná
"I am going for a while, I'll be back, you will cook."

i ch basatna chora kachká ibojodeja
And then he left those children behind.

sersa chora ibojwashanebwa
Truly then they cooked.

bwen ndokna   65
Fine, no one came.

ndoknasna ah chore ibojareparana shekwatxena
As nobody came, ah, then they looked around for tracks,

jwashekwastotama ndemajana natsana
so they could follow the track where he had gone.

bojaborlaka tojtotona
"Look how he fooled us, he must have left again."

ntxamo kaibojeniana
How did they speak to one another?

i ch wabtxe yojarepara yojarepara   70
And that brother was looking around, he was looking around.

wickedness and is most often punished severely. This theme reflects a strong emphasis
among the modern Kamsá on the sharing of food and drink.

ase chorna anye stjanasha yojtsamuntsuntsna ch iñesna
But then hair was scattered all around there.

akach unachayá kache bebta serta antewela ibojtsatajtse
The one who brought them, that father, truly had been eaten by the
   old hag in the mountains.

**a de la warda chorna ch basatna taitana impasena anye bwiñe
   kutsatamuntsuntsna**
Heaven forbid, then those children saw their father's blood spilled
   about there.

wela ndayá bayá tbojtsesaka
The witch or some beast had eaten him.

bweno   75
Fine.

chora chatena kachentxe yojataye
Then those two spent the night there.

ibsana ch ibsana kayé a vera xkotetontxe reparanan
The next day, right away that morning: "Let's have a look around,

ndayá bayá taixochasaka a vera
or else some beast might eat us."

ar mojtsaka boyabasa yojiya
"Yes, go ahead." The boy went off.

a chorna tangwa yebunentxa bnoka inashingo   80
Then he came upon an old cottage far in the distance.

yojinye yojashjango niñetxiñe chentxe yojashjango
He looked about, he came to a tall tree, he came there.

**tsbananokana yojarepara de ombre betsantxetetañe ch tangwa
   yebunentxe**
From above he looked around, my word, smoke was coming out of
   that old cottage.

i chorna ana chore choye yojontxá janaka
And then, then he started to walk over there.

yojabokna ora chokena ch welana inetsoshabiamenañe[67]
When he arrived there that witch was spinning thread,

---

[67]line 84: *inetsoshabiamenañe*, "she was spinning thread there." This is the primordial task assigned to female figures in the myths; to this day it is the job of
women to produce the woven fabrics, especially belts and ponchos, that are worn by
members of the community.

betsoshabiamenañe impas bshetanuja betsoshabiamenañe wenana wenana[68]   85
spinning thread, with her eyes completely shut, spinning thread slowly, slowly.

yojobekoná a chentxa a la warda chentxa chinche bacheshá iowajajona torchenaka[69]
He approached there, heaven forbid, a wooden bowl full of little cakes was kept there.

aray chorna ch boyabasana inetsomañe ch welaja orna
Damn, then that boy, when the witch was sleeping,

yojamashingo tsoye i ch torchena
he went inside there and those cakes,

trabajosa diosbe pobre jisomenana
it is hard to be so poor in God's world,

nye shabwangwanatemañe yojoftsajonwama ch torchena yojobenaye[70]   90
he just stuffed as many of those cakes as he could into the arm holes of his cusma.

nyetxá yojwamba ch tamboye kenatabojoyiye ibojawiye ch torchena
He took all of them to that camp, he gave them to her, he gave her those cakes.

ch welaja totsomañe i chata ch torchena ibojtsosañe chokena
That witch was asleep and those two ate those cakes there.

i chorna ibojtsosañe orna kwando ch torchena bebtebe minyekase inamna
And then they ate them, when those cakes were of their father's flesh,

y chkase ch basatena nye ibojtsosañe
and like that those children were just eating them,

a de la warda i chká ibojtsosañe ch torchena   95
heaven forbid, and like that they ate those cakes.

i chora nye yibsana shembasana a vera bwatjá
And then, just the next day, the girl: "Come on, let's go."

[68]line 85: *wenana wenana,* "slowly, slowly." The pacing of this line of text captures the languor of the scene.

[69]line 86: *torchenaka,* "little cakes." These cakes are prepared in Kamsá kitchens from corn flour and they are favored as treats by the children.

[70]line 90: *shabwangwanatemañe,* "the armholes of a cusma." The *cusma* is the traditional male kilt; around the waist is a space which serves as a pocket for carrying odds and ends.

kabana serta ibojwasta ch wabena ibojatasto
Finally, truly that sister followed him, she followed him.

choye ch tangwa yebunoye ch welabioy esa shembasana
There at that old cottage, at that witch's place, the girl,

i ch boyabasa chkajema tsbananoka mntxá yojtsawaubjautsanaye
and that boy, small like that, to reach up high had to stand on his
    tiptoes,

waubsajanaye ch torchen jokiñama orna   100
when he stood on the tips of his toes to reach those cakes,

ah bshoka ch wabena shembasa kutsobchaka
ah, inside the hallway, that sister, the girl, laughed.

a de la warda chore ch wela tempo yojtsobxená
Heaven forbid, then that witch woke up right away.

ah iye nyets utata yojtstabayika a la warda yojtstabaye
Ah, and she just grabbed the two of them, heaven forbid, she
    grabbed them:

aka mwentxe mwentxe ndoñe batawatjushematana
"You, here, here don't be afraid,

kam mwentxe xoisomiñeshemata   105
right here you may stay."

i tempo jwachentxañe yojatantea[71]
And right away she felt their necks:

ooh nyetxá flakoshemata kwaxunemuna
"Oh, you are much too skinny,

tsundata kam mwentxe kam mwentxe xoisomiñe moiseiñe
you two, here, here you will stay, we will live together."

niñubja yojawaka lempi tsexañe lempi tantxoye yojobomedidaye
She went to bring a stick, she measured their width and their
    length.

**yojtsebwajonaye de ombre nye tondayana torchen chká jutsosañ-
ana**   110
She had those cakes stored there, my word, and without knowing,
    like that they ate them.

yojataye chká jwajamanamna mntxá jatantiayana jwachentxañe
They awoke, like a mother she slept with them, like so she felt
    their necks:

---

[71]line 106: *jwachentxañe yojatantea*, "she felt their necks." This motif is accompa-
nied by a dramatic gesture on the part of the narrator: he runs his own hand around
the front of his neck.

plakwa ndayá bemnana inyetska
"Skinny." What, she kept feeling them all over.

ajá ibsana tojibinynaye jimediana tojabinyna jimedidana
Aha, the next day they awoke as she measured them, they awoke as
she measured them:

ar bejtsobochaye ntxamo betsemanana
"Well, are they growing? How are they?"

asa mo ungaté yojajetana orna ch wabtxe tsaubjañe
    inamena[72]   115
Then on the third day, when that brother awoke, there was a place
for the cuyes,

choy yojatamashingo jareparana orna ah bebtebe betxaxe
    betsjonyañe
when he entered there to look around, ah, father's head he found
there.

ch yojtsabwajonyaye ch welana ch bebtebe betxaxe
She had hung it there on the wall, that witch, their father's head.

chabe mntxensa chatena ibojoyebmwanata bebtebiana
The two of them were swallowing his flesh, their father's.

chana como a lo tonto nye kachká ntxamo masna nye imenetsey-
    enunga[73]
He, just like a fool, like that, what else could they do, they just continued living there.

chká kadaté tsemedidayan tsemedidayan   120
Like that every day she measured them, she measured them.

ajá unganatesna ah jitantiana jwachentxabe
Aha, after three more days she felt their necks:

kwajtsemenyekajema chora yojayana
"Now you are really fat." Then she said:

mantena tsundatena mantena xochjawaubjka buyeshe
"Today, you two, today you will bring water,

i che btse batebá xmochjaixne
and stand that large jar up inside the hearth.

xmochjwabwexniye buyeshe tsobebiamaka   125
Place the water inside for a bath,

---

[72]line 115: *tsaubjañe*, "a place for the cuyes." Kamsá kitchens often allow space in
one corner for the *cuyes*, the Andean guinea pigs kept for eventual eating.

[73]line 119: *como a lo tonto*, "just like a fool." This Spanish phrase has the sense of,
"without knowing it."

ana jutsobebiama xmochjwabobwexniye[74]
you will prepare water so I can bathe."

iye yojontxa jtebanana buyesh
And they began to carry water.

yojtsotbana ora torchena chore ch basatena torchena ibojisokañe buyesh jwabkukanoye
As they carried it, then those children took along cakes to the place where they got the water.

ch torchena tombantema jatastetonana
Crumbs from those cakes fell to the ground,

ch basata podeska ibojtsaye orna nyetxá imenachnujwana   130
as those children fooled around just passing back and forth.

i ase ch jwanga tempo imnastetona ch torchena
And then those ants, right away, the cakes fell,

i tempo ch jwanga tempo imojtsosañe torchenatema orna
and right away those ants, right away as they ate those bits of cake,

chore ch basata ch wabtxe yojtoshekojojoye ch jwanga[75]
then those children, that brother, was stomping on those ants.

chore ch jwana yentxakwenta yojobema yojoyibwambaya[76]
Then that ant became like a person, he spoke like a person:

ndoñe chká xmatabomanasna kabochjabwayena   135
"Don't do that to me, I am going to warn you."

chore ibojotsaye orna serta yojoyibwambaye
Then he told them that truly they were to die.

mnté chté tsundata jobanteka
"Today, this day you two are to die.

ch buyeshna xochjwabwexniye i niñuxe uta palankuxe xochjwa-pronta
You will prepare that water, but a stick, get two boards ready.

ana ch torchena inyetomba maka bngabiama jabunjasamasna
Now go bring another cake for us to eat.

---

[74]line 126: *jutsobebiama xmochjwabobwexniye*, "you will prepare water so I can bathe." As we shall see, these words are more accurate than the witch knows.

[75]line 133: *yojtoshekojojoye*, "he was stomping on them." The narrator here gives a few illustrative stomps on the floor, virtually transforming Justo's parlor into the witch's den.

[76]line 134: *ch jwana yentxakwenta yojobema*, "that ant became like a person." Such transformations are common in these myths, showing that they transpire before Wangetsmuna's sounding of the trumpet (see m3).

kbochjabwayina si no mnté chté tsundata jopochokate   140
I will explain it to you, otherwise today, this day, the two of you will
   be finished.

kutsemna kwaxjomenyekaná
Today it is, now you are fat."

bweno
Fine.

ai serta torchena ibojtaftseka
There truly they went to bring cakes.

ibojtisá ora yojauyana ch palankuxe tseboprontanana
When they returned he told them: "Have those boards ready."

i chore choka ch jwanga yojabwayina   145
And then those ants advised them there:

eso sí mora kmochjamanda chentxa morna ndoñe mas buyesh
"Yes indeed, now she will tell you there, 'No more water now.' "

i chorna yojamanda jwajwinyinyiama bwayaxaka
And then she told them to blow on the fire with their mouths,

ventadorshana ndoñika ana wayaxakaka[77]
not with the straw fan, but with their mouths.

i chká kmochjamanda ora xochjayana
"And when she tells you to do that, you will say:

kach btse mama xmobwatumbaka   150
'But Grandmother, show us how.'

iye kejtsatsejbena orna i xochjaproba jatsungewanaye
And when she crouches down: 'Show us how to blow on the fire.' "

i jetutserepitiana ar txamo
And they repeated this: "Please, how do we do it?"

a chora chana ch welana yojontxá jangowana ffft ffft ffft[78]
And then that witch began to blow, ffft ffft ffft,

**yojtsinguwaye ana chan jobshetaise ana jobshetaise jobshetay-
anase jutsingowayana**
she blew with her eyes closed, with her eyes closed, with her eyes
   completely shut she blew.

---

[77]line 148: *ventadorshana*, "fan." This is a fan of woven straw used to enliven the
embers in the hearth. Taita Mariano was accustomed to making these in his old age.

[78]line 153: There is suppressed laughter on the narrator's part for the next five
lines.

**achká yojtsetombana bshetanana yojtsashinyetombana ch welá
bayá orna[79]**   155
Like that when she was stretched out with her eyes closed, she was
stretched out by the fire, that witch, that beast,

chutata eso sí ch mateba ibojtsaspalankaye
those two, yes sir, they turned that pot over with the boards,

asko ch welá impase imojtsebwexkjaye la warda yojabwexkja
then they spilled the water right on that witch, heaven forbid, they
spilled it on her.

i tempo chunchu yentxá yojwatuntsuntsana
And right away her guts were slipping out,

ch bwawanayeka ibojtsbwexkja ch yentxaye
they spilled that boiling water on that person.

i chore ch jemata i chore ibojtsena binyiana ibojtsachá   160
And then those two, then they took off like the wind, they ran.

ibojtsachá orna tempo ch welá sachamatiyuja yojaisakaye
As they ran, right away that witch grabbed a gourd bowl,

i sachamate kwashajaka mntxá yojisenatebaye[80]
and with that gourd bowl like that she covered herself:

maishukona yakona shemata maishekona mesketolla mesketolla[81]
"Come back, come back, little girl, come back, sweet things, sweet
things."

yojtsekamena i chata nye ibonachaye
She chased after them and those two just kept running.

**ch welana mntxá ch sachamatiujaka mntxá yojtsayatenatbana chun-
chu yentxá[82]**   165
That witch like that with that gourd bowl was holding her guts.

i yojwakamiye i chata ibojtsachaye
And she chased them and those two ran.

ibojtsachaye orna btse bejaye inamna
As they ran there was a large river,

[79]line 155: *bayá*, "beast." There is ambivalence in this myth regarding the status
of the witch; here she is called a beast, while in line 159 she is called a person,
yentxaye. She is a marginal figure, human in her form and in her ability to speak, but
alien in her consumption of human flesh.
[80]line 162: *mntxá*, "thus." Here the narrator gestures the witch's vain attempt to
cover her mid-section.
[81]line 163: *mesketolla*, "sweet things." This term is not Kamsá; I was told it is
Inga, the Quechuan language spoken by the neighboring Ingano community.
[82]line 165: *mntxá*, "thus." Again the narrator imitates the witch attempting to
hold her loose guts in place.

ch btse bejay ibojabokna orna chorna chokna inetsebxanañe
as they arrived at that large river, then he sharpened it there,

**shabwangwaniya shabwangwana inetsebxanañe tatxniyaka tsubk-
wakwatjo[83]**
the rainbow, dressed in a cusma, with a cusma on, he was sharpening an ax.

a chora betsko ibojetserwa   170
Then quickly they begged him:

diosmanda por diosa betsko xmotsechnungo taita bakó[84]
"For God's sake, by God's will, quickly let us pass, Father Uncle,

welá xnukamena bayaka
a witch is chasing us."

chora apontada taitabakona shembasa btsa yojtsemna
Then that crafty father uncle, the girl was already full grown,

apontada taitabakona inayana
that crafty father uncle said:

xmatá musheshe xkojta musheshena kbochjaochnungoka[85]   175
"Come and make love to me, make love to me and I will let
you cross."

nye ka chama chká yojayana i serta yojtsechnungo
Just like that he spoke and truly they crossed:

nye diosmanda xmaftsochnungo bwenoka
"Only please let us cross." "Fine."

**tempo ch tsubkwakwatjo katoy yojenchentxe chewabnuxe yojo-
bema**
Right away that rainbow made a bridge from one side to the other,

btse niñekwema yojtsatabena
like a long pole he placed himself there.

ibojtsachnungwata nyets utata chungwana orna   180
They crossed over, those two, to the other side then.

chore i tempo yojtabobwatatxená ch bayá i chuja
Then right away she appeared, that beast, and she said:

---

[83]line 169: *tsubkwakwatjo*, "rainbow." The rainbow is a mythical figure generally portrayed as a handsome young man. In this line it is made clear that he is a Kamsá, for he is wearing his *cusma*, the traditional men's kilt.

[84]line 171: *diosmanda por diosa*, "By God, for God's sake." This is a traditional phrase of entreaty, a touch of ritual language applied to such requests. The term of address that occurs later in this line, *taita bakó*, is another marker of respect.

[85]line 175: *musheshe*, "make love to me." This is a ribald stroke that has somehow survived the rigid code of "decency" imposed by the Catholic fathers.

bakó atxe xmutsechnungo ch txabe yakonashema xmuntsebiachá
"Uncle, let me cross, those sweet little things got away from me,

jutseshichiñamá cha yakonashema misketolia misketolia maishe-
     kona[86]
so that I can catch them, sweet things, sweet things, come back."

yojtsekamena orna
She was still chasing them.

chore i ch tsubkwakwatjo kachká ibojatjwaka
     jutamesheshanasna   185
Then that rainbow gave her the same response, that she should
     make love to him:

batamama kbochjuchnungoka[87]
"Aunt Mother, then I will let you cross."

i chuja i tempo ibejatsjajna juxnana ch welajnaka
And she, right away she threw herself on the ground face up,
     that witch.

inye ndoñika
But he didn't pay any attention to her.

yojatebe sertoka aray ch shbenoka chentxe yojtsenatabena
He lay down, truly, damn, but when she was in the middle there he
     pulled up,

i chuja buyeshoka imojashbwetxika   190
and she fell into the water.

i chore ne borla chorna ne borla kaba shbeniñe imojashbwetxe
And then, no fooling, then, no fooling, still short of the end, she fell
     into the water.

bwajushoye ch xmuntsebushawá a xmuntsebushawá
By the edge: "They threw me into the water, they threw me into the
     water."

tambello barioye achkoye chana yojtxena[88]
On the Aponte side, there she came out.

chore yojaordena adelante ch taitabakona eso sí more yojtutebiya
Then he told her, "Go ahead," that father uncle, yes sir, now he laid
     himself down again.

---

[86]line 183: Once again the witch's speech betrays an Inga accent.
     [87]line 186: *batamama*, "Aunt Mother." Note the formal address occurring
throughout this encounter at the river. Ceremonial speech among the Kamsá re-
quires accomplishing all personal address through a limited set of kinship terms.
     [88]line 193: *tambello*, "Aponte." Aponte is a town at a day's walk across the
highlands.

i tsuntsaka yojtsetabenakaye i sersa tsuntsaka
yojtsetabenakaye   195
And in the middle he pulled himself up, and truly in the middle he
pulled himself up.

i sersa tsuntsaka yojtsaye orna chora serto yojtsenatabena ch
wabnuxoye
And truly as he pulled up in the middle, then truly he pulled away
that bridge.

i chuja parsama imojtotashbwetxeye ch welaja
And a second time she fell into the water, that witch.

i chorka yojaordena eso sí ndetxebeka lo que se pueda
jutsatechunganjan
And then he told them, yes sir, to throw rocks, as many as possible,
at her.

kach taita bakó parejo imojenabojoto
That father uncle likewise threw them at her.

imojtsatechnganja ch welaja impas   200
They really stoned that witch.

i chentxe nyetxá xmuntseboshayá chentxe nyetxá xmuntseboshayá
And there just: "They threw me in the water," there just, "they
threw me in the water."

impas ch bejaiñe tambello benache ultimoka
In that river by the end of the trail to Aponte,

chimbonaka kwabaina chentxe atxe tsutsonyiñe[89]
Chimbona it is called, I have seen the place,

ndayentxe cha yojopochokan antewa
There she finished her life, in the old days,

ch bejaye kwabaina kwabaina buntsutaye kwabaina ch
bejaye[90]   205
that river, it is called, it is called, the Hail River, that's how that river
is called.

i chentxa cha ibojtsetjoye impasa
And there she drowned forever.

---

[89]line 203: *chentxe atxe tsutsonyiñe*, "I have seen the place." The narrator interjects
a piece of autobiography which lends credibility to his account, reinforcing the implication that these events should be taken as factual.

[90]line 205: *buntsutaye kwabaina*, "the Hail River it is called." Elders like taita Mariano recall the place names for innumerable creeks, rivers, cliffs, gorges, hills, and
the like, a form of traditional knowledge that is fast vanishing as modern developments change the landscape and reduce the intimacy of the human connection to it.

ajá
Aha.

chorkokayé tsubkwakwatjona a bweno orna yojayana
Right then the rainbow, fine, then he told them:

tsundatena mntxaka tsundatena xochjá poblungabioy pobloy[91]
"You two, thus, you two will go among the Santiagueños, to
    Santiago.

chkoye xochjastjango chkoye shekwatxe tjañe shekwatxe
    jayana   210
Now you will descend to that place on a foot path, you will go there
    on a foot path."

chore yojantrega boyabasa tongentseshe bojajna gwardasion[92]
Then he gave that boy a wad of protective cotton,

i shembasa kachkaka tongentseshe
and the girl likewise some cotton.

boyabasa beshna bestxoka jutsobwajwana ibetna
The boy was to place the cotton by his head when he slept,

i shembasabe shekwatxoika gwardasion tongentsesheka
and the girl by her feet, that protective cotton.

ndaybayana chawana tsache bayana inye kachká bayá
    jobemanasna   215
Whatever beast might go about, large or small, if they did like that,

chká jobowiyanama sin miedo jitsojajwanaka
they could protect themselves, they could sleep in peace.

iye chká ibonaye ibonaye pronta chata katabunjanobra
And like that they walked and walked, that's just what those two
    did,

pobloye jutsashjangwana chuta basajemata
until they arrived at Santiago, those two children.

i ajá mor kokayé asta morsa ch pobloikunga nyetxá opunga mond-
    isomiñe poblungaye[93]
And aha, now, even today those Santiagueños are very tricky, those
    Santiagueños.

---

[91]line 209: *tsundatena xochjá poblungabioy,* "you two will go to Santiago." The rainbow assumes a role similar to that of the thunder deity in the Wangetsmuna cycle,
sending the two orphans into the world.

[92]line 211: *tongentseshe bojajna gwardasion,* "a wad of protective cotton." Cotton
also figures as a spiritual substance in the Wangetsmuna cycle, though it plays a different role in the two stories.

[93]line 219: This line shows that there is no love lost between the two native
American communities in the Sibundoy Valley.

choikna shbwayana inamena kotxe sawatja kotxe inajakena jatash-
oka 220
There was hunting in that place, wild pigs, pigs were found in the
swamps,

ch bochinana shachenowata bomná ch kotxe
the mature ones, five years old, those pigs.

uh kexunga ndoñe imondobena jashbwana
Ah, the dogs were unable to hunt.

i de la warda ana ch kexe ch tongentseshna uta kexateka ara chata
tojujana
Heaven forbid, that dog, from that cotton those two brought out two
dogs.

ooh pronto ch kotxe jashbwana i ajá
Oh, right away they hunted those pigs, aha.

kabana pobloikunga imojeniana morna mntxá mochjamaka 225
Finally the Santiagueños said among themselves: "This is what we
will do.

ch kexata mwentxe chabokedamana
Those dogs will stay here with us.

ch basatena ndmwanye basata betsomñana
Those two children, who are those two children?"

taiyotatxumbosna
They didn't know.

ch basata jutsabayana iya ch kexata chabokedaka
They would kill those two children and the dogs would stay with
them.

i serta chkaka ch kexe chunga yojaunatsa shbwayoye 230
And truly like that they took those dogs out hunting.

iye ch basajematna tsoka ch yebunokna yojtsebaye
And those poor children, inside the house they killed them,

nyets utata yojtsapochokaye
they finished the two of them off.

iye betsko yojtsajwe diosbe tsoka inamna
And quickly they buried them, inside the church it was,

jajwena diosbe tsoka nyets utata yojtsajwe
to bury them, inside the church, they buried those two.

tempo shbwayoka ch kexata ibojenianana 235
Right away at the hunt those dogs felt a kind of pain.

iye ibojtsatoñika ndetse shbwaka ibojtsatoñe
And they returned, without hunting they returned.

iye chorna ibojatashjango ch kexata chorna nye ndokasna
And then those dogs arrived, then they found no one.

ibojtsabajtoye a bajtoye ch buxaxa ch diosbe bxoka
They were scratching, scratching, at the wall by the church door.

ch buxaxa mntxá bajtoyana obligada shangustana yojatebjoye
With all that scratching at the door, the sacristan had to open up.

ibojamashingo ndayentxe ibojtsejwenentxe   240
They entered where they were buried.

betsko ibojtetontxa a bajtoyana a bajtoyana ibojtsejwenata
Quickly they started to scratch, to scratch, where they were buried.

i chentxe chutata yojaubwakna yojaubwaknaye
And there they removed those two, they removed them.

i chora iye ibojatontxe jabwertanana ch tombanankwenta jaja-
jwama ch añemasajemata
And then they began to turn them over, to bury them again face
down, those poor souls.

i obligada ch yentxanga chká imojobedesa imojatsjatsaka
imojatsjats
And they forced those people like that, they obeyed them, they
turned them over, they turned them over.

iye chorkokayé nyets utata chentxe yojisjatsaka stutxoikana   245
And right away there, those two, they turned them over on their
backs.

mwentxe kanye paloma i kach kexata palomata
Here one dove and those dogs, as doves,

ibojtsaysobemañe iye katai palomungna ndoñe seloye[94]
they flew off as two pairs of doves, but not to heaven.

i chentxa katunjanapochoka
And there they came to an end.

ch palabra welabiana nyetxase
That's the end of that story about the witch.

nye nyetxase tijatsparla   250
Just as it is I have told you.

esa es una cuenta de la vieja antigua
This is a story of the witch of old.

[94]line 247: *ndoñe seloye,* "not to heaven." A curious detail, suggesting a reluc-
tance to assimilate this story to the Christian worldview.

(m12) bngabe taitabe parlo
The Tale of Our Father

As performed by María Juajibioy in Kamsá, October 1978

María Juajibioy overcame her shyness with a concerted effort; it is unusual for a woman, and a woman of child-bearing age at that, to perform mythic narrative in mixed company. But she is the daughter of a distinguished elder, taita Bautista Juajibioy, who is known around the valley for his stories of the old days. As a child she often heard her mother and father discussing these things, and now this friendly outsider is asking for a story, and her husband, Justo Jacanamijoy, is urging her on. Her performance came out in a subdued tone of voice, but it developed a coherent sequence of episodes centered on Our Lord, the syncretic deity of Kamsá folk religion.

The mythic narrative she performs reveals a process of fragmentation and regathering of narrative chunks, the kind of shuffling of motifs and episodes that Franz Boas witnessed and described on the Northwest Coast (see Boas 1891). The narrative episodes treated here, the inquiries made to farmers, the failure to share a hen, the healing of a blind woman, are all found elsewhere in the Kamsá corpus, sometimes in association with other episodes not included in doña María's tale. Doña María's tale evinces the Christian overlay in its tone of moral righteousness. Our Father rewards those who exhibit courtesy and punishes those who are rude. When farmers reply that they are planting "the father's kindness," a verbal gesture of humility and respect, they are rewarded with a standing field of corn. But when they haughtily reply that they are planting "rocks," they indeed harvest what they have mockingly claimed to sow.

The central narrative motif here is Q.1.1, "Gods in disguise reward hospitality and punish inhospitality." Lévi-Strauss (1969, 256) notes that "myths concerning a supernatural being who, in the guise of an old man, a cripple, or some other poor wretch, puts human generosity to the test, are found throughout the length and breadth of the New World." Both European and American prototypes can be located with ease. Perhaps most prominent in the Americas is Cuniraya Viracocha's questioning of various animals as he travels toward the sea in pursuit of his beloved (see Salomon and Urioste 1991, 46ff).

The planting episode occurs widely in Europe and America. A few tale types with Eastern European variants provide rough parallels: 750 **, "The Discourteous Sower," and 850 B, "My crops will survive here without God's blessing" (in which crops only appear in the footmarks of the deity). Robe (1973, 122) discusses, as Type 752 * D, "The Virtuous Youth," three close parallels from New Mexican collections. Among the Quechua-speaking Yura of Southern Bolivia, a figure known as *tyusninchis* (Our Lord) puts questions to farmers as he flees the *yawlis* (devils). He asks those who answer well to tell his pursuers that he passed by as they were planting. The next day their corn and potatoes are ready to harvest. When the devils hear that their quarry passed by when the farmer was planting, they assume he is months ahead of them and give up the chase. Rasnake (1988, 144) characterizes this as "the most popular tale of this genre" among the Yura. Laughlin (1989) provides a parallel from Zinacantán, and he states that this episode is "surely the favorite throughout southern Mexico and Guatemala." He notes that "the 19th-century folklorist Oscar Danhardt determined to his satisfaction that the story of Christ and the farmer originated in the Balkan countries and was brought to Europe by the Crusaders" (Laughlin 1989, 274). Is Europe also to be credited as the source of a Tupi version in which the demiurge asks planters what they are doing? A Tembe (Northern Tupi) version has the man who gives a rude answer finding branches fallen on his field, while the man who is polite finds manioc (Lévi-Strauss 1973, 312).

The punishment for hoarding food appears elsewhere in the Kamsá corpus (see m30). Américo Paredes (1970) includes a version of Type 779 C*, "The Hard-Hearted Son," wherein a son who refused to share corn with his parents is punished: "a serpent came out and wound itself about his neck and strangled him" (Tale 40, p. 125). Paredes (1970, 219) observes that "tales of this sort are much more popular in Mexican oral tradition than published reports indicate." The restoration of sight brings to mind biblical parallels and also 750 B in which "a pious beggar is received in a poor man's house; the peasant's only cow is killed for him. It comes to life again (or new cows appear")." Thompson (1961, 255–56) locates variants in Spanish and Spanish-American tradition.

It is probable that a variety of deities, Wangetsmuna, Our Father the Sun, and the Christian Jesus, have coalesced over the centuries into the protagonist named here, *bngabe btsá* or *bngabe taitá*, "Our Lord, Our Father." Various bits of evidence point to the emergence of a syncretic deity combining elements of the former traditional religion and elements of Christianity. The elders who light a candle to Our Father the Sun at high noon also attend mass on Sunday as devout Catholics. Like other peoples experiencing a conversion to world religions, the Kamsá Indians manage to sustain this bicultural religious focus. They understand each named deity as one statement of what might be thought of as a spiritual deep structure, ultimately defined by the ongoing accommodation of clashing religious systems. Arthur Demarest (1981, 46) describes "a generalized celestial creator god" as "a widespread and ancient pattern" in the Andes. The Andean high god has characteristically been a diffuse figure, possessing diverse attributes and appearing in various guises. The incorporation of the Christian deity into a pervasive Kamsá religiosity can be viewed as a continuation of this Andean pattern.

bngabe btsá kem lware inan ora inabwachanaka[95]
When Our Father walked in this world he went about visiting the
  people,

inopasana chká tojanajabwacham
he went about like that to visit the people.

iye yojashjango kanye yentxabioy imojtsashuntsanentxe
And he arrived at one person's where they suffered from hunger.

chorna yojatjay ndayá xmobojenaka
Then he asked: "What do you plant?"

chorna imojojwá taitabe karidad sindobojena[96]   5
Then they answered: "Father's kindness we plant."

i asna inyoy yojatjá
And then he came to another place.

ibsan chká ch botamán imojojwá chentxe botamán xubwachan
  yojtsetsan
The next day like that, they answered well, there a beautiful field of
  corn was standing.

i inyoy yojatá i choka yojtatjay ndayá xmobojenaka
And he went to another place and there asked again: "What do you
  plant?"

chentxe rabiaka imojtsujwañe tmojauyán
There they responded in anger, they told him:

ndetxexe sindobujena as ndayase mas   10
"We are planting rocks, what else?"

i ch kaus ibsanté nde ombre nye ena ndetxexe inabtsejametona
And because of that the next day truly nothing but rocks were piled
  there.

inyoy yojatá bngabe btsá chokna twambian imnawabwanay
He went to another place, Our Father, there they were cooking a
  hen.

i chorna ch bngabe taitá inashjango
And there Our Father arrived.

i chor betsko imnetsenauyaná betsko metsaitume kejatoñe ora
  mochjase
And then quickly they said to each other: "Quick, hide it, when he
  leaves we will eat."

[95]line 1: *bngabe btsá*, "Our Father." One of many ways of referring to the Lord,
btsá means "adult" or "father."
[96]line 5: *taitabe karidad*, "Father's kindness." In Kamsá ritual language, the Spanish loan *caridad*, "charity," is used with frequency to signal the proper attitude of humility, which traces all good things to the Lord's kindness.

i as serto ch twambian imojetsabwetume   15
And then truly they hid that hen.

i ch bngabe taitá yojatoñe ora imojontxa jutsukama jasangama ora
And when Our Father left, when they began to open the pot so they
    could eat,

ndoñe jonjopodia txa yojtsetoton ch tapexe
they couldn't do it so tight was that lid.

i la fwerzam yojopodia jutsukama ora
And when they managed to open it with force,

choykana mtxkwaye inontsunja ibnetsotamorshundamaná[97]
a snake lept up from there and wrapped itself around the neck of
    one of them.

ch ndonanjay kaus chká yojapasa   20
For not sharing with him like that it happened.

i asna ibsan inyoy yojatá ch bngabe taitá kanye jtanjema inoyen
And then the next day Our Father went where a blind woman lived.

chentxe yojashjango
There he arrived.

i ch jtanjema nye kanye twamba ibnabojakena
And that blind woman kept only a single hen.

ibojtsexbwa jonanjam bngabe taitabioy
She brought it out to offer it to Our Lord.

i ch bngabe taitana txa yojochwaye   25
And Our Father was very thankful.

ibojamanda que ch plumashunga ndoñe ndoñe jtxenan
He told her that those feathers, do not, do not, throw them away,

ndoñe jawashanan sino que biakwiñe jwajajwán
don't throw them away but instead place them inside a basket,

i inye biakoka jetsjatsan i ibsanté jawashanan
and cover them with another basket and the next day throw them
    out.

i asna chká yojaobra
And then like that he worked a miracle.

ibsanté nyetxá twambunga boxenana imenachashjajanaka   30
The next day there were hens, good things, walking around in the
    patio.

---

[97]line 19: *mtxkwaye*, "snake." The snake is a powerful actor in Kamsá belief, associated with the native doctors and with the thunder deity.

bngabe taitá chká milagro ibojabemaka
Our Father like that worked a miracle.

i asna ch jtanjemabioye ibojamanda
And then he gave orders at the blind person's house:

kekatswanatema base chorrer jatema kobujenase chentxe metso-jobia
"Over there a small stream is running, go wash your face there."

i chká ch jtanjema yojobedesia yojajtsojobiama
And like that the blind person obeyed him, she went to wash her face.

i chorna tojetsano jobebiye i tbojatabinyna   35
And then she went to wash her face and her eyes opened.

nye nyetxá sinditutatxumbo
Only so far do I know the story.

(m13) |wlslo
The Judgment

As performed by Mariano Chicunque in Kamsá, October 1978

The world's mythologies are replete with tales of judgments, those catastrophic punishments inflicted by the divinities on erring mortals. In biblical tradition, as in many other religious traditions (Dundes 1988), it is a flood that cleanses the earth of its flawed inhabitants; in the *Popol Vuh*, a sacred book of the Mayan Indians, there are several judgments as the gods attempt to create life forms that will worship them properly. In one judgment, household objects rise up and wreak havoc on the people (Tedlock 1985). Incan tradition is replete with tales of floods (Lammel 1988), and this same motif is prominent in Mapuche tradition as well (Faron 1963). The Sibundoy judgment involves a tempest and a devastating earthquake. It occurs in the midst of revelries associated with Corpus Christi, a particularly ebullient celebration in Spain and its New World extensions, including the Sibundoy Valley of southwestern Colombia. According to Fernando Horcasitas (1988, 188), the Mesoamerican versions of the flood myth rarely mention a cause; the Sibundoy account departs from this pattern by imputing unchecked revelry and the failure to heed Christ's warning as the motives for the Lord's wrath.

As in many imaginative constructs, it seems that an actual occurrence may well underlie this tale of general calamity. The shards of pottery taita Mariano recalls seeing as a child might indicate the existence of a settlement that underwent destruction in the early decades of the nineteenth century. We know that volcanic activity and earth movement increased during this period; the nearby city of Pasto, for example, was leveled in 1834 in a tremendous earthquake that shook the mountain walls throughout the region (Bonilla 1972). But even if historical fact is implicated in this tale, it is clear that human fancy has transported the bare facts to a higher plane of understanding.

As taita Mariano tells it, *bngabe taitá*, "Our Lord," descends to the rooftops and warns the people to temper their merriment. The narrator paints a picture of mad revelry, with dancers and musicians holding forth under the influence of chicha, much as the Kamsá carnival is celebrated to this day. When the people ignore this warning, lightning and thunder crash upon them, a reminder of the syncretic association of Our Lord with the celestial deities in Kamsá thinking. Shortly thereafter the earth opens in a severe earthquake, destroying everybody save a few more devout souls who were gathered in the church where they heard two black dogs talking about the coming judgment. Taita Mariano displays a certain diffidence toward the content of his narrative, wondering out loud about the details but in the end adducing oral tradition and implicitly the wisdom of the elders as adequate insurance:

> **no se ntxamose inamanana**
> I don't know, how was it?

> **pero siertona chká xmunjaftseparlá**
> But truly like this they have told me about it.

This mythic narrative combines Christian and traditional elements in weaving an account of the Sibundoy judgment. The injection of a strong moralistic perspective—the people are destroyed "for their wicked ways"—is decidedly Judeo-Christian, while the action of the thunder deity and the conversing of the two black dogs has its origin in Amerindian tradition. The dogs are presented with a characteristic insistence on their animal natures in spite of their ability to speak as humans speak. As they walk along conversing with one another, one of them complains about the stinginess of his owner:

> **ko atxebe patrona ndoñe ch xmunjwaprobá mntxenaka**
> "Here my owner didn't let me taste any meat."

These dogs have prior knowledge of the coming judgment, and a few righteous people, those who were at church instead of at the celebration in the plaza, overhear the talk of the dogs and receive information concerning three safe places.

The narrator locates his story in an earlier historical period in the Sibundoy Valley, when the town of Sibundoy contained only a small tile church, and when the valley was highly inaccessible to outsiders. The story takes us back to an early moment in the tangled web of Indian-Spanish interaction; it focuses on the incompatibility of native lifeways and the new orthodoxy, and attributes superior power to the latter. We are told that the Indians would carry a monk from Pasto to deliver the blessing, a graphic representation of the relationship that emerged between the natives and their conquerors in colonial times (see Taussig 1987). Our Lord unleashes the judgment as a response to what might have been considered (by the Spanish missionaries) as "pagan revelry." Yet, in spite of this tilting toward the dominant hegemony, it is those dogs conversing as people—hardly a Christian motif—that provide the only hope of survival.

In this fashion, "The Judgment" achieves a remarkable blending of Catholic and non-Catholic components. Was this story an item of propaganda fostered by the Spanish priests and then reshaped in the mouths of Kamsá storytellers? The Catholic fathers might have perpetuated "The Judgment" to reinforce their prohibition of Corpus Christi celebrations in the valley. We know that the Capuchins sought to eradicate the entire calendar of indigenous festivals and that they were successful in doing away with all of them save carnival, which remains the one surviving period of traditional revelry. If "The Judgment" was intended as a stern lesson in Catholic faith, this lesson has been partly vitiated by the introduction of key native elements.

In the closing section taita Mariano draws on his own experience in attesting to the veracity of the myth. As a small boy he observed the forced labor of his elders as they excavated the site of the convent in Sibundoy. He recalls many broken fragments of a previous settlement being removed from the earth, and he takes this as proof that an earlier people existed in the town of Sibundoy and were violently destroyed in an earthquake. As the elder states, *bwertata chká jwisio inetsobema*, "It was strong like that the judgment they received."

antewano de un terremoto te voy a contar
An old one, of an earthquake I am going to tell,

de un terremoto que había pasado en este pueblo anterior
of an earthquake that happened in this town long ago.

anteo anteona bngabe tabanokna tonday yentxanga yemondemuna
Of old, in the old days, there were no people in our town of
    Sibundoy.

iye española katanjaftsejebo tejiyebunatema
And the Spanish constructed a small tile house of God,

base yebunabe yojoftsejebo españolna   5
the Spanish made their small house of God.

bweno
Fine.

i ch española chngana shatjoye ndoñe
And the Spanish, they didn't go to Mocoa, no,

lo mismo ndoñe benache ndoñe imundenabwache
since there was no trail, they didn't visit there.

**ndoñe yendotatxumbo ndomoye shatjoye inetsomañanana ndoñe
   yendotatxumbo**
They didn't know where Mocoa was, they didn't know.

bweno   10
Fine.

chngana chká ch shekwatxe jwabanchiñe
Like that they made a narrow track barely the width of a foot,

ch karniserioka ch peñukwema ntxamo inetsomañana
by the place known as Karnisero, those cliffs, how was it?

chká imenanga shatjoye i chnga tmojoftsatobjo
Like that they went to Mocoa and they opened a path.

iye bngabe tabanoka inamna ch tejiyebuna
And our town of Sibundoy was just that tile house of God.

aray cuando de olpena santo diosa   15
Damn, when all of a sudden, saintly God,

no se ntxamose inamna anteona
I don't know, how were they in the old days?

ana ah korobxamena bachna josmayana bastoka wabainoka[98]
So on Corpus Christi day they would carry a monk from Pasto for
   the blessing.

ndayá ko bngana nye moká jtschamuñengán
What was it, here the people would just be partying.

chngana buyesha waubkukanunga a sentoyika
They were just drinking chicha underneath.

no se ntxamose inamanana   20
I don't know, how was it?

pero siertona chká xmunjaftseparlá
But truly like this they have told me about it.

ana chká josmayana ch korobxa[99]
So like that they were celebrating Corpus Christi day.

---

[98]line 17: *bachna josmayana*, "they would carry a monk." It was the custom in the
Central Andes for Indians to carry missionaries and other Europeans on their backs
across the mountainous terrain.

[99]line 22: *korobxa*, "Corpus Christi." One of the most splendid of Catholic festivals, especially in Spain and its New World colonies. It coincides roughly with the
summer solstice and likely replaced harvest festivals established for that time. In the

chentxana chkaye chká iye korobxe yojtsemna korobxena
There, like that it was Corpus Christi, Corpus Christi day.

chentxa ch lamentasionentxe lantsayunga imojtsetamboñeray[100]
There in the middle of the plaza the dancers were playing the drums.

yojtsenana tamboñera iye ch meyesenaka ah jtsajatetanana[101]   25
The drums were sounding and the trumpeter, ah, he was blowing.

i lempe chká yojtsemna orna
And when it was just like that,

a chorna seloikana konforma mwentxe yojtsenana
then in heaven it sounded just as here,

fshantsoka i choika seloikna chká kompletamente konpormaye
on earth and there in heaven, like that just the same.

iye mntxá bngabe taitá ch lantsayungabe tsantsaka inabaitebemana
And so Our Father descended right in the middle of those dancers.

iye ch lamentasionentxe yojabototona momtsemiokakwenta[102]   30
And he came to rest above the plaza at about the level of the rooftops.

iye chentxasa ntxamosa yojoyebwambayana chabe palabra
And there how he had spoken his word!

iye impasa imojtetotsjwañunga
And they just returned to what they were doing.

iye yojaboyeibetata yojatakunyá iye impasa jwisio katunt-sanobema
And it started to get dark, lightning flashed, and the judgment was upon them.

ana ch tejiyebuna ch yebuna impasa lempe yentxanga lempe kwentadna
So that tile house of God, that house was quite empty of people, except for a very few.

Sibundoy Valley, Corpus Christi was celebrated with great merriment until the Capuchin Order prohibited the public ceremony.

[100]line 24: *lantsayunga imojtsetamboñeray,* "the dancers were playing the drums." Sibundoy festivities bring people into the plazas where they simultaneously make music and dance. A steady beat is kept on drums of various sizes and tones. For the Indians, the music and dance, under the friendly influence of large quantities of chicha, creates a revival of the ancestors (see McDowell 1987).

[101]line 25: *meyesenaka,* "the trumpeter." Sibundoy musical tradition includes an indigenous trumpet, consisting of a horn attached to a long, hollow pole. This instrument has disappeared from the valley since mid-century.

[102]line 30: Here the narrator invokes the actual setting of the performance as a token of the story setting: he points to the rafters of don Justo's house to indicate the level to which Our Lord descended.

ana kexe uta kexata ftsengata bnatna ibonatatmenguse   35
But a dog, two black dogs, went by conversing with each other.

ndmwanye yentxanga jwesia bominajemunga
Those people of good will noticed them, they heard them.

chjemunga imojatwena bayena tstsnaye utatoka
They heard them as they came speaking with each other.

imojarepara ndayá kasna
They looked around: "What's going on?"

asna kexata ftsengata biayetsenatsetsenaye
Then two black dogs came along talking to one another like people.

chora chora yojobekoná ntxamo ndomoyeka   40
Then, then, he approached: "How's this, where to?"

ch kexe yojoyibwambaye kompleto konforma
That dog spoke exactly as we do:

ko atxebe patrona ndoñe ch xmunjwaprobá mntxenaka
"Here my owner didn't let me taste any meat."

chnga yojoftsenaye jtsachetama
They were saying that they should flee:

mnté jwisio jente lempe jtspochokaté kutsemna
"Today is judgment day, the people will be completely destroyed."

taiteko nye kach komoká   45
Lord, that's just how it was.

ana atxejema xmotsechaka
"But have pity, take me with you."

bweno motsacheta
"Fine, let's get out of here."

komena ungañika utañena palmuxe koshakwana palmuxentxeka[103]
There were three places: two palms, with grass by the palms,

ya yanyoka mase bnokna ntxnajushoyeka[104]
and another place further on, by a *motilón* tree.

chenache jotobongwamuse   50
There they could be safe.

---

[103]line 48: *palmuxe*, "palm tree." This is *Ceroxylon hexandrum*, characterized by Bristol (1968, 593) as "a tall palm in 'natural' borders, endemic, very sparse." He notes that its trunk is used for house construction, its leaves in religious ceremony, and its fiber for net bags.

[104]line 49: *ntxnajushoyeka*, "by a *motilón* tree." The *motilón* is a fruit-bearing plant found sparsely in the Sibundoy Valley. Probably *Physalis peruviana*, according to Bristol (1968, 582), it is "distributed widely in the American tropics and has been cultivated in many places."

bwenosna
Well then.

chjemana nye bwetajemunga xkwesabwayenaka
"But I am giving this warning only to a few poor souls."

ch yentxá yojayanaye i ch kexona yojaftsabwayenaye
He spoke to that person, that dog warned him.

i kwentadna imojtsachetaye
And a few of them fled.

iye iye ch alredador ch palmuxa rededore inawatekukjana ch
   shunga   55
And, and there around the palm, all around, those leaves had
   fallen,

jotsashunga inawatekukjana ntsatxa chiñe
so many leaves had fallen there.

chentxe chana nye konye jatabonjon jatabonjoyana
There it just trembled, it trembled,

iye o ndoñe fshantsa jashtutxenana jashtutxenanana
But the earth didn't open there, it didn't open.

iye ntxena joshoka lo mismo nye kwentadajemunga kata-
   munjantebungwa
And at the *motilón* tree the same, only a few poor souls were able to
   escape.

lo de masna impasa jwisio yojtsobema   60
All else completely underwent the judgment,

i chentxa lempe tojanopochokaye
and there everything was destroyed.

atxe basajema chentxa skwela podeska
I was a child in that rough school.

ko nye diosbe yébuna nye ena btsajushayebuna
Here there was only a church with a thatch roof.

atxe tijuftsabwatemana diosbe yébuna batesa chká chentxana mil
   novecientos diez
I knew that church, a long time ago, around the year nineteen-
   hundred and ten,

ora tokjanashjango bachnanga   65
when the Catholic Fathers arrived.

iye chora chora diosbe yebunentxna kwentadungena
And then, then only a few people came to the church.

padre estanislaona o ch mexama imojtsobungwaná
Father Estanislao gave mass but they didn't come.

kaseona yojatxataye i chnga imojontxa jatrabajan chentxe
He gave them punishment and they began to work there.

jtsetrabajayan chentxe jtselimpiayana ch konvento jajebwama
They would work there clearing space to build the convent.

ndayám chká imojontxana ara konventena btsashayebuna   70
Why, like that they started the convent in a large thatch house.

pero diosbe yébuna btsashayebuna
But God's house was a large thatch house.

atxe tijoftsinye chentxe
I saw it there.

iye chentxa ko ndoka remidio ko sertosa asentoka jajoutjwama
And there without remedy they started to remove earth,

mo nyetxá jajotjwama chokse
then they just removed earth there.

choka jonynana teja chkebé che chanunga lempia asentoka   75
There they found tile and other things below the surface.

sin embargo chká serto yojanopasana
But anyway, like that it really happened.

asa atxe chká tijoftsinye asentoka
Even I found things way under the earth.

chká ch nye pedasunga tasunga chká inetsena
Like that only pieces of cups, like that they were shattered.

bwertata chká jwisio inetsobema
It was strong like that the judgment they received.

**ana ndoka remidio siertamente jwisio tojoftsobema bngabe taban-
oka   80**
But without remedy truly the judgment they received in our town of
    Sibundoy.

ana nye bngabe taitá chká yojoftsoyatatxumbwa
So Our Father just surely let them understand,

cha towaisabona ndoñe txabiamase ana lempia jtsepochokana
he might return if we aren't good and completely destroy us.

ana ko chká yojtseibetata impasa chká yojtsepochoka
But then like that it got dark, and like that he utterly destroyed
    them.

pero ch sitompokausna ana chnga mase nye impasese
But for their wicked ways, so it happened to them, utterly.

nye de lo masa katamunjantebungwa ch palmixiñe   85
Only as for the rest, they managed to save themselves by that palm,

iye txenajoshoka katemunjatebungwa
and by that *motilón* tree, they were able to save themselves.

chká atxe xmunjaftsekwentá jwisio yojobema bngabe tabanokama
Like that they have told me about the judgment that happened in
   our town of Sibundoy.

achká tstatxumbo
Just so I know the story.

6 Tricksters and Suitors

This part of the collection features a crew of imposters and their deceptions. At one extreme, their antics are a source of amusement; at another, they border on the grotesque. These dissemblers move within the late ancestral period, before the moment of demarcation between animal and human personae but after the essential contours of social life have been established. There is still a hint of the exemplary in these mythical events, but the mood has shifted toward the picaresque, and these tales exude the flavor of fable in many cases.

The first four mythic narratives in this section depict humorous deceptions, utilizing laughter as a means to moral instruction (see Toelken 1969). "About the Rabbit" (m14) and "About the Squirrel" (m15) unleash the classic bag of trickster ploys known widely throughout the world's societies, yet each of them provides a specifically Kamsá ingredient. The rabbit, it turns out, is another of the animal-people, and he changes shape by casting himself to the ground and rolling around in the dirt there. The depredations of the squirrel activate the indigenous political system, when bear as governor of the community marshals the entire apparatus of state in an unsuccessful attempt to subdue his relentless nemesis. Etiological nuances in these tales of tricksters have more a literary than a cosmological feel to them.

"The Tale of the Weasel" (m16) features the portrait of a false shaman. Weasel poses as a native doctor, even producing a facsimile of shamanistic behavior for the benefit of deer, who has mistakenly sought her medical intervention. But as in the other attempted deceptions in this group of myths, there remains a telltale clue, some incongruous element to spoil the fabrication. In this instance it is her ludicrous call for culinary helpers instead of the spiritual helpers that would ordinarily be summoned on such occasions.

"Mashangola" (m17) initiates a sequence of mythic narratives concerned with attempts to procure a mate. The deer and his father go through the proper channels to solicit his intended mate, but when she turns out to be a frog the match is canceled. The remaining mythic narratives included in this section portray suitors in a variety of guises, whose suits with very few exceptions are unsuccessful. Most of them feature animal-people attempting to worm their way into human society. These suitors, either female or male, approximate human appearance and conduct but retain some uncouth feature that marks them as animal and thus unacceptable as mates in the human family. The owl is unkempt, the bat is ashamed of his tiny face, the hawk is given to collecting snails in the garden.

In several instances these intruders are presented as doctors, that is, as persons skilled in the manipulation of spiritual forces. These powerful figures have been sent by the deities to convey precious knowledge, such as the ability to turn the wilderness into a garden by merely shouting down the mountainside or to prepare massive quantities of chicha from only a few grains of corn. It is either a failure in communication or the perception of radical otherness in the suitor that moves the family to prohibit the marriage. Typically the intended spouse favors the match and arrangements are almost final when a suspicious sister or parent sounds the alarm. In "About the Owl" (m18) it is the sisters who note the apparent laziness of the suitor and discourage the match. In "About the Sparrow" (m19) the intended mother-in-law finds the intended bride combing her hair in the patio when there is work to be done. It is the father in "About the Bat" (m20) who discovers that his daughter's suitor is a bat-person and calls off the marriage.

There is an inherent dilemma in the cluster of myths involving animal-people suitors. On the one hand, the pretenders often come bearing remarkable knowledge, knowledge that has the potential to transform this harsh existence into an earthly paradise. On the other hand, these suitors are portrayed as uncanny intruders who cannot be allowed to join the human family. The narrators sometimes lament the loss of this knowledge but on balance it seems that destiny must take its prescribed course lest the spiritual potency of these anomalous creatures overwhelm the arena dedicated to human society. Meanwhile the lure of an easier route to plenty, of a release from life's labors, is longingly contemplated in these myths about suitors.

The need to fend off the advances of the animal-suitors is expressed most forcefully in "The Tale of the Young Woman" (m22). Here the suitor is strange to the point of revulsion: when asked by her intended mother-in-law to help with the planting she insists instead that she will become the desired food crop herself; later it becomes clear that she has taken the form of a centipede and in that form received a blow from the older woman's digging stick. This mythic narrative decisively aligns the older woman's virtue as a planter with a "good hand" to her good labor in unmasking this imposter. In both of these arenas, it seems, she is contributing to the perseverence of human society.

This widespread theme of powerful spirits as suitors achieves a special concentration in the *montaña* area along the eastern flank of the Andes. Among the Shuar, for instance, garden woman brings food into existence by mere utterance until she is discouraged and leaves (Guallart 1978). A characteristic difference emerges regarding the treatment of this motif among highland and lowland peoples. In several lowland mythologies, unions between animals and humans are consummated. For example, among the Yekuana of the Guiana region "marriage to an animal spirit, even if dangerous, brings with it the chance to acquire power" (Bierhorst 1988, 71). Kamsá mythology presents a turning away from these possibilities, perhaps in keeping with the claim of the Sibundoy peoples to be *indios civilizados*. Civilized Indians, who dwelt in stable villages and received the Catholic faith, were accorded legal rights denied to *indios salvajes* (savage Indians) in the Spanish colony (Bonilla 1972). The Sibundoy peoples lay claim to civilized status even as they relish the lowland incrustations in their culture (McDowell 1989).

A series of mythic narratives pursues the theme of courtship in reference to amorous bears. In one instance, "About the Lively Bear" (m25), the clever young woman is able to outwit the seductive bear and send him running off into the distance. In another, "About the Bear" (m24), the bear is successful in carrying off his human mate, but she eventually returns to human society and the bear destroys their offspring before he himself is destroyed by the soldiers. A third take on this theme, "Juan Oso" (m26), has the bear-child survive, come of age, and achieve success in war. These variants point to a matrix of tales about bears who seek human mates not through trial marriage but through outright abduction. The most famous of these, the Juan Oso story in which the bear raptor is successful and begets a viable son, appears to be the odd one within this particular mythology of indigenous America.

(m14) koñeshbiana
About the Rabbit

As performed by Mariano Chicunque in Kamsá, November 1978

"About the Rabbit" clearly belongs to the great international parade of trickster stories featuring apprehension of a food-stealing critter through the device of a sticky doll, yet just as clearly it uses this familiar motif to paint a thoroughly Kamsá canvas. This string of trickster episodes contains narrative elements that occur widely throughout the world, but that seem to be particularly popular in the Americas. The closest European parallels fall into Type 74 C and of course Type 175, "The Tarbaby and the Rabbit." Hansen (1957, 7) identifies a version, 74 K, that has many of the ingredients of m14, and locates variants in Argentina, Chile, Peru, Cuba, and Puerto Rico. Boydstun (1947) finds variants of Type 175 continuously from Argentina to Venezuela. Américo Paredes (1970, 212) observes that "this is a very popular tale in Mexico" and that "it is the tricks played on the coyote after the escape from the tarbaby that are enjoyed the most." Robe (1973) locates more than fifty variants in Mexico and Central America. The American variants involve a wax doll—most likely not a "monkey" as Franz Boas (1912) claims in a variant from Oaxaca. (I suspect that he mistranslates the Spanish *mono*, which can mean "monkey," but is better rendered "doll" here).

Rabbit's arrogant behavior when confronted with the mute doll could be taken directly from African-American or European parallels, but his curious oscillation between human and animal forms connects this trickster figure to the mainstream animal-people of Kamsá mythopoeic thought. This narrative affords a view of the transformative process that turns a young man into a rabbit and a rabbit once again into a young man: he gets down on all fours and rolls about in the dirt to bring off the change in outward identity. Taita Mariano's plot accomplishes a very clever bending back upon itself: in his human form, the young fellow blames the rabbits for devouring the bean plants, while in his animal form, he is the true culprit.

As is customary in Kamsá mythic narrative, it is the elders, drawing on their stockpile of traditional knowledge, who devise the winning plan. They bring forth the sticky doll in order to catch the rabbit in his deception. This doll is cognate to the tar baby but its stickiness derives not from tar but from resin found inside bee hives. The heat of the sun loosens this resin, and taita Mariano tells us that the doll is glistening at mid-morning just as the rabbit approaches with his basket of table scraps. The narrator takes evident delight in portraying the imperious rabbit accosting the intruder he finds in the garden, and this episode is a favorite among Kamsá children. Rabbit rages in the authentic tonality of a cocksure bully: *morna koisetatxumbo more kbochjatoskunjaka*, "Now I will show you something, now I will kick you!" At this and other humorous junctures in the story, taita Mariano can barely retain his own composure; the storyteller's grin breaks into laughter from time to time during the performance.

But this narrative pierces beyond the comic in the harsh fate that apparently awaits this carefree trickster. The owners (unlike the audience) are not amused at his antics; in fact, they are visited by anger (line 75) and resolve to destroy the rabbit with a heated iron brand. A shift in the emotional vector of the story occurs and is clearly marked in line 79, when the narrator refers to the rabbit as *chjema*, "that poor fellow," using the empathy marker *-jema*. Circumstances have converted the laughable rabbit into an unfortunate prisioner awaiting his execution.

However, trust good old bear to revive the comic ambience. Rabbit formally solicits bear ("Father Uncle") to take his place, exploiting bear's gluttonous tendencies, and foolish bear falls for the ruse. This exchange of words reveals that Kamsá ritual language, a form of polite speech, can be used to deceive in the schemes of unscrupulous actors (see McDowell 1990). The narrator emphasizes the point by playfully referring to bear as "uncle," taking his cue from the irreverent rabbit. When the owners arrive they are distressed to find that the culprit has made his escape; they scorch bear for good measure and send him off to deliver the infamous rabbit.

The final episode shows rabbit in characteristic form, calling his pursuer into the shade of a garden, then eluding him by crawling into a hollow log. Bear is able to grab only rabbit's tail, and ever after, we are told, rabbits have only a stub of a tail. Another fateful consequence of rabbit's scheming is the prohibition against taking up his human form. From that day on, rabbits have been required to remain rabbits, and tailless at that. The etiological tags have a distinctively "literary" feel in this story; here they appear to be thrown in to achieve closure rather than to explicate cosmic process as in so much of Kamsá mythic narrative.

koñeshbiama mntxá
The one about the rabbit, like this.

koñeshna ntxamsa inamenana anteona
The rabbit, how was it in the old days?

nye lempse yentxanga inetsomiña nye lempe yentxanga
They were just people, they were just people.

chiyeksa chká chngnana bianga inamenámena[1]
And so like that they were able to speak.

**pero inopasana ch anteona ch basana inamna por ejemplo xexon-
    kwenta inamna[2]**   5
But it happened in the old days, that little fellow was, for example,
    like a son, he was.

ajá i ch btsetsanga imenawaubojena tsumbejwá
Aha. And those parents had planted beans,

tsumbejwá lo de mas saná nye ch reswardo inajena
beans, and all other kinds of food, by the edge of that plot they were
    planted.

ana ch basa jimandana motsajajoka jtsetsajajwana[3]
So they would send that little fellow: "Go to the garden to spread
    these scraps."

[1]line 4: *bianga*, "speakers." Consistently the distinguishing feature of human beings is their ability to speak; the animal-people confound things by also being able to speak.

[2]line 5: *xexonkwenta*, "like a child." Refers to a common living arrangement wherein a youngster will reside with a family in return for helping out with the chores.

[3]line 8: *motsajajoka*, "go to the garden." The *jajoka*, garden, is a cultivated plot that stands near the house; it is a major source of the household food supply. Often bounded by lines of eucalyptus trees, its verdant abundance and dancing corn stalks are emblematic of the traditional Kamsá lifestyle.

i ch basura sebarokuñe juftsatswamana juftsasmayana jwabotbot-ama ch tsumbijunga⁴

And he would place that garbage in a basket and carry it to the garden to fertilize those bean plants.

koñesbiamaka bueno   10

The one about the rabbit, fine.

i cha chká de ombre jiuyanbana ch sebarushá wasmana jajoye ch tsumbijwá jwabotbotamaka

And like that he really carried the garbage on his back to the garden to spread around those bean plants.

yaye jtabobwambayana ah lempe tmojsasañe ch koñishunga

And he would go and tell them that the rabbits had completely eaten those plants,

lempe tonday nye lempe washsasniñe twatomiñe

completely, nothing left, nothing at all, they were completely eaten.

bueno

Well.

nye chká kada ora betsekwentayamina yojoyamba ya nye   15

Just like this he came to inform them every time, he told them just so.

i chorna stonoye ibojwasto imojarondanga⁵

And then they followed behind him, [narrator laughs] they kept an eye on him:

ntxamo ndayeka chká bejtsopasanana

"What's going on here, why is this happening?"

kwando cha serto yojashjango jajoka orna

When he truly arrived at the garden,

ch sebarushana yojetsabwajwa ch chaboka

that basket of garbage he placed to one side.

i chorna ch btsana ana nye ndiabwena koshajaye ch fshansiñe   20

And then that fellow, without any leave, just fell on all fours to the ground,

yojojanduwowo i koñesho ijobemaka⁶

he rolled around in the dirt and turned into a rabbit,

---

⁴line 9: *jwabotbotama*, "to fertilize." This plot detail offers a glimpse of Kamsá composting technique, part of a widely acknowledged horticultural mastery (Bristol 1968)

⁵line 16: [narrator laughs]. The narrator here starts to display openly his amusement at the antics of the story protagonist.

⁶line 21: *ijobemaka*, "he became." From the root, *bema*, meaning "to make." Thus

ah koñeshe kobemaye a lempe yojtsashsasa lempe
ah, he became a rabbit and completely devoured everything.

chorkokayé yojtotó batsaye a cha i yojtotojandowowoye fshansiñe
Right away he got down to work, and he rolled about on the ground
   again,

i chora yojtatobema yentxaká
and then he became like a person again.

chorko chusha yojwaka lempe yojaftsobotboto   25
Then he took up that load, he spread it all about to fertilize the
   plants.

iya yojiyita jobwambayám
And he went to tell them about it.

ooh nye konforma nyetxá jwashsasniñeka
Oh, just like that he was eating it all up.

bwenosna
Well then.

ch patronunga ya imojtsetatxumbo chká wamaná inamna⁷
Those owners already knew that he was that sort of fellow.

mntxana imojeniana   30
Like that they were talking among themselves.

bweno
Well.

chore inje ibsana yojuiyambo orna imojauwiyana
Then the next day, when he went to take it, they said:

bwenoka chká yapa betsashsaikausna
"Well, since he is eating so much,

bnga btsetsanga toftsejajo choka muñeko⁸
we elders have left there a doll,

jtsemna a ver ntxamo chakontjetxiyesna   35
so we can find out just what is going on,

ana nose ndayá chká bewashsayana
so just what is it that is doing all this eating?"

"he made himself" or "became" a rabbit.
   ⁷line 29: *patronunga*, "owners." This Spanish borrowing denotes the adult members of the household. It implies a service relationship on the part of the other people living or working within the household.
   ⁸line 34: *bnga btsetsanga*, "we elders." As usual, it is the elders, *btsetsanga* (also
meaning "grandparents"), as the repository of traditional knowledge, who come to
the rescue. *muñeko*, "doll." The Spanish borrowing is used; it indicates a human-like
figure, an effigy.

asna a ver mareparaka
Then: "Go have a look."

bwenoka serto yojá
"Fine," truly he went out.

chorna ana ch íngabe betsetsañe jajoka[9]
Then that sticky doll was just standing there in the garden.

ya yojtseshamé junya orna impase ibonetsobosesañika   40
Already the sunshine was warm, the doll was glistening.

yojawajajwa sebarishá iye chore primer yojá ch íngabe
He set aside the basket and there right away he came upon the doll.

yojtsemenentxe ibojauwiyanaka mojwanaka[10]
He approached it and spoke: "Answer me!"

ndoka jojwanaka
There was no response.

pero tjayana mojwanaka
"But I tell you, answer me!"

ndoka   45
Nothing.

bwenoka kbochantsepegaka
"Fine, I'm going to hit you."

nye ndoka i sersa ibojapegaka
Just nothing, and truly he hit him.

kwando ibojapegay kukwatxe mntxá ibojtsanjo[11]
When he hit him, his hand stuck like this.

aray mojwanaka
"Damn, answer me!"

i kachká mntxá inyoy katxeka ibojatspega   50
And then he hit him with the other hand.

iye nyets utatxe yojtsatanjoná del todoka
And both of them remained completely stuck.

bweno
Well.

[9]line 39: *íngabe*, "sticky doll." This variant on the tar baby is made from a sticky substance extracted from bee hives, not the honey, called *tsingajax*.

[10]line 42: *mojwanaka*, "answer me." The narrator delivers this line in a fierce voice, simulating the rabbit's arrogant demeanor. Throughout this episode (through line 61), the narrator's voice is animated as he dramatizes rabbit's encounter with the mute sticky doll.

[11]line 48: *mntxá ibojtsanjo*, "like that it stuck." The narrator gestures by striking the open palm of one hand with the closed fist of the other.

ndayám chká xkjama
"Why have you treated me like this?

morna koisetatxumbo more kbochjatoskunjaka
Now I will show you something, now I will kick you!"

ibojatoskunja kanyoy katxeka iye ibojatanjoka   55
He kicked him with one foot and it also got stuck.

inyoy katxeka ibojatoskunja ibojatanjo
With the other foot he kicked and it also remained stuck.

chorna nye del todo choye yojtsataujona
Then he was completely stuck there,

ch ingabioye yojtsanjona del todo
He was completely stuck to that doll.

bweno
Well.

chorna chore yojayana kbuntetsejantsaka   60
Then he spoke to him there: "I am going to bite you."

**chorna chana nye kabá jajantsama ndoñe orna chora ndweñunga
  imenabebaneka**
Then when he was going to bite him, no, then the owners came
  along.

chora ch ndweñe yojabashjango
Then that owner arrived.

**ndoñesna kwandemuna koñeshosna kachaka btsá chká kwako-
  braka**
"So it wasn't the rabbits, it was this fellow, you've been doing
  all this."

chora yojtsatanjona ntxamo cha nye ndoka
Then he was stuck there, what could he do?

bweno   65
Well.

chorna ndoka remidio chká ch anteona
Then without remedy that's how it was in the old days,

chkase ch pegapegaka inawabaina chká inamanana[12]
that was the sticky doll, as it was called.

jatajanjana ana uta bnutsana jatajanjuse ana ndiabwena
They whipped him twenty times, they whipped him without mercy.

---

[12]line 67: *pegapegaka*, "sticky doll." Here we get the Spanish word, reduplicated
from the root *pegar*, "to stick," with a Kamsá focal marker (*-ka*) tacked on to it.

chora jutsjabjonanaka
Then before they let him down,

i nyetxá imojachibunja uta bnutsana   70
they gave him twenty lashes.

i ase chora cha yojutsjabjona nedombre yojtsoweltaka
And after that they let him down, upon my word, they turned him
    loose.

ajá ndoñe ch koñesho chká kwakobraka
"Aha, so it wasn't the rabbit that was doing all this.

bweno kwatajna tsoyika
Well, let's go inside."

imojisebetxe chusha imojisoshaná imojtanga tsokana
They picked up that load and spread it about, they went inside.

i chokna rabia ibojwabwache ch ndweñungna   75
And there anger visited those owners.

imojtetsajonyaye chana yojtsajonyana
They left him hanging there, he was hanging there.

iye ch patronanunga imojá
And those owners took off.

i yerubja jajwinyiyam cha jtsenechentxa jtseitanam[13]
And they went to heat an iron brand to stick through him and
    kill him.

cha imojangana iye chjema chentxe yojtsajonyana
They took off and that poor fellow was just hanging there.

chká imojoftsajonyayunga   80
Like that they just left him hanging there.

bweno
Well.

i ndoknaka ndoknakaye
And nothing happened, nobody came along.

i ndeolpe chore yojtabokena osoka
And suddenly then the bear appeared.

chore ch oso ibojauyana
Then that bear said to him:

i taita sobrena ndayek chkaka[14]   85
"And Father Nephew, why are you like this?"

---

[13]line 78: *yerubja*, "iron brand." This detail is imported from the post-colonial
period, since it was the Spanish who brought this technology to the Sibundoy Valley.
[14]line 85: *taita sobrena*, "Father Nephew." Note the use of fictive kinship terms

a ko ndoka omena chká xmuntsema del todo chká bentsabasna
"For no reason at all they have done this to me, but I won't be able
   to handle it all.

karay taita bakó achká btsá i komna masa i kmaba
Damn, Father Uncle, you are large and can hold more.

sanama tokjanga jwakama tabanoye tokjangasna[15]
They have gone to bring food, to Sibundoy they must have gone.

malaya bakó xkwatetseswelta
Please, Uncle, let me go,

iye bakó katetokeda ch kwenteñose   90
and uncle can stay in my place.

saná michanjiyiboye atxebiama bakó ch kwente koisosañeka
They are going to bring food, and in my place uncle can eat."

i ch oso cha ch ubojemana nye yojowena[16]
And that bear, that poor numbskull, he just listened to him.

serta ibojaswelta
Truly he let him go.

i chana lwaroka chká swelto yotsatsana
And in his place, loose, he just stood there.

iye ch bakó chentxa yojtsobatemana[17]   95
And that uncle just waited there.

ajá i ndoñe bna ora imojabushjango
Aha, and it wasn't long till they arrived.

ch yerobja tashanganganushe imeniyeboye
They brought that red hot iron brand.

saná kana yerubja imeniyeboye jutsejwinyama
Instead of food they brought an iron brand to burn him.

nyetxá rabiaka batxetema
They were very angry with that poor little fellow.

---

used throughout this episode as a sign of mutual respect, especially amusing in light
of rabbit's duplicitous intentions.

[15]line 88: *tabanoye*, "town (Sibundoy)." From the outlying veredas, the Kamsá
people travel to town to secure those foodstuffs that are not produced in and
around the homes and gardens. Thus rabbit's claim arouses in bear hopes of some
special treats.

[16]line 92: *ubojemana*, "numbskull." From the Quechua (Inga) root, *upa*, meaning
"dumb" and by extension, "foolish." The root is assimilated to Kamsá through the
addition of the empathetic suffix, *-jema*, and the narrative suffix *-na*.

[17]line 95: *bakó*, "uncle." Note the narrator's playful designation of bear as "uncle," picking up on rabbit's duplicitous use of this honorific.

tempo kushe ch boboshe yojabotuchemena iye tempo 100
Right away they came to scorch that fur, right away.

a chora ndoñe chká xbatsemana
Then: "Don't do that to me.

sempre atxe ndoñe cha ketsatsemuna atxena ndoñe
Hey, I'm not the one, he's the one, not me.

cha yanaka chkoye tokjuftseboknaka
He took off, way over there he disappeared."

ase mateshacheka
"Then go and catch him."

ana chora ch osona yojoftsebochá   105
And then that bear took off,

basetxatema jwinyna yojaftsebokna orna
He was a little burned when he came into view.

chore cha kachentxe kack bekoñe yojachembo
Then in that place nearby he spoke:

taita bakó taita bakó motsobosana btse jajoye motsobosana
"Father Uncle, Father Uncle, come to the shade in this big garden,
    come to the shade."

chore cha ibojtsakamena jutseshachama jutemashingwama
Then he chased after him to catch and deliver him.

yojtsaiyika   110
He ran off.

tempo kweboshoye tronkoshoye yojetsojweka
Right away he went inside a hollow trunk.

iye chorna ch osona waskwatxá inamna
And then that bear, rabbit had a long tail,

chorna nye chjwa yojaushache kwatatábena ch waskwatxejwa
then he grabbed it and he pulled off that tail.

i chká maná ya yenyoka yejtoitana
And like that he hid in that place.

**i komo cha koñeshona impase chorko yojtsechañe
    impasama**   115
And rabbit then completely got away, completely.

cha chteskana yentxá ndoñe ycntobcma chká ochjajnayekausna
From that day he could not become a person, for behaving like that.

**chentxana ch kausa ch koñeshunga tonday waskwatxijwa ndwabo-
    menunga**
From that day, because of that, rabbits are without a tail.

nyetxase ch antewana koñeshbiana komena
That's how that old one about the rabbit goes.

(m15) iyendonabiama
About the Squirrel

As performed by Mariano Chicunque in Kamsá, October 1978

Trickster stories are among the most popular of mythic narratives in the Sibundoy Valley. The current favorite is *koñesh*, rabbit (see m14), but there is evidence that squirrel was a puny but clever hero to earlier generations of Kamsá children. The common butt of each of these tricksters is the bear, not the formidable seductive bear but the round bear, the foolish oaf. This mythic narrative is set within the framework of the indigenous governmental system, the native *cabildo* or community council. The institution was imposed by the Spanish as a means of indirect rule and persists today as the organ of community self-government. The cabildo consists of its leader, the *gobernador,* and his several officers including the *justicias,* roughly comparable to constables in the British system. At the service of the governor are the *soldados,* armed troops who are called out if the need arises. All of these layers of authority will figure in taita Mariano's humorous narrative.

Bear, as governor of the community, is tricked by squirrel into smashing his own testicles. This trickster motif, like the others related in this narrative, is common to Amerindian trickster cycles (see Sherzer 1990, for a version from the San Blas Kuna of Panama and an account of parallels in indigenous Mexico and in Colombia). Later squirrel fools the constables sent out to bring him to the cabildo, and then the soldiers sent out to apprehend him. He even manages another deception on the bear, luring him into emitting a tell-tale fart. Squirrel remains carefree and composed, prone to dash through the trees with his triumphant cry of "chuj chuj chuj chuj chuj."

When the governor marshals his soldiers, squirrel recruits the wasps, large ants, and bees to fight in his cause. One of the delightful scenes in taita Mariano's narration is the squirrel parading around bravely, behind the lines, taunting the beleaguered forces of the governor: *a ver atxe are mabunga atxe xmabuftseshache atxe kach eskoltakakaye,* "Let's see, come on, come and take me with my rifle."

There are numerous Amerindian parallels to all of these trickster episodes. The motif of the crushing of the testicles occurs in Mesoamerican as well as South American settings (see Sherzer 1990, 94). The tell-tale fart occurs widely in folk literature, as Type 66 B, "Sham-dead Animal Betrays Self." A close parallel is found in Juan Rael's collection from New Mexico, with coyote as the dupe and rabbit as the trickster. Robe (1973, 14) cites nine variants from Mexico and Central America.

The army of wasps and other insects occurs in the *Popol Vuh*, when the enemy lords launch an attack on the Quiche citadel at Hacauitz (Tedlock 1985, 195-96). Laughlin (1988, 136) presents a Zinacantán variant, "War Between the Cricket and the Jaguar."

Trickster stories always precipitate a reversal of cultural norms. Here we have the classic case of a small animal outwitting a larger one. But this mythic narrative implicates the political framework as well, by pitting the irreverent squirrel against the local authority figures. It would be hard to find support for a revolt against the indigenous authority system in these amusing anecdotes, though this story does highlight, in its humorous vein, tensions that emerge in the implementation of local authority.

xkwatsparlá iyendonena
I will surely speak of the squirrel.

chká chana ako iyendona ndoñesa iyendona
Like that, wow, the squirrel was not a squirrel,

pero yentxá ch iyendona yentxá i ya ch biyange imenamna[18]
but a person that squirrel, a person, and they were able to speak as humans.

oso kachebé ya bweno iyendona jinyasa btse niñekwema[19]
Bear, that round one, fine, then he saw squirrel sitting on a large trunk,

inashajaye kwemiñe inetsotebemañe iyendona btsana   5
where a tree had fallen, he sat there, that squirrel person.

orna chorna cha chentxe yojtabokna ch oso
Then he arrived there, that bear,

i osona goberna inamenaka y ch oso bweno[20]
and bear was governor of the community, and that bear, fine:

ndayakama taita sobrenaka ana kojomestema tswasaka[21]
"Why, Father Nephew, are you eating those berries?"

chkaka taita bakó kekatjabmwanaka
"As you see, Father Uncle, would you like to swallow some?"

---

[18]line 3: *biyange imenamna*, "they were speakers." It is the ability to use human language that defines the human being in the Kamsá scheme of things.

[19]line 4: *kachebé*, "round one." The nominal classifier , -*bé*, for round objects, signals a humorous treatment of bear here.

[20]line 7: *osona goberna*, "bear (was) governor." The Kamsá community is governed by its council, known as the *cabildo*. The chief officer of the cabildo is the *gobernador*, elected annually by the adults members of the community in consultation with the priests.

[21]line 8: *kojomestema*, "berries." These are known as *shuftá* in Kamsá, *uvillas* in Spanish. According to Bristol (1968, 597), this is *Physalis peruviana*, a perennial herb found in some houseyards. Their edible fruit is much prized by children.

aiñe a ver cha tatsebiaka yojtabotebema ch oso   10
"Yes, let's see," and then he sat up there, that bear.

i serta ch jayanana ch bnga wasungebetemoikana
And truly so to speak right beside our testicles,

chana chká apontada mntxá jatschebwanaka
like that he aimed well and struck there.

ase jatakana i serta ibojoiyena
Then he picked it up, and truly he passed it to him.

chká serta cha ch apontado inetsayambañe choye ch intxayá
Like that truly he cleverly had placed the fruit there inside his
    clothing,

ch shoftaka ana shoftá inamna   15
those berries, they were berries.

i chusha ibojoiyé ch oso yojwasaka i chore ibojoiyana
And he gave them to that bear, he ate them, and then he said:

taita bakó ntxamo nasana kenotamnaka
"Father Uncle, how does it taste? Is it good?"

aiñeka asa taita bakó kekochjatasaka
"Yes." "Then Father Uncle, will you have some more?"

aiñeka ibojatiye yojatasa
"Yes." He gave him another, he ate it.

kenotamnaka aiñeka   20
"Does it taste good?" "Yes."

chorna a ver asena kach taitabakobetema mntxá btsa betsomeñeyna
Then: "Well now, those of Father Uncle are so large like that.

a ver atxe mntxá mwentxa xkobontsé
See, I just strike myself here."

chkasna ibojenye nye wasungebexentxe yojenochebwá
So like that he watched, he struck right beside his testicles.

ase ndayá yojwaka ndetxetema pero chan ndayá pikaro[22]
Then, what, he picked up a rock, but that guy, what, a tricky fellow,

cha bninye chana inenopegaye   25
he showed him, he hit himself.

chana i ch osona nde ombre ch puñitebeka yojabema
And that bear, I swear, he made a fist,

[22]line 24: *pícaro*, "trickster." The Spanish word is used here; it is interesting to
note that the Kamsá sometimes label Spanish-speaking Colombian nationals as
pícaros, in reference to the "tricks" they have played on the Indians.

shmnebé chká yojtsenachebwa impase[23]
he soundly struck his eggs like that.

ch tatsebiokana joxnana yojenotsatxe
From up there he tumbled down, he fell backwards feet in the air,

chká ch wasungebé yojtsenopega
like that he struck his own testicles.

aray chorka chuja ch iyendona yojisobema 30
Damn! Then that one, that squirrel, he ran off,

i ch betiye shjoye yojontxá jtsechañana
and up high in the trees he began to dash about:

chuj chuj chuj chuj chuj chuj chuj chuj
"Chuj chuj chuj chuj chuj chuj chuj chuj."

iye impas ndokená
And then he just vanished.

i osona añemo yojisekaye
And bear recovered his strength.

yojtá ese justisia yojichamwá cha jobetxamnaka[24] 35
They went, those constables, he sent them to bring him,

ch taita sobrena jobetxama
to bring that father nephew.

aray ch justisianga serta imojangaka aye amanita imojenyenaka
Damn! Those constables truly went and easily they found him:

ah bweno a ver xmanatsa ndayám tstseita
"Ah, fine, well, take me with you, what am I needed for?"

yojayc nye bekoñe
He followed close behind.

iye xkweisebwache xjtsatsebwache 40
And: "I need to stop off here, I need to visit the bushes."

yojamengo ch jamengwama i bastxatema yojamengoye
He turned to enter the bushes and as he entered just a little,

i tempo cha iyendona yojisobema
right away that squirrel took off,

i ch betiye yojatebechañe impas
and he was dashing about high in the trees.

---

[23]line 27: *shemnabé*, "egg." This familar metaphor, referring to the testicles as eggs, operates in Kamsá as well as in Spanish (and English).

[24]line 35: *justisia*, "constables." These are junior officers of the cabildo under the governor's command.

ntxamo mase jtsakamenana nye iyendona yentsotatxumbo
They couldn't pursue him further, they didn't know what to do
    with the squirrel.

a la finalna nya pronta ngobernuna yojtisechamwa   45
At last just right away the governor sent them again:

ndayeksa nya ndoñe nya pronta mojtsajnaka
"What happened? You couldn't catch him? This time several will
    go."

iye pronta imojtatinyena ch iyendona iye txababé inetsasañe
And right away they found him, that squirrel, he was eating wild
    cherries:

a vera xkwetsebmwana añemo xkwetsekusa chja
"You see, I have to finish eating to have the strength to follow you,

anya kbochjauseto
but sure, I will come with you."

pronto imojwanatsaka i chora yojatstatxumbona   50
Right then they took him along and then he inquired:

ndayamsa nyetxá xmaftsengwayika
"Why are you always looking for me?"

ako taitá mandado xoká komna del todo xoká jtsobanama resuos
"Well, father governor is sick, very sick, in danger of dying.

nye jwatsesaiyamas ndayama masnaka
Just to go see him, that's all."

bwenoka a ver xmanatsa
"Fine, then, take me with you."

imojaushjango orna cha shjokana nyetxasa opunga
    imenamna   55
When they were arriving by the patio, they were so uncouth,

imojoshjango orna yojayana
when they were arriving, he said:

a ver mobwambaye che ijtá tswanachá ch sobrena tswanachanga
"Let's see, tell them that we have brought the one who was missing,
    we have brought that nephew,

ase ntxamo chaujayanaka tsoikana tokjayanaka
then what will they say from inside?" he said.

chká kasna vera taitá mandado mo mandá a ver cha osinyiaka
    yojayanaka
"In that case, then, Father Governor, send a fart to me here,"
    he said.

i serta ch goberna oso tonto kwetosinyia yojosinyiaka 60
And truly that governor, the foolish bear, let out quite a fart,
he farted.

chore yojayana chubja ch iyendona
Then that one, that squirrel, spoke,

chentxe i shjoka yentxá inetsomiñe²⁵
there in the patio, he was a person:

ah ndoñe kwando xoká oh nyetxá jabwache tojatotsesinyia
"Ah, no, since when does a sick person fart so loudly?

cha o chatse xoká aray apontado kwaxmunjwanatse
And you tell me he's sick. Damn! For some other reason you
brought me here."

tempo chuj chuj chuja jtsongwebjajaye yojatebechañe 65
Right away: "Chuj chuj chuj," he flew off, he escaped them again,

ch ngobernabe cha shjokana cha yojatechañe impase
from that governor's patio he surely fled.

nyc ndoñe imonjobenaye ajá
There was nothing they could do with him, aha,

impas kachká imojtsonyayuja kachkay imojatonyaye
so like that they just left him alone, they let him be.

bweno
Fine.

bateskokayé ngoberna ch oso yojtisechamwa 70
After some days the governor, that bear, he wanted to send them
again:

a vera morko nya pronto joshjangwan xmochjanga nya prontoka
"Really, now, this time for sure you will bring him, go for me."

chore chnga imojtsoyatxumbwa ndoñeka ana ndoñe jobenayiñika
Then they told him no, since there was nothing they could do
with him.

**chorna a ver asna asna soldado chkasnaka soldadoka chkasna
chabe opanaka**
Then, well, then, with soldiers, like that with soldiers, like that for
that bad fellow.

serta soldado imojá soldadungeka
Truly the soldiers went, those soldiers,

---

²⁵line 62: *shjoka*, "patio." On the lee side of Kamsá houses there is a rectangular
area that is kept free of plants or weeds; this is the patio.

i ch iyendona chana yojtsenotatxumbo   75
and that squirrel, he found out about it.

i chana soldado ana ko yojtangwango soldadonga
And he went about finding his own soldiers,

eso sí soldado ana ko tojuwangaka soldadunga tojuwanga iye
   sechetxiyangaka
yes indeed, soldiers, those bees, soldiers, the bees, and those large
   ants.

i chore chnga iye nyetxá propio soldado imojtsemna
And then those were his own soldiers.

aray nyetxá shekwatxiñe nyetxá sechetxiyanga nyetxá tojowanga
Damn! Right to the feet, those big ants, those bees,

eso ndoñe borla serto ntxá tsetotjwana   80
no fooling, truly they went to sting.

yojtsarebajaye ch propia soldadnaye
He defeated them with his own soldiers.

i chore ch iyendona eso sí chana yojtasemaye ch kach skopetaxá
And then that squirrel, yes indeed, he carried his rifle:

a ver atxe are mabunga atxe xmabuftseshache atxe kach eskoltakakaye
"Let's see, come on, come and take me with my rifle."

yojontxá bxaka tsobuxpasiañe tsobuxpasiañena
He began parading about, parading about, in front of his door.

ch iyendona yojtabwananaye   85
The squirrel was stronger.

i ase ch tojowanga i ch iyendonabe soldadunga imojojabwachiná
And then those bees, those soldiers of the squirrel, they attacked
   without mercy,

xubjenache jwebiunache etsetotjo i ese mwiñe jwaxenache
   sechtxiyanga[26]
they stung their ankles and faces and even here to the buttocks the
   ants came.

impase yojtachamoye i pronto ch iyendona
They really made them run and right then, that squirrel,

ko ndoñe imonjobenaye jwanatsanaka
there was nothing they could do to bring him in.

_____

[26]line 87: *mwiñe*, "over here." The narrator points to his own behind at this
moment.

chkase ch antewana tstatxumbo ch iyendonabiama   90
Like that, the old tale as I know it, the one about the squirrel.

(m16) mamaxbe parlo
The Tale of the Weasel

As performed by Mariano Chicunque in Kamsá, October 1978

"The Tale of the Weasel" is one of Mariano Chicunque's little gems; he tells the story with dramatic flair, relishing each nuance of humor and irony. The weasel and deer are (or were) prominent in the fauna of the valley, the weasel loathed for its penchant for carrying off plump hens (that is, for sharing human appetites), the deer much pursued for its meat. This myth returns us to the ancestral period when animals and people were not yet clearly differentiated and animal-people walked the earth. The narrator makes this curious fact explicit: *mamaxna shemaka, shema inamna mamaxna* ("The weasel, a woman she was, a woman that weasel"); and in reference to the deer, *ku yentxase inetsomniyeka*, ("he was like a person in those days").

The precise identification of the animal referred to as "weasel" in these narratives is as yet uncertain. The Kamsá narrators I recorded use the terms *mamax* and *osungatxiye* to refer to this animal in Kamsá; Alberto Juajibioy provides the Kamsá labels *alwasero* and *chukuro* and the Spanish word *comadreja* (Juajibioy and Wheeler 1973). It is possible that these labels identify a cluster of small carnivorous mammals rather than a single discrete species. One interesting clue emerges in a narrative not included in this sample since it overlaps extensively with the two versions of "Wangetsmuna" (m2, m3). I refer to "The Death of Wangetsmuna" performed by taita Mariano Chicunque, in which Wangetsmuna perishes at the end instead of returning to his grandfather's abode.

In this version of the cycle the weasel accompanies Wangetsmuna during his final days, and taita Mariano provides an account of a curious episode that does not appear in the other versions. This animal, named the *chkuro* and translated for me as *comadreja* or "weasel," spills corn flower on himself and remains forever marked with a white streak on his face or head. A glance at Emmonds and Feer (1990) indicates many possibilities for identifying the animal source of this mythical figure. Positive identification is impeded by the failure of the Kamsá labels to coincide with the local names listed. In any case, the mythical weasel (whoever she may be) is an important actor on the stage of Kamsá narrative.

The ancestral or spiritual weasel and deer are important figures in traditional Sibundoy cosmology. Weasel generally plays the part of a crafty, conniving story character in Kamsá mythic narrative. She is the one who steals fire from the culture hero, Wangetsmuna, and makes it available to the other animals (see Juajibioy and Wheeler 1973), thereby precipitating the transition out of *tempo crudo*, the raw time. It is weasel who accompanies the culture hero Wangetsmuna, in one version of this cycle, as he finishes his journey into the world. In the mythic narrative weasel appears as a native doctor with transparently improper intentions. Deer appears in Kamsá mythic narrative as a somewhat naive young man: in one myth he chases after an inappropriate mate (see m17); in the following myth, he solicits help from a highly inappropriate source. But these humorous cameos aside, deer is a powerful spiritual actor in the traditional worldview: the ancestors taught that his appearance in a dream warns of spirit sickness (McDowell 1989).

Stylistically, this performance is nicely framed, running from an opening announcement ("Well, the one about the weasel") to a closing rite ("That is the story, by Our Lord") and clearly organized into a logical sequence of dramatic units. The introductory material in the first five lines yields to the onset of action with the arresting phrase, *a de la warda serto ndeolpe* ("Heaven forbid, truly all of a sudden. . ."), signaling the narrator's reverence for what is about to happen. The next section (lines 6-19) presents deer's solicitation and weasel's response. The third section (lines 20-26) portrays weasel's peculiar curing chant, with the repeated elements *tsetxá tsetxá seboyuxe seboyuxe tamó tamoka* ("Sauce, sauce, onion, onion, salt, salt"). In the fourth section (lines 27-34) deer rejects these ministrations and escapes from weasel's clutches, despite the doctor's protests that *anya chka kutsiañe sinjayánaka* ("Just so it is, just as I'm speaking"). The fifth and final narrative section (lines 35-45) describes the father's reaction on hearing of his son's experience at the weasel's. The boundaries between these narrative chunks are clearly articulated by lexical items (*bweno*, "Fine", *a chor*, "and then. . .") and by phrasing devices such as pause and intonational closure.

In general, the narration procedes in a leisurely fashion and we sense that the narrator is savoring each successive moment in the plot. There are frequent parallel locutions—*ana inaxoka ch mongojoka, mongojo inaxoka* ("And so that deer came down with something, the deer came down with something")—as the story gradually wends its way to the key episodes of reported speech. These are performed as realistic impersonations; the narrator takes on the persona of the speaking protagonists and convincingly reproduces the accent and tonality of their speech. We find ourselves immersed in the speech universe of the Kamsá Indians and vicariously in the presence of the myth's protagonists. These dramatizations not only draw us into the story by animating the plot; paradoxically, their humor also produces some ironic distance on social life and its machinations. We enter the story about weasel and deer only to emerge a little wiser about the ways of human beings.

"The Tale of the Weasel" is a multi-faceted verbal art object that can be understood and enjoyed from a number of angles. It is, for one thing, a debunking of spurious doctors. In this aspect it falls into a familiar category of traditional narrative extolling or exposing the reputed skills of local medical practioners (see Paredes 1965; Graham 1981). Weasel looks every bit the part of the native doctor: she has her curing branches in hand, and she commences to dance and chant much as they do. But there is something "fishy" about her performance: in fact she is planning to "eat" her client (and the sexual undercurrent is not to be missed here—the narrator tells us, *ah yojtsoboxe,* "Ah, how she wanted him!"). The myth warns of charlatanism in the realm of traditional medicine, a sentiment that is echoed in Sibundoy protestations against the more flamboyant practices of the native doctors, for example the practice of extracting *capachos,* "spirit bundles," from the guts of their patients. It also delivers a precedent for disrupting a false curing session: *batamama inya chka tainayanaka* ("Aunt Mother, I think you got the words wrong") says the deer as he puts his clothes back on.

At the same time, this myth can be appreciated as a fable whose primary moral might be something to the effect, "know thyself," with a secondary impulse along the lines of "listen to the elders." It is deer's lack of self-knowledge that leads him into the hands of his predator. Deer's father is incredulous on hearing that his son has gone to weasel for a cure, and the narrator nicely captures the old man's bemused inarticulacy: *ah kach ke chká achkach chká tatxumbwá ch mamajema* ("Ah, so that's it, so that's how it is, that weasel a doctor"). The father drives the message home in giving this advice to his son:

txam bngajemanga jutsesañam inetsemna
We poor creatures are for eating,

i cham tschikaka
and so she thought to feed on you.

asna ndoñe mas choy ndoñe mas kichabataka
Now don't go back there, don't ever go again,

ar ndoñesa nyetxana chawajabanaka
"Lord no, just take it easy."

Mariano Chicunque's skillfull handling of the key episodes of reported discourse suggests another significant hearing of this myth, as a meditation on Kamsá ways of speaking. Stylistically, this performance is notable for the care taken in rendering two special Kamsá speech codes, the curer's chant and the ritual language. In other words, there is a strong ethnolinguistic bent to this story, for the plot turns on the correctness or otherwise of a speech act, the doctor's curing chant. As it happens, her words are not the appropriate "singing to the spirits" that should establish her pedigree as a curer and invoke the spirit helpers; instead she invokes a set of culinary helpers (salt, onion, hot pepper) in anticipation of a good meal. Here the successful accomplishment of the speech act is frustrated by its inappropriate content. In contrast, the words exchanged between doctor and patient accurately mirror the ceremonious discourse appropriate to such occasions of formal entreaty. Each speaker makes use of the ritual language register, a special form of Kamsá discourse associated with public ceremony. The terms they use to address one another, *batamamá* ("Aunt Mother") and *taitsobren* ("Father Nephew") signal the presence of ritual language, since in this discourse mode all personal address is accomplished through the use of fictive kinship terms. Moreover, the words used by deer to entreat weasel's help contain several ritual language nuances: *achka tkmoftselesentsia shnanatem kwabwatemaka,* "So it happens God has bestowed upon you the knowledge of the good medicines." Note the invocation of a divine charter for human activity; the weighty logism based on the Spanish-derived root *lesentsia;* the use of the diminutive *-tem* in conjunction with the word for medicine: all of these invest this speech with the aura of ritual language. Further, the audio tape reveals assimilation of this phrase to the chanting intonation of Kamsá ritual language speeches. The crafty aunt mother continues the deception by responding in kind to the young man, using an empathy marker associated with ritual language, *ar señoraka,* "By our Lord" and addressing him as *taita sobrén,* "Father Nephew."

"The Tale of the Weasel" thus portrays (and mocks) two special uses of the Kamsá language, one a poorly executed "singing to the spirits" and the other a well executed but poorly timed entreaty for medical assistance. These demonstrations alert us to the fact that discourse can be treacherous, even when executed in accordance with the traditional speech charter. Spurious doctors can feign "singing to the spirits" (though perhaps not convincingly) in an attempt to exploit (in this case, devour) their patients, and people can employ ritual language discourse in misguided or even deceiving projects. This story is inherently humorous, portraying the encounter between a naive petitioner and a bumbling predator; its humor is enhanced by the narrator's skillful impersonation of these protagonists through a realistic representation of their speech.

bweno mamaxna mntxá
Well, the weasel, like this.

mamaxna anteo tatxumbwá inamna
The weasel in the old days was a doctor.

mamaxna shemaka shema inamna mamaxna
The weasel, a woman she was, a woman that weasel.

eh mal tsepasana ana nye mamaxbioy janaka
Ah, if I'm feeling sick, then its off to the weasel's,

batamamá choy batamamá jutserwanaka cha mamaxna   5
aunt mother, there to aunt mother, to ask for help from that weasel.

bweno
Well.

a de la warda serto ndeolpe ana inaxoka ch mongojoka
Heaven forbid, truly, all of a sudden, that deer came down with
    something,

mongojo inaxoka
the deer came down with something.

ku yentxase inetsomniyeka
He was like a person in those days.

i yojá jutserwa xokanama jashnamaka   10
And he went to ask her to cure him of his sickness.

iye chorna ch batamamá ch mamaxna ibujinyen
And then that aunt mother, that weasel, he found her,

ch mamax inetsotbemañe ch batamamá ibojarwa²⁷
that weasel was sitting there, he entreated that aunt mother:

achká tkmojoftselisentsia shnanatem kwabwatemaka
"As it happens, God has bestowed upon you the knowledge of the
    good medicines.

chama tsabó mal tsepasa tseshnamaka
For this I have come, I am not feeling well, I need a treatment."

ar señoraka   15
"By Our Lord.

achka mal kopasa taitsobrenaka
So you are not feeling well, Father Nephew.

a ver mwentxe mabotbemaka
Then come and sit here.

a ver na mojenoyenaxeka ch yentxayá
Let me see, take off those clothes."

yojenoye inaxeyeka
He took his clothes off, he undressed.

ah tempo yojotsabana ch beuntjatiyeka waibainushcka²⁸   20
Ah, right away she picked up the curing branches, as they are called,

---

²⁷line 12: *ibojarwa*, "he entreated her." Based on the Spanish root, *rogar*, "to beg."
²⁸line 20: *beuntjatiyeka*, "curing branches." A standard feature of native medicinal practice is the use of curing branches, generally from a palm or wild bush. The

yojontxa jabachenjanaka
she began to brush him.

ah yojtsoboxe ch mamaxna batamamana[29]
Ah, she wanted him, that aunt mother weasel,

ah tsetxá tsetxá tsetxá seboyuxe seboyuxe tamó tamoka[30]
Ah, "sauce, sauce, sauce, onion, onion, salt, salt."

yojtseboxe
She wanted him.

ii txa yojshekwan xokabé[31]   25
And so she circled around and around that sick fellow,

chabwajanaka yojshekwanaka
from one side to the other, she circled around him.

a chor sempre ch mongojo ch bobonse baka ibojtsawenan
Then that deer, that young man, he didn't like what he was
    hearing.

chor nye ndiabwen tojtoshabwangway
Then without asking permission, he dressed himself again.

iye chore ibojoyana
And then he said to her:

batamamá inya chká tainayanaka   30
"Aunt Mother, I think you got the words wrong."

anya chkasa kutsiañe sinjayanaka
"Just so it is, just as I'm speaking,

anya chkasa kutsiañeka
that's just how it is."

ah nye mejor xkwaftsatoñeka
"Ah, but I had better be on my way."

kachká ibojesonyaye ch tatxumbwaye nye yojtsatoñe
Then he left her behind, that doctor, he just took off.

bebta ibojauwenaye   35
Later his father heard about it.

native doctor shakes these to create a rhythmic pulse and he also brushes the patient's body with them.
    [29]line 22: *yojtsoboxe*, "she wanted him." Note the delicious ambiguity here be-
tween sexual and culinary appetite.
    [30]line 23: *tsetxá tsetxá tsetxá seboyuxe seboyuxe tamó tamoka* "Sauce, sauce, sauce,
onion, onion, salt, salt." Part of the curing routine involves a chanting or singing to
the spirits, normally to invoke spiritual helpers.
    [31]line 25: *yojshekwan*, "she circled around." The native doctors walk and some-
times dance in a circle around their patients.

ah kach ke chká achkach chká tatxumbwá ch mamaxjema
"Ah, so that's it, so that's how it is, that weasel a doctor."

chká xunaborlanika
"Here's how she made fun of me:

ah kach tsetxá tsetxaka xojtsebachunja
ah, that 'sauce, sauce,' she brushed me with the curing branches."

aja chor bebta ibojojwá
Aha. Then his father responded:

aku bngajemunga sasnunga mondemenamse   40
"Be careful, we poor creatures are food for her.

chkasa tamó tamoka seboyuxe tsetxá tsetxaka
That's why 'salt, salt, onion, sauce, sauce.'

txam bngajemanga jutsesañam inetsemna
We poor creatures are for eating,

i cham tschikaka
and so she thought to feed on you.

asna ndoñe mas choy ndoñe mas kichabataka
Now don't go back there, don't ever go again.

ar ndoñesa nyetxasa chawajabanaka   45
Lord no, just take it easy."

esta es la conversa
That is the story

nyetxá tijatsparlá ar señor
just as I have told it, by Our Lord.

(m17) mashangola
Mashangola

As performed by Mariano Chicunque in Kamsá, December 1978

The impact of this mythic narrative is contained in the very name of its
female protagonist, Mashangola, an unwieldy, awkward combination of
sounds to the Kamsá tongue and ear. It appears that two great Amerindian mythological themes are condensed here into an entertaining
tale of courtship, revealing another face of myth as it operates within a
living narrative tradition. It may be that this narrative charts the
progress of myth into folktale, as sacred elements give ground to the
humor and pathos of the human circus. The theme of the frog bride is
central to some Amazonian and North American Indian mythologies.
Claude Lévi-Strauss (1973) devotes considerable attention to this theme
and its permutations, which he views as an indigenous commentary
on appropriate and inappropriate mates. Likewise, the hiding contest

between a large animal and a smaller one appears in a number of my-thologies of the Americas. Yet taita Mariano's rendition of these themes avoids these cosmological threads and instead focuses on the amusing and embarassing standoff between the suitor's party and the party of intended bride.

It is tempting to hear an echo here of a widespread Amerindian cluster of motifs concerned with the choice of appropriate mates. Sug-gestive parallels occur among the Arapaho, in which the sun chooses a bride who doesn't squint when she sees him, but this bride turns out to be "a frog which was hopping along in front of the door and urinating at every leap" (Lévi-Strauss 1978, 208). This episode is followed by a farcical contest, a test to determine "who makes the greatest noise in chewing."

Kamsá mythic narrative abounds in the portrayal of intended mar-riage, usually through unsuccessful trial arrangements. This tale por-trays the formal model for arranging a marriage, through the suitor's solicitation of the intended bride. Mariano Chicunque often situates his narrative plots in realistic social and sociolinguistic settings. In this nar-rative he creates a persuasive simulation of the solicitation process as it actually occurs in Kamsá society. First the young man speaks to his fa-ther, asking him to arrange the marriage. The father agrees and accom-panies his son to the home of the intended bride. The narrator doesn't mention it, but generally these visits involve the exchange of chicha and other ritual gifts. Note how the narrator preserves the convention of surrogate address here, as the young man speaks to his intended in-laws only through the voice of his father.

Much of the discourse in these events is couched in the ceremonial expansiveness of Kamsá ritual language, and taita Mariano does a splendid job of mimicking the proud yet importuning voice of the young man's father. These words may be taken as exemplary of such addresses: *chká atxebe xoxona kamna nyetxá dios tbojaftselisensiana,* "Like this my son has truly with God's help come of age."

ana mntxá kem palabra kbashekwastona,
And so he has truly followed in their footsteps.

mntxá ndoñe kanye vuela jisemniye,
So now he would no longer live alone,

mntxá matrimonio jatoma palabra jtsebinyana,
so he would enter into marriage, he would take the vow.

bndatabe xexonaftaka i atxebe xexona mntxá jenebiangwan,
Your child with my child will be united.

Several features mark this discourse as Kamsá ritual speech. The attri-bution of all human accomplishments to God is characteristic of the con-ventional humble stance adopted in such speech-making. The notion of "following in the footsteps (of the ancestors)" is perhaps the central theme of all ritual language speeches; it asserts fidelity to the example of the ancestors, and following this example is thought to be the one sure guide to a happy and healthy life. Missing from this transcript entirely is taita Mariano's accurate reproduction of the aural texture appropriate to these verbal performances, featuring a rapid pacing and a leveling of pitch contours into a chantlike intonational pattern.

mntxá inabinyam ndoka remidio ana sapna botamana bersiayá inamna botamana
So it once happened without remedy that the frog was a beautiful singer, beautiful.

tsxtoka tsxtasha inawamna anteo chká kostumbre inamna[32]
There was the wooden platform, the wooden tower, in the old days such was the custom.

janyama o jtsejanyama tsunekwangabiama ndayá
They would go, they would go there to scare off the parrots.

tsxtasha tsxlashoka cha jtsotcbemañana txa botamán javersiayana
The tower, on the tower she was sitting, how prettily she sang.

i ch bobonse ch mongojona chabwajana inetsachnojwana inetsachnojwana   5
And that young man, the deer, he was passing by there, he was passing by there.

chká inetsewinana ch botamana versiayá
Like that he was hearing that beautiful song.

inetsemnana jinyana ndoñe ibondinye
As for seeing her, he wasn't able to see her.

asna ndeolpna bebta ibojatiana
Then suddenly he spoke to his father:

taitá ka ana choka shembasa nyetxá botamán versiayá
"Father, over there a woman sings such a pretty song.

choka tsxtoka inye betsowinana   10
There on the tower I always hear her.

malai cha xkatayebwambañe jobwamayamaka[33]
Will you please speak to them for me about marriage?"

---

[32]line 2: *tsxtasha*, "wooden platform." Until recently the Kamsá would build wooden platforms by their cornfields; when the parrots came to the valley, a person would be stationed on the platform, making noise and throwing objects, to keep them from pecking at the corn.

[33]line 11: *jobowamayamika*, "to speak for me." It is customary for the parents to arrange for a marriage, once the young people have shown an interest in one another.

bwenoka asna a ver chjá a ver
"Fine, then, I will go and see to it.

asna parejo chkasna bochjá
Then surely like that we two will go."

bweno xkochjwanatseka yojoyejwa ch bobonse
Fine. "Yes, take me there." The young man was pleased.

ibojataka i ana aiñe imojenyen ndoñe ndokna   15
They went together and yes, they found them, the place was not
    empty.

tempo janyoy yojtsatoñe chana
Right away they went to look for her.

i chor rasón imojatstxetaye btsá
And then the father explained things:

chká atxebe xoxona kamna nyetxá dios tbojaftselisensiana[34]
"Like this my son has truly with God's help come of age.

ana mntxá kem palabra kbashekwastona[35]
And so he has truly followed in their footsteps.

mntxá ndoñe kanye vuelta jisemniye   20
So now he would no longer live alone,

mntxá matrimonio jatoma palabra jtsebinyana
so he would enter into marriage, he would take the vow.

bndatabe xexonaftaka i atxebe xexona mntxá jenebiangwan
Your child with my child will be united."

ar señorika ibojojwaka
"By Our Lord," he responded.

i chor tempo ch bebmá yojoyanaka
And then right away that mother spoke up:

ooh kachká bwenamente sobrena taitá taitanga xmutsepadesena
palabra bwenamenteka   25
"Ooh, it is in vain Father Nephew, Fathers, that you have traveled,
    truly in vain.

podeskajema tsabembenañe podeskajem
Our poor daughter is very ugly, very ugly.

---

[34]line 18: "Like this my son has truly with God's help come of age." This and
the next four lines are delivered in the chantlike prosody of Kamsá ritual language.
The reference to "God's help" is a standard formula in this speech register (see
McDowell 1983).

[35]line 19: *kbashekwastona*, "he is following in their footsteps." This is one of the
central formulas in Kamsá ritual language. It carries the sense of following the example of the ancestors, both traditional and Christian.

chká janyok chká inetsoversiañejema podeskajemaka
Like that she goes there, like that she sings to scare the birds, the
   poor ugly thing."

i chor ch boyabasa ibojaieksigia bebta ibojamandaka
And then that young man insisted, he requested of his father:

anya taitá xmiañe ch btsetsata nya stetsinyeka[36]
"But Father, please tell these parents I would like to see her."

i chká ibojauyana   30
And like that he spoke to them.

orna sierta ch bebmá yojayana
Then truly that mother said:

bwenosna bominye xmochetsebwajo xkochemboka
"Well, then, you will set your eyes on her, I will call her."

chora serta shjoye yojoftsebokna shjokañe yojachembo
Then truly she stepped outside, from outside she called:

mashangola mashangola mabowenaka
"Mashangola, Mashangola, come here."

yojtsechembwana ch sembasana mashangola   35
She called for that young woman, Mashangola.

chorna i chká xmochetsinyeka
Then: "And so you will see for yourselves."

ah yojabatsebokna orna a sapobja yojabetsatobokeñeka
Ah, when she appeared, it was a frog that came into view,

tsontsunjenañe tsontsunjenañe yojabetsatobokiñe
hopping, hopping, she appeared in front of them.

impasa ibojtsaboté ndoñe jobwamaye palabrana impas
He completely rejected her, he called the marriage off.

xmutsepasentsiaka i yojtsoyatxumbwa tonday palabra   40
"Please forgive me." He denied her, there was no agreement.

bweno
Fine.

chorna nye kachkan ndemanamna
Then so there would be no bad feeling,

chore i ch bobonsna chorna jwabney ibojateshebe
then, that young man, then, he lost his bearings.

---

[36]line 29: "But Father. . . ." Note how the son speaks through the father as his
emissary in this circumstance.

i yojatayana jenapostiana ah
And he said that they should bet, ah,

joitananaka mongojna joitanana sapo   45
deer will hide, frog will hide:

ar taixochjinyenaka
"So, perhaps you will find me."

ah o nya amanita jtinyenamaka
Ah, just with ease she found him.

sapo tojoitanana ooh nyan ndoñe jinyenaneka
The frog went and hid, ooh, he couldn't find her anywhere.

impas cha ibojwaboté tsachetxá kwandaisengway
He just gave up searching for her so much.

chan nye chká moy choy jtsoitañena   50
He just like that looked here and there, she was hidden.

impasa chteskana cha shembasana jaibwambayana tojanjaban
So forever from that day he spoke no more to that young woman
   about marriage.

chana mongojobian i sapobian
That's the one about deer and frog.

nyetxá tojaftsekwenta nyetxa koman
I have told it all, just as it is.

(m18) koskongobiama
About the Owl

As performed by Mariano Chicunque, in Kamsá, December 1978

The owl is a suitor who appears to be lazy but in fact possesses a remarkable gift: simply by shouting across the mountainside he can transform the wilderness into a garden. The Sibundoy Indians construe him
as a messenger of the gods, sent to implant his priceless knowledge
among humans. As one friend told me, "If only we had listened to him,
imagine how we would live today!" But there is something uncouth
about the owl as a suitor, some insistent perversity that leads to a break-
age in the line of communication and rejection of the proposed matri-
mony. The owl is unkempt and uncivil, lacking the industrious habits
appropriate in a young man looking to marry. These stories leave us
with a sense that unions between supernaturals and humans must be
thwarted, even at the cost of denying earthly paradise, if the world is to
remain orderly and hence hospitable to human purposes. These myths
are about paradise glimpsed rather than paradise lost; they affirm the

necessity of the harsh realities that mark the human destiny, even as they flirt with the possibility of alternative arrangements.

The owl is described as a doctor, which indicates that he has unusual spiritual powers, but he comes across as an odd little fellow, reluctant to join in the companionship of his adopted family. His lack of civility is a sign of his physical otherness. Most revealing is the detail about chicha pouring out the back of his neck, which marks him clearly as something other than human. Also of interest is his proclivity to speak in Inga, the language of the neighboring indigenous community. The owl's diffident response, *noka singallalla pingawaka,* "I am just ashamed of my little nose," is a tolerable facsimile of the speech of these neighbors. (It is worth noting that Ingano suitors do occasionally arrive seeking marriage with Kamsá women). When the match is rejected by the nervous and contemptuous sisters, the owl undoes his miraculous labor, transforms into his animal form, and disappears forever. The narrator makes this transformation graphic by mimicking his animal call: "ko ko ko ko ko."

The special talent of the owl, the ability to turn a forest into a garden, is poignant indeed in this agricultural community that has had to win every parcel of its arable land from the creeping forests and the swampy lowlands. Like the story about the sparrow (m19), this myth fastens upon a central facet of Sibundoy subsistence and depicts a moment in ancestral time when human beings stood at the threshhold of receiving an easier path, only to lose out in the end. In this instance too it is the rash behavior of the human hosts that triggers the loss of this labor-saving knowledge. But if these myths recommend a milder and more patient demeanour, they stop short of endorsing the proposed marriages with animal-people, who confirm their unsuitability by assuming once again their animal forms and habits as the story draws to a close.

Taita Mariano dwells on the strained familial relations in his performance of this myth. He quotes the young woman's relatives at length as they seek to fathom this extraordinary visitor. We hear the mother encourage the owl-person to sit with them by the fire, the father provide careful instruction about the work he wants done, and the women rant and rage about his shortcomings as a mate for their sister. Taita Mariano has a knack for getting these voices right, so the performance is a rich portrait of routine verbal interaction, as well as a rendering of Kamsá spiritual beliefs.

koskungobiama mntxá
The one about the owl, like this.

ndoka remidio mntxá xkwetseparla mntxá tstatxumbo
Without remedy like this I will tell it to you, just as I know it.

koskungana ko yentxase inetsomiñe[37]
The owl used to be like a person,

tempona nye yentxangasa imnobiyamenaye
in the old days they could just turn into people,

i chká shloftxna jobemana tempna inamna chungna anteona   5
and like that they could be birds, in days gone by, those guys in the
  days of the ancestors.

bweno ndoka remidiona ch koskungana tatxumbwanana[38]
Fine, it happened that owl was a doctor,

ndoñesa imondetatxumbunga yanyingna
but the others didn't know it.

**cha chká inana koskungna chká shembasen jongwangwan jobwa-
  mayama inana**
He went about like that, the owl, like that looking for a girl to marry,
  he went about.

**i bweno i chana kachká tongentsaja rwanajwa wakuftsayaná jut-
  sashjajwanana chana**
And fine, like that he always arrived wearing a cotton poncho, that
  one.

i ckká asena koskungna ch wamben taitá jabokná jayanana   10
And then like that the intended father-in-law would say to the owl:

sobreno mabo iñoye mabo xboniye
"Nephew, come by the fire, come warm yourself."

ndoñe nye des lo payika[39]
"No, but thank you anyway."

ndoñe ntjobekonan
He wouldn't come nearby.

bweno
Fine.

**ibojoftseté shemabasaftaka iye ibsana kachusa ch mamaxe yojay-
  ana**   15
He spent the night with that woman and the next morning that old
  woman said:

---

[37]line 3: *ko yentxase*, "like a person." Kamsá narrators generally pause over the
mystery of these dual figures, the animal-people, who simultaneously display
human and animal characteristics, or else move between human and animal
incarnations.
    [38]line 6: *tatxumbwá*, "doctor." This means the owl possessed special spiritual
knowledge.
    [39]line 12: *des lo payika*, a thanking formula derived from the Spanish, "Dios le
pague," "May God reward you."

sobrena metsawardá wabwananatema[40]
"Nephew, wait for some food to heat,

kochjetsemwanasa xkochaisabashejonase
you should eat something, or will you leave us so soon?

**ndoka remidio atxebe shembasana okupado kobomana buyish-
tema**
As it happens my little girl is busy making chicha,

japormama komnaka
for chicha must be made."

ase chora niñatema ndayá buchjatamungasa   20
And then: "With kindling, what, we will soon have something
cooked,

metsawardá sanatema metsabmwaná
wait, we will have some food,

mabo metsotebema moye
come, sit over here."

i txenuxe imojabwajwa jaftsotebemanaka
And she placed a wooden stool there for him to sit on.

i ndoñeka ay nya ndayeksa sobrena
And "No." "Ay, why Nephew,

nya atxebe shembasaftaka kmojtsebobinyana   25
you only spend time with my girl,

ndayeksa ndoñe ndayamsa ndoñe kochján jobekoná iñoye
why not, why don't you come over here by the fire?"

chore yojoyibwambaye ingatsache ka koyimbwambá[41]
Then he spoke, in Inga he spoke to them:

noka noka singallalla pingawaka yojayanaka
"I, I am just ashamed of my little nose," he said,

ntxamo chká yojayana noka singallalla pingawaka
Just exactly like that: "I am just ashamed of my little nose."

nye chká yojayanaka   30
That's all he said.

aye chore shembasá ibojeniana
Then he was conversing with the girl:

[40]line 16: *sobrena*, "Nephew." The polite form of address to a younger man.
[41]line 27: *ingatsache*, "the Inga language." The narrator is explicit here about the
owl's speech, which is Inga, the northernmost dialect of Quechua, spoken by the
Ingano community sharing the Sibundoy Valley with the Kamsá community (see
McDowell 1989).

bwenoka as morna nye betsko añemo chjabema mamitá perdona jatjaiñeka
"Fine, now let's quickly make the arrangements to get married."

bweno
Fine.

chorna yojatopasa ah chorna serta btsetsanga jatrabajama inaun-gamena tejashaka
Then it happened, ah, then truly the parents had some clearing to be done on an unworked piece of land,

inaungamena tejash jatrabajama i bna   35
they had an unworked piece of land on the mountainside to clear, and far off.

chorna cha ch boyabasana serta ibojontxa peongaftaka jatsaye jatrabajam[42]
Then that young man, truly the father was about to have some workers do the clearing,

chora ch boyabasa yojtsoyatstxumbwaka bangena
then that young man told him not to call many:

ndoñika bangena ndoñese nye kanya chkasna
"Not many, no, just by myself like that,

xmenyinyiye ch tjañe ndmwañe jatrabajana
show me the mountain where the work is to be done."

yomena tjañe jatejabemana   40
It was pure forest that had to be cleared:

xminyinyiyisna bangene ndoñe
"Show me the place, and don't bring a lot of workers."

ah taiteko yetsangameñana beka btsañe
Ah, Lord, it was a large stretch of mountainside:

xntsangamiñe
"I haven't cleared it yet."

ch wamben taitá jaboknà parejo ch shembasa parejo imojanga ibojinyinyiye
That intended father-in-law went along with that girl, they went to show him the place:

mojano mojano mojano mushe nyetsaxe xnangamena   45
"Here, here, and here, all of this is uncleared,

[42]line 36: *peonga*, "workers." From the Spanish, *peón*. Refers to crews of young men and women that can be hired to help with heavy tasks such as clearing land, in return for food and drink.

pero jabojatxama nye tsatxatema dios tbojayudan
but just get it started, do what you can, God help you.

nyetxá nye jabojatxama chkaka ase mokana ijkmangemena
Just get it started, like that, then this part needs it the most,

a mokana jutsobwatejabemana tsumbetena jtsobojiyama chkaka
clear to here and plant beans like that."

ase bweno
Then, fine.

asna ase a vera mntema ndoñese ibsa kbochjabayadaka   50
Then: "So let's see, not today, but tomorrow I will help you."

bwenoka ibetatana juyisashjango
"Fine." It was getting dark so they returned home.

chorna chká imojtsobjajana nye chká yojtetayana
Then like that they called him, but like that he answered again:

noka singallalla pingawaka
"I am just ashamed of my little nose."

nye ibojeyitsojajwa shembasaftakaka
He just went off to sleep with the girl.

kachté yojayan sanatemna aiñe nye ch bokoyina
     imojaoshbokeina   55
The next day: "Want some food?" "Yes." They gave him some
     chicha.

moika yojtsebwachkukjanaka chká yojoftsobxiye[43]
But it just came running out the back of his neck as he drank.

ibojwanatsa choyeka i chana ndoka chana yojtotebema
They went off there together, and he, nothing, he just sat down.

imojtetoñunga saná imojwabwa ora imojá jobetxama jasama
And when they had cooked lunch they went to call him to eat.

inetsotebemañika
He was just sitting there.

karay chora chana nye betsotebemañe   60
Damn, then: "He just sits around,

ndayeka chan nye betsotebemañe ndoñe i chan jatrabaja ntxamoka
why does he just sit around, wasn't he supposed to be working?"

---

[43]line 56: *yojtsebwachkukjanaka*, "it came running out the back of his neck." Here
the narrator gestures to the back of his own neck, thus using his body as a prototype
for the body of the mythical owl. This detail is a clear indication that this character is
not a human being. This motif occurs also in m22, in which it is the rainbow who
evinces this characteristic.

chora yojayana atxebiamna jetiñe kachoye ch taboye i jabobonyana[44]
Then he said: "I will take a look for myself this afternoon."

kokayé xmochjawenaye taitá chawabobonye
Then: "Tell them for me, Father, come and see."

ase chana nye jojoyanaka tojoye
Then he just let out a yell, he shouted,

iye tsachiñe tojwenana ntxamo tbojtsangamenaka dweñoka   65
and as far as the sound carried the hillside became just as the owner
   wanted it,

lempe trabajaniñeka achká chanaka
completely cleared, that's how he was!

karay i serta imojanga orna ooh lempe botamana tsumbiyubja
Damn, and truly when he went to look, what a beautiful field of
   beans,

bobemanana trabajaniñe bwaketufxnana
weeded and cleared, the lower branches trimmed,

chká montón montón yojtsakjana nyetxá botamana trabajaniñeka
like that in piles, everything piled, just beautifully cleared.

bweno   70
Fine.

a vera chorna nye cha ndayek
And then: "So what about him?"

i nyetxá imojeniana ndayeka ntxamo nyetxá tojatstrabajaka[45]
And so they spoke among themselves: "Why, then, did he really
   work so hard?"

a vera chkasna
You see, like that.

ase yibse ndoñe nyeté chkase mochjiyerwa
Then: "Tomorrow, not the day after, we told him."

ase i chora ch btsá lo mismo yojtetotbemaka ibejtutstbemana   75
Then that man sat there again, he just remained sitting there.

iye serta txatjayana maloka txatjayana mal inamnaye
And truly anger is harmful, their anger was harmful.

---

[44]line 62: *chora yojayana*, "Then he said." It is evidently the intended father-in-law who says this.

[45]line 72: *nyetxá tojatstrabajaka*, "he really worked hard." These voices are of the sisters, and they are sarcastic in tone.

batxa imojeneyanunga ndayeka chan chká chinchiñe tojatrabajá
They spoke quite a lot among themselves: "Why like this did he work so hard?"

ibojeniana mwana sekera krischiana ndayá⁴⁶
They said: "Is he even a human being or what?"

cha inamna ibejtsenajnanaye
They were speaking nervously among themselves.

bweno   80
Fine.

chorna a vera shema jabokná mojarepara ch trabajaniñe
Then they sent his intended wife to have a look at his work,

ntxamo yojtsopasana
to see how much was accomplished.

ooh yojá ora santo dios nyetxá botamana tsumbe botamana txematxe
Ooh, when she went, saintly God, all beautiful bean plants, beautiful corn plants,

kalabaxexe ndayá che bnga pobrunga moye
squash, all the things we poor folks need,

yingotema limpe lo que es saná limpe bochenana   85
roots, all that is food, everything ripe.

yojobobonyika ch tjana chká manuñe
She saw all this on that mountain slope.

bweno
Fine.

chora imojenawatjana ndayá cha la warda taiteko
Then they were frightened: "What is he, God preserve us?"

karay asa chká kenata o mamashe o nda ch tstxatjayá
Damn, then like that a sister, or the mother, or who was that angry one?

yojtsetxatjayika a ver nye chká jutsotebemañana   90
She became angry: "Let's see, so he just sat there like that?

nye chká ntxamo chkana bida kwanjatsebomna
Like that, how will they make a living?

---

⁴⁶line 78: *krischian*, "human being." The Kamsá have borrowed this word from the Spanish, and likewise use it as a general term for "human beings" as opposed to "animals" and "spiritual beings."

nye chká jatrabajam jiwasasam jitotbemaṣe
That's how he works, to find food he just sits there.

ndayám chkaná nye karay mejora ndoñe jobwamaiñe
How will they make it like that? They just better not marry."

imojtsawiyana áraye chká imojenakwentá
They prohibited the marriage, damn, like that they spoke among
    themselves,

ch shembasa ch boyabasafta   95
that girl with that young man.

chore yojayana bwenoka xmojtsaboté
Then he told them: "Fine, you have decided against me,

xmojtsaboyunjasna ase nye isatoñe yibsana
if you don't want me, then I will just leave tomorrow."

yojaftsebokna kachuse ya yojtoyoyeka
He went out, that fellow, then he yelled.

yojoyoye mokna tjañe inetsomiñe konforma
He shouted, here the mountain became what it had been,

tjañe yojtiseboshjona   100
it became forest once again.

chora yojtsaisongwebjoñe iye choka shloftxe cha
Then he flew off, and there he was a bird like that:

ko ko ko ko inyebetsama
"Ko ko ko ko," as they call.

i chká choka yojesongwebjo impase
And like that he flew off there forever,

kwatsetsayiye ijwesongwebjó impase
they spoke to him and he flew off forever.

chora ch txematxe tsumbe bochiniye tonday   105
Then there was nothing of that corn, those beans.

ajá chká ibojenákakan
Aha. Like that he scolded them:

ndayám chká ndayama kutxatjaye
"Why like that, why did you get so angry?

chká kwaborla ch koskungoka
Look what the owl has done to us."

nye nyetxá tijatsparla
That's all there is, just as I have told it.

y ese es la historia del koskungo   110
And that's the story about the owl.

(m19) shloftxebiama
About the Sparrow

As performed by María Juajibioy in Kamsá, October 1978

This myth is among the most popular in the Sibundoy Valley, among Kamsá and Ingano alike. María's version is a distillation, a personalized vignette extracted from the surrounding mythopoeic environment. In its full-blown versions this myth recounts a crucial episode in Kamsá cosmogony. The young woman is presented as a messenger of the gods, and she has arrived to teach humans how to prepare chicha from only a few grains of corn. The older woman is anxious to have chicha on hand because she and her husband are hosting a work crew on their land that day. The older woman returns to find the young woman combing her hair in the patio and the bushels of corn still full; she assumes the worst and severely scolds her son's intended wife. The rash behavior of the older woman saddens the young woman, who transforms into a sparrow like bird, dips into the chicha, and flies away.

This story revolves around the mystery of procuring large quantities of food from a slender food source, as Christ does in the famous "loaves and fishes" episode. In *Sayings of the Ancestors* I produce in English translation an Ingano version that is explicit about the loss of an intended paradise where a single grain of corn could have produced a full barrel of chicha. A fairly close parallel occurs in one episode of a long Tucana myth, in which a young girl produces five large jars of beer from only one ear of corn. As in the Kamsá variant, the mother-in-law mistakenly scolds the younger woman, who then turns into a macaw (Lévi-Strauss 1978, 26-27). In a Zinacantán narrative, thunderbolt girl "picks a net of corn" and with this slim picking "the corn filled a corner of the house." Laughlin (1988, 270) traces this motif from Oaxaca to Guatemala, and finds a parallel in the *Popol Vuh:* Blood Girl, mother of Hunter and Jaguar Deer, "found only one stalk of corn. After praying for help, she tore the tassel off an ear of corn. And abundant ears of corn filled her net" (Edmonson 1971, 83-84).

The Sibundoy elders point to the appearance of this common bird as proof of the story's veracity: this sparrow has smooth head feathers (she had been combing her hair) and ruffled body feathers (produced by her dip into the chicha). The capacity to brew chicha from only a few grains of corn is lost forever, and people must now plant and harvest large quantities of corn, and woman must grind it endlessly on the mortar, in order to prepare chicha, the symbolic fluid of life in the Sibundoy Valley. This myth, in its complete form, belongs to the group of Sibundoy myths relating how the intended establishment of a paradise on earth was frustrated by a breakdown in communication between human beings and the messengers of the gods.

María Juajibioy takes this mythic framework and constructs an action-centered version that has removed the cosmological trappings of the complete myth. Her account centers on the conflict between the two women protagonists; it highlights experiential, emotional components such as the anger of the intended mother-in-law and the sadness of the younger woman. María's version preserves the remarkable transformation of woman into bird but relates this incident outside of its cosmological setting. This focus on novelistic elements and the loss of surrounding cosmology illustrates one prominent response to mythic potential within a narrative tradition. This response involves seizing on the dramatic moments embedded within such plot structures as dramatic archetypes in their own right. Maria's recasting of this myth illustrates the polyvocality of mythical traditions, which are pliable to individual needs and perspectives. In María's personalization of these mythical elements we encounter mythology evolving into folktale.

kanye tobiaxe inashjango bobonsebiama kanye imenoyenungabentxe
A young woman arrived where they lived with a single young man.

i ch wamben mama jabokná chká yojashjangwám ibojwabwajwa arob mats jakakjamaka[47]
And that intended mother-in-law, when she arrived, had stored an arobe of corn to make chicha.

i chuta btsetsat ibnetsoñe inyoy[48]
And the two parents went off to another place,

ibojtashjango orna ch mats nye konforme inetsajajoñe
and when they returned the corn was just as they left it.

i ch wamben mama jabokná txa tbojetsetna   5
And that intended mother-in-law became very angry,

yojetschembumbaka
she really shouted at her,

i chká kausna ch tobiaxna ibojongomia
and because of that the young woman became sad,

i shlobtxe yojesobem
and she turned into a bird.

---

[47]line 2: *wamben mama jabokná*, "mother-in-law to be." If the trial marriage is successful, she will become the young woman's mother-in-law. *arob*, a traditional dry measure equivalent to twenty-five pounds.

[48]line 3: *inyoy*, "to another place." In other versions it is made clear that the family had invited a work crew to help with their land, and thus incurred a serious obligation to provide chicha.

i ch bokoy inakakja chenache yojesoshufbatajchkaye
And she had made the chicha, she splashed about in it,

i yojesongwebjwa i yojesongwebjoy 10
and she took flight, and she took flight,

yojtschañese
she disappeared.

i ch wamben mama jentjareparakas chká yojtsetxatjay
And that mother-in-law without looking, like that she became
angry.

i tobiaxna aiñe inakakja[49]
And the young woman, yes, she made the chicha,

ch bokoyna list inetsabkjañe
that chicha was ready to drink,

nye ntjontjexeká inachembumbe 15
but without looking she scolded her.

chká kaus ibnaftsongamé
Because of that she became sad,

ch bokoy tojanutskakjaye
she had really prepared the chicha.

i tojesanoshubabatajchkakaye
And she splashed about in the chicha she had made,

i tojesanongebjoñe
and then she flew away.

nye nyetxá 20
That's all.

(m20) murselakobiana
About the Bat

As performed by Estanislao Chicunque in Kamsá, May 1978

We have in this myth an attenuated version of the "About the Owl"
(m18), a story about a male suitor who keeps to himself in order to
disguise his animal nature and who is finally rejected by the family.
Lacking here is the element of the animal-suitor as a messenger of
the gods or as a doctor with remarkable knowledge that could alter the
circumstances of human existence. Another difference between this tale

---

[49]line 13: *i tobiaxna aiñe inakakja*, "And that young woman, yes, she made the
chicha." In other versions it is made clear that the young woman was able to make a
whole barrel of chicha from just a few grains of corn.

and many others is that the father of the intended bride is the one who unmasks the spirit imposter. The narrator gives ample coverage to the wise counsel of this capable father as he steers his daughter away from the odd suitor that has caught her fancy. As these tales of suitors accumulate, it becomes apparent that we are dealing with a cluster of mythical elements on the theme of ambiguous suitors, a prominent concern in both European and Amerindian storytelling (Thompson 1961; Lévi-Strauss 1978). Kamsá storytellers make use of this cluster of narrative elements, recombining them in different permutations within this branch of the corpus.

As interesting as the tale itself is Estanislao's introduction to it. The narrator is at pains to establish a link to tradition, and he avers that the tradition was once far richer, as the present remnants would suggest. Estanislao's introductory lines exhibit traces of Kamsá ritual language, evident in the choice of lexemes, in the grammatical apparatus, and in the chantlike tonality of his voice. Note for example the parallel tendency in line 3: *atxebe nemoria atxebe jwabna,* "in my memory, in my understanding." Kamsá ritual language is constituted by precisely these kinds of parallel constructions. Estanisalo and Justo are approximate age-mates; their relationship is friendly but slightly formal. This was the first myth that Estanislao performed for us, and he frames it gracefully with opening and closing enactments of respect.

murselakobiana morna mo chjatenakwentá
The one about the bat, now let's speak of it among ourselves.

ndoka remidio nye pobrebe barina[50]
So be it with all due respect,

nye atxebe nemoria atxebe jwabna yojtsemna nyetxana
just as it exists in my memory, in my understanding.

a vera nyetxa nye testigotemena[51]
Even though it might be only a small remnant,

xkwaisenobweye ch mursilakobiana   5
I will tell you the one about the bat.

murselakna ana obebenkwayá
The bat arrived as a suitor.

taitá i mamana ibomnana pero bnga krischana
The father and mother were still alive, but human beings like us,

---

[50]line 2: *ndoka remidio,* "without remedy." These opening lines are couched in the tonality and diction of Kamsá ritual language; note that the same gesture closes the narrative act.

[51]line 4: *testigotemena,* "a small remnant." Estanislao indicates that the myths still remembered are only a small fragment of what was once available.

propio krischan bebmana ch tobiaxbe mamana krischan
a real human being the mother, the young woman's mother, a human being,

tobiaxbe bebta ibomna taitana krischian
the young woman's father was still alive, he too was human.

pero ch bebinkuna ana murselako wabaina propi nombrena   10
But that nephew was a bat, as they are properly called.

chana jitiñe jiboknana obebinkway
He would arrive every evening, that suitor.

i asna ch tobiaxna jitobjana jitobjana
And then that young woman would call him, she would call him.

chorna bebmanajema ibojatiana
Then that poor mother said to her:

ndaykausa chana nye jutsostutxañanaka
"Why is he always with his back to us?"

nyekasa kutsamañajema nye jutsebstutxayana   15
"He is just like that, he just likes to turn his back to people."

malaisa jobia stenye ndayeksa chká inetswatjaka
"I would really like to see his face. Why is he so shy?"

bebmana kwatiyana bebenaka
The mother surely spoke to the daughter:

bembe malaisa mntxoye kutobwertana stuwabwatemanaka
"Daughter, I hope he turns so that we can get to know him."

chorna chana ibojatjwa uwatujema komenaka
Then she responded: "He is very timid."

kachke moka betsopasañamsa ko nye betsowatjaka   20
The fact is that he was shy because he barely had a face.

karay ibsana jitsaisobokuñana
Damn, first thing in the morning he was up and gone,

itojitsejetatena orna jitsatstbemanajemana
and then at dusk he would be sitting there again.

ch pamilla jokedamana ntxamo ketsemankana
He wanted to become a member of that family.

sempra bebtena jatsnotisiana sikera krischan taikunamena
But the father kept wondering if he might be a human being,

o bayujema chaondotsomiñeka   25
or could he be some kind of beast?

a vera kachama ntxamo mwatutsemana nya yapa respeto staperdiajem
"Now let's see how it goes for us, without being rude,

kejadeskansa ora itukana chajabonyeka
when he is sleeping, quietly I will go take a look at him."

a chora ibojajwebubonye orna biena ibojabwertana orna
Then when he went to take a look, when he turned him around,

ache murselakoko chena inetsomiñe ch obebenkwayanaka
that suitor turned out to be nothing other than a bat.

ah chorna ibojojwá bembena chká uwatjajema komenasna   30
Ah, then he told his daughter: "So that's why he is so shy.

ntxamosa moisemanaka chana ndayentxana mwana
What are we going to do? Where is this one from?

ndoñe krischana kwakundemunasna ndayama kachkaka chana
He is not even a human being, why one like him?

mejorana nye mo kanye persona batsmunasa
It would be better since there are people around.

mallajkta ombrena imutsómiñe sobrante imutsómiñe
There are plenty of men around, they are in abundance.

mejorna barie mntadilijensia   35
It is better to go looking elsewhere,

ch bayujeman ndoñe txabaka
this little beast will not do.

mejorna ndayiñe mochobodilijensia barie
It is better that we go looking elsewhere,

mntxá kompañero mochongwangosna
like that we will find you a companion."

mojemna mo bayujema tal vesa iwabmunaka
Then that poor beast must have heard them.

ndoka remidio chorna ibojtsaboté murselako betsemenkausa   40
Surely then they rejected him because he was a bat.

ibojajwebonye kausna ah del todo bashejobiatem tonday ndojobia
Because he went to look at him, ah, he had a tiny face, no face at all,

i chama imojtsaboté i chorna chjemena wabotená yojtsekedá
and for this they rejected him and then he remained unwanted.

nye nyetxasa ch palabrana komena
Just like this is this story.

nye nyetxá chusna kenatsmuna
That's just how he is, that fellow.

ndoka remidio   45
Without remedy.

(m21) gavilanbiama
About the Hawk

As performed by Mariano Chicunque in Kamsá, December 1978

This narrative provides additional insights into the institution of trial marriage, which forms the customary foundation for these myths of suitors. "About the Hawk" features most prominently a shrill chorus of dissenting sisters who rail against the intended match. The animal-person in this instance is the hawk; only at the end, when the family has rejected his suit, does he reveal his animal identity by picking at snails and then calling, "pex pex," from the limb of a tree. This hawk, unlike some of the other animal-suitors, does not appear to possess special powers, though he does excel as a hard worker and thereby captures the support of his intended father-in-law.

The sisters' dissent is rendered persuasively in this performance. We can hear the contempt and sense the anger in their derisive voices, even as the parents are leaning toward endorsing the marriage: "That lazy fellow is no good. Why should we be cooking good things for him? We should just give him garbage to eat. He should return to his own people." Tensions attending the introduction of a spouse into the tight-knit Kamsá family are portrayed vividly in these stories; this one proposes that passing the grade with the sisters of the intended bride is a significant hurdle. Of course, the reversion of the animal-suitor to his or her animal form ultimately confirms the impossibility of the proposed match.

gavilanbiama mntxá
The one about the hawk goes like this.

gavilan lo mismo shembasabiama inashjajwana[52]
The hawk also arrived looking for a woman.

are gavilana konporma nye ntsekona bobonse txabe bobonse inetshjajwañe[53]
So the hawk, just like a young man, a handsome young man, would arrive.

iye bwena
And fine.

chorna lo mismo ch shakwana ibonetsangmenana[54]   5
Then those weeds had really taken over.

[52]line 2: *lo mismo*, "the same." This narrator had just finished his performance of "About the Owl" (m18).

[53]line 3: *bobonse txabe*, "handsome young man." This suitor is not reclusive, nor does he exhibit signs of his animal nature.

[54]line 5: *shakwana*, "grass, weeds." The Sibundoy Valley floor is very fertile, and the climate provides plenty of rainfall; as a consequence, the grass and other undergrowth comes up strong and fast. Two weedings are associated with a single corn-growing cycle.

jashtsama nyeyama o tsumbijwa jtsabanama
To clear away the weeds by those bean plants, or else to lift them,

ndayama ch btsetsanga inetsungemianana
whatever, those parents were in need of help.

a vera pareja motsatá mashame trabaja chintema koiseshbwangaka
"Let's see, you go together, go do some work, those plants will
   wither."

ay yebojataka
Ay, they went off together.

iye jetiñoye jwasam ora yojobwache bebmá   10
And in the afternoon around lunch time the mother payed them
   a visit,

yojá jawenayamaka
she went to call them.

lo mismo ch btsá kachká tatsebioka biatotebemañe
That fellow was just sitting there on top of a log,

i ch shembasana btsetsañe etsenokwentañe
and that young woman stood there conversing with him.

shakwana konforma ndoñe batxana ndoñe yendotetxenaka
The weeds were the same, no fewer, nothing had been cut.

bweno   15
Fine.

chtena ibojeniana katana
That day those two spoke to one another:

ar chjawanta ndayá biamana a vera yibsa
"I will wait to see what they might do tomorrow,

a vera yibsa ntxamo ndayá chaojiyetsamaka
let's see tomorrow what they might accomplish.

kam mwentxe chabote ya yibsa bochjiyarwasa
Let him stay the night here, tomorrow we will ask for help.

iye kachkuntxamena ndoka bwatechamo   20
And let's not say anything to them now."

bweno
Fine.

a vera ibsana a vera diosmanda ch chuse nya pwerte xnangemena
So the next day: "For God's sake, those weeds, we really need your
   help."

bweno ibojeyaka
Well, they went off again.

aray chté kokayé de ombreka ooh nyetxá ch btsayé nyetxá yojoshkona
Damn, that day right away, my word, ooh, that fellow walked all around that area,

shbwanganiñe lempeka   25
he completely sized it up.

ah jtiñe nyetsto ora yojawasa iye i lempe pochokaniñe yojatsmunaka
Ah, by midday when they ate lunch, he had completely finished the work.

bweno
Fine.

chora chamna dweñe agradesido ana tokjapochoká
Then that owner was grateful that the work was done,

mokna yotsomañana
for all he was doing there.

bweno   30
Fine.

chora ch mayora bebta asna mejor nye jtsabwamayiñe chkasnaka
Then that elder, the father: "Perhaps thus they should marry."

i chora iye kach lo mismo bebmá kenatunga ndayunga bemenana
And then that mother, like those sisters, there were several,

i chká jiyana jatrabajama i chká jtsotebemañana tatsebioka
and like that they spoke: "So they went to work and they just sat there on top of a log.

ndoñe bensetrabajaye nye chká
Like that they didn't even work.

nye chká jtsasañana nye chkaka   35
Like that they just ate, like that."

bwenoka
Fine.

chorna ch chnga ch wabotenunga bejtsabotena bejtsetxatjaye
Then those sisters were rejecting him, they were angry.

asta wawenana ndoñe kosa txabá ch araganabiama
You could hear it: "That lazy fellow is no good.

ndayá botamana wabwanayanasa
Why should we be cooking good things for him?

nye kejopodeká muchjwajwatxiyesa   40
We should just give him garbage to eat.

mas vale chaotsatoñe kachabioye
He should return to his own people."

pero ch inya yojayana
Then another one said:

a ver ntxamo jobowamayama tojtsemenasna ntxamoka
"What's this about being all ready to marry? What is this?"

bweno
Fine.

i la misma cosa ch katana ibojenakwenta   45
And the parents were saying the same thing to themselves.

imojtsabotenaka chkaka
Like that they were turning against him.

bwenosna asna asna mnté depedida xkwetse
"Well then, then I will leave today.

xkwetsesoborodea jajañe
I will go take a walk around the garden.

akana ndoñe batabonasna nye atxeka
You shouldn't follow me, just by myself."

ase chana choroxunga inakjanaka[55]   50
Then he had piled up those snails,

chuxe cha chuxe chana inetsoftakoñe choroxunga
those, he, those, he was picking at those snails.

ayekna chká imojinye choroxunga chkaka
Then they saw all those snails, like that.

bweno ase imojeniana choroxe ftekoyana
Well, then they were saying: "He was picking at those snails.

ndoñe mejora ndoñe mamitá perdona jatjayiñe[56]
No, it is better not to celebrate this wedding.

ndoñe kaochanjobwachika   55
There will be no marriage,

chana nye chawaftsatoñika chawaftsatoñika
he will just have to leave, he will have to leave."

orna chká imojenakwenta
Then like that they spoke among themselves.

---

[55]line 50: *choroxunga*, "snails." These are small white snails found in Sibundoy gardens.

[56]line 54: *mamitá perdona*, "the Mother's pardon." This is the term used in Kamsá to describe the marriage celebration. In this ceremony the young people ask the Virgin Mary's permission to marry.

ibsana achako nya palabriñeka
The next day he was in agreement with them.

i ibsana mo atxeka kmojatosintia
And the next day: "You are unhappy with me,

ntxamose ndoka remidio atxe chjatolwariñe   60
what else can I do, without remedy, I will leave for another place."

chkasa a chiñe konpormaka yojoftseboshjona trabajaniñe
Like that he left the work just as it was.

chana yojtsana nyetxá limpio txa ch janyetxina choroxe
He walked over there, it was full of ground bits of snail.

ndeombre choroxe sayay inamna
Upon my word, he was one who feasted on snails.

i chore cha yojtsatobemañe gavilana
And then he was sitting there, a hawk,

i tsbananoka pex pexeka   65
And from above: "Pex, pex,"

chká yojtsandontjnaye tsbananokaka
like that he screeched from above.

yojisongwebjoñe gavilan impas
He flew off, completely a hawk.

ndokená bebinko intutsemuna shechayana
There was nothing left of that son-in-law who did the weeding.

ana cha chnga gavilana katunjanaobra
So he just turned himself into a hawk,

ch gavilan kasamentero ch kasament palabra inabinyana   70
that hawk suitor, the wedding was more or less arranged.

chuxe komna nyetxá tijaparlá
That's how he is, just as I have told it.

(m22) tobiaxbe parlo
The Tale of the Young Woman

As performed by María Juajibioy in Kamsá, October 1978

A mythic narrative corpus can exist in multiple statements, some of them gravitating to the personal and anecdotal. María Juajibioy has a knack for isolating choice moments in the mythology and elaborating them into striking narrative vignettes. She has stripped this myth of its cosmological surround in order to focus on the dramatic encounter between the older woman and her son's intended bride. Familiarity with the general corpus of Kamsá mythology leads us to wonder if the centipede-woman might have arrived bearing precious knowledge, as is the case with "About the Owl" (m18) and "About the Sparrow" (m19). Her statements that she herself will become specific food crops might indicate that she possessed knowledge of an easier route to the finished product of agricultural labor. But such details do not interest our narrator, who prefers to center the story on the two women, and on the dangerous proximity of the the spirit realm.

"The Tale of the Young Woman" places us once again within the context of Kamsá trial marriage. In this version, a young woman has come to the home of an available man to test the waters; the assumption is that if she gets along well and proves to be a good worker, the marriage will be recognized. In María's vignette, the older woman observes the social forms appropriate to this situation. She addresses the intended bride as *sobrena* (line 18), from the Spanish word for niece, but in Kamsá the appropriate term of address for a daughter-in-law. The young woman responds with the respectful term of address toward an older woman, *batá*, "Aunt" (line 19). But something goes awry in this verbal exchange. When the older woman makes the legitimate request for help in planting *barbacuano*, an edible root, the younger woman responds with what appears to be a flippant dismissal: *xwatsetsejaja jomuxenaka*, "I myself will become barbacuano." The narrator observes: how could the older woman beg her? (line 8). It would be the obligation of the younger woman to comply gracefully with this request.

Our suspicion that something is amiss is confirmed when the older woman returns from planting corn only to find that the centipede she struck with her digging stick was in fact the very same younger woman. Just as the centipede was damaged, so too the younger woman has "her head all banged up" (line 15). This breach of the boundary setting apart the mundane and spiritual domains becomes apparent to the older woman, who exclaims: *ak ndoñe krischian*, "You are not a human being" (line 23). The centipede-woman is a throw-back to the animal-people of the ancestral period, but her emergence in this contemporary setting is weird and unsettling. She represents a crossing of cosmological boundaries: much as the centipede is a creature of the field who sometimes enters the house, the centipede woman is a duplicitous spiritual actor capable of taking both human and animal forms.

The Kamsá Indians have been praised for their agriculture from the first European contact (Bonilla 1972), and to the present day they continue to plant and harvest lush gardens. The men play an important role in clearing the land, weeding around the sprouts of corn, beans, squash, cabbage, and other crops, and bringing in the harvest, but it is the woman's job to actually place the seed into the earth. To accomplish this, the women walk about a prepared garden plot, the seed in their hand, opening and closing the site for each seed with their long-handled digging sticks. These sticks consist of a handle and a pole some five feet long to which is attached a short metal or rock "foot" that makes contact with the loose earth.

A great deal of traditional custom and belief revolves around the practice of agriculture among Sibundoy Indians (McDowell 1989). Much lore attaches to the act of planting, stressing its importance in the overall scheme. The most important factor is the "hand" of the woman who does the planting. Women who have "a good hand" are valued; the birds and mice will not bother their seeds, thus assuring an abundant harvest. It is customary for women to partake of the visionary medicine under the supervision of a native doctor who "cures" their hand. A woman must avoid toasting or grinding grains of corn on corn-planting days or their hand will be "ruined" and the seeds will not yield a good return. In this conceptualization, planting is not merely a "routine" activity but is rather a key moment in the cycle of food production, and one charged with spiritual significance.

María Juajibioy speaks of planting on good authority. She is in her own right a reputable planter of corn seed. Her account of the recalcitrant centipede-woman is a cautionary tale warning of the dangerous proximity of the spirit realm, a domain defined by its mutability, always lurking at the edges and interstices of routine experience. It is likewise a tale featuring the woman planter as heroine, for it is her appropriate behavior that unmasks the centipede-woman and prevents an unnatural union between her son and this denizen of the spirit realm. Kamsá mythology presents the development of civilization in the Sibundoy Valley in terms of the gradual taming and banishing of the transformative spiritual beings, who persist on the margins as sources of power and danger. The woman protagonist (like María herself) is a keeper of civilization by virtue of her planting hand, but in addition she cleverly foils an unwarranted incursion of the spirit realm into the sphere of productive human society.

kanye tobiaxe inashjango bobonsbiamaka
A young woman arrived at the home of a young man.

i ch wamben mama jaboknán ibojauyan
And that intended mother-in-law said to her:

xkatjesaboye jenaxaka[57]
"Come plant *barbacuano* seed."

i ch bebinkwa jabokná ibnetsjwañe
And that intended daughter-in-law answered her:

[57]line 3: *jenaxaka*, "barbacuano." *Colocasia esculenta*. According to Bristol (1968, 593): "annual herb purposefully propagated in gardens, introduced from the Old World, common. Tubers edible."

xwatsetsejaja jomuxenaka[58]   5
"I myself will become *barbacuano*."

asna bibiaxá xmetsabojeka[59]
Then: "Plant some *achira* for me."

inye chká jatjwañana xwatsetsejaja bibiná
Again she responded like that: "I myself will become *achira*."

i nye ndoñese juwenan ntxam tbojtserwanka
And she just wouldn't listen, how could she beg her?

chorna ch wamben mama jabokná inetsoñe jawashuntsam
Then that intended mother-in-law went out to plant corn.

inetsashuntsañokna santopeso ibninyenaka[60]   10
Where she was planting corn she found a centipede.

i as cha chuwashuntsantxeka ibnetsutsjanganja[61]
And then as she was planting corn, she struck it with her digging stick.

nye natjumbañe inetsashuntsañe
She just calmly continued planting corn.

yojabuchoká orna yojtá tsoy
When she finished she returned to the house.

chorna ibninyen ch bebinkwa jabokná imp̠asajem
Then she found that intended daughter-in-law in bad shape.

intsatotebemañe betxaxena txa lisianajem   15
She was sitting there with her head all banged up,

umochkwanajem ibojinyem
she found her with her head covered.

chorna ch wamben mama jabokná ibojatjay
Then that intended mother-in-law inquired:

---

[58]line 5: *xwatsetsejaja jomuxenaka*, "I myself will become barbacuano." The verb implies an act of self-transformation from one state into another.

[59]line 6: *bibiaxá*, "achira." *Canna* aff. *edulis*. According to Bristol (1968, 593): "perennial herb, purposefully propagated in gardens, introduced, abundant. Edible tubers."

[60]line 10: *santopeso*, "centipede." Apparently a Kamsá adaptation of the Spanish word for centipede, *ciempies* or *cientopies*.

[61]line 11: *chuwashuntsantxeka*, "planting corn with the digging stick." The root for the verb "to plant corn" contains the root for "hunger," (*shuntsa*), capturing the intimate connection between nourishment and corn in the Sibundoy mentality. The women plant corn by opening a shallow hole in the ground with their digging sticks (*jenantxeka*)—these are straight poles, several feet long, with carved tongues sharpened to open the ground.

ndayek sobrená chká biyatsmanaka[62]
"Why, Niece, are you like this?"

chorna ibojojwá ndoñe kach batá chká xkondwabonaka
Then she answered: "Didn't you, Aunt, do this to me?"

chorna ibojauyán ndayentxe chká tkunbjamaka   20
Then she said to her: "Where did this happen to you?"

orna ibnojwá ndoñe ch jajoka jenantxeka xkonjutsjanjanaka
Then she responded: "In the garden, didn't you strike me with the
    digging stick?"

**chorna ibnojwá jenantxeka ndayá santo pesontxe chká tijuts-
janganja**
Then she responded: "I struck a large centipede like that with my
    digging stick.

as ak ndoñe krischian nkondimunaka ibnauyanaka
Then you are not a human being," she said to her.

nye nyetxá sindutatxumbo
That's all there is just as I know it.

(m23) tsubkwakwatjobiama
About the Rainbow

As performed by María Juajibioy in Kamsá, October 1978

María Juajibioy gives us here another vignette that appears to derive
from a very personal process of selection and crystallization within a
narrative corpus. We witness the encounter between two sisters left behind to look after the house and their dashing visitor, the rainbow. The
young man enters in fine form: he carries with him the flute that reveals
his festive character, and he is decked out in a poncho with beads
around his neck. This is an attractive young man. Immediately he is offered chicha, the essential gesture of Kamsá social life, as a sign of ap-
preciation and welcome. But there is something odd about this visitor:
as he drinks the chicha, it pours out the nape of his neck.

The alert younger sister tries to warn her older sibling: *chan kristian
tainamena mo bayuj yomnaka*, "Would he be a human being? Maybe
he's a beast." She poses·a question that emerges as paramount in all
of these animal-suitor myths, regarding the fundamental distinction
between human being (*kristian*) and animal (*bayuj*). But the older girl is
enamored of the handsome visitor, so much so that she walks out with
him into a nearby river, apparently drowning and transforming into the
rainbow's companion. The rainbow is an important figure in Kamsá

[62]lines 18, 19: Note the use of formal terms of address, Niece and Aunt, exchanged between these two women.

mythology; he appears in "The Tale of the Two Little Children" (m11) as
a lesser deity who gives instruction and aid to these culture heroes.
María's vignette does not contribute to our knowledge of this figure: it
confirms his manifestation as a handsome (and lustful) young man, but
we learn nothing more about his place in the Kamsá scheme of things.
As is her wont, María concentrates on a moment of social intrigue, leaving aside most of the details that connect these episodes to the thread of
Kamsá cosmogony.

In the aftermath of this telling, Justo stated that the existence of the
two rainbows, one strong, the other more faint, confirms the veracity of
this myth.

btsetsata ibnetsoñe tabanoy tajayam
The parents went to Sibundoy for a fiesta,

i bembeata ibnokedá shanyata
and the two daughters remained behind to look after the house.

chorna inaboy kanye bobonse alegra
Then along came a lively young man,

inabay flautan waruanaye i wachakirana inashjango[63]
he came along with a flute, he arrived with a fine poncho and lots
    of beads.

chorna ch wabochená chan ibnontxá ushubkayán bokoy[64]   5
Then that older sister, she began to give him chicha to drink.

i ch wabentsá ibninye
And the younger sister saw it,

ch yojtsebtmana i ch yojtsaytsebwachkekjan jochentxoika
when he drank the fluid just passed out the nape of his neck.

chorna ch wabochená ibnawakakán
Then she scolded that older sister:

chan kristian tainamena mo bayuj yomnaka
"Would he be a human being? Maybe he's a beast."

i asna ch wabochená nye yojtsotjayanañe   10
And then the older sister didn't like hearing that.

---

[63]line 4: *flautan*, "flute." The Kamsá make and play wooden flutes of different
sizes, made from local reeds. During carnival season those who can play them wander about from house to house, making music and joining in the festivities (see
McDowell 1987). *waruanaye*, "wearing a fine poncho." The root here is *ruana*, a
French word (designating, I believe, a textile company) that has been appropriated
into Colombian Spanish to name the ponchos worn throughout the highland sectors
of the nation. The striking quality of this poncho is carried in the Kamsá prefix, *wa-*,
an intensifier. *wachakirana*, "fine beads." Chakira are seed and also glass and ceramic
beads worn by men and women around the neck and indicating social status.

[64]line 5: *ushubkayán bokoy*, "she gave him chicha to drink." This act is the cen-
terpiece of Kamsá social etiquette; as don Justo once said, "Where there is chicha,
there is love."

i ch bobonse inetsaysobokne i chká inayetso flautañe
And that young man walked out of there playing the flute.

i bejay inamna nye chentxe inetsenatjombañe
And there was a river nearby, she just went there with him,

i tobiax ibnawakamiye i chanaka chentxe nye inoxobuntsá bejayoy
and the young woman followed him and she just entered the river
   there.

nye nyetxá
And that was that.

i as monbetsechamo ke chatja chata tsubkwakwatjoka[65]   15
And now they say that they are the two rainbows.

nye nyetxá tsindotatxumbo
That's all that I know of it.

(m24) osobiama
About the Bear

As performed by Mariano Chicunque in Kamsá, November 1978

One of the most popular narratives in Spanish-American tradition is the
Juan Oso cycle, featuring the exploits of a youth who is the offspring of
a union between a bear and a human female. I have selected from
Kamsá tradition three versions of this prototype: in the mythic narrative
immediately following, the bear-child is destroyed by its raging father.
In m25, "About the Lively Bear," the clever young woman manages to
avoid the bear's seductive intentions, so the conception of the bear-child
is forestalled. Only m26, "Juan Oso," presents the more familiar plot fo-
cused on the growth and development of the mixed-species child. These
materials suggest that the Juan Oso tale emerges from a narrative matrix concerned with seductive bears and that it should not be accorded
preferential status, at least not in the Amerindian context.

This tale is assimilated only with difficulty to two European types,
Type 301, "The Three Stolen Princesses," which veers off into the hero
descending into the underworld and his rescue of the stolen maidens,
and Type 650 A, "Strong John," which places emphasis on the remarkable strength and unruly character of the bear-child. It is an immensely
popular tale in Latin America, where greater emphasis is placed on the
coming of age of the bear-child and his adventures as a young man,
often in war. Boas (1912, 254-57) notes "the most remarkable distribution
of this tale among Western American Indians" and views this distribution as a product of early Spanish contact and subsequent transmission
northward from tribe to tribe. But this may be an unwarranted privi-
leging of the European variants; I find it more probable that seductive

---

[65]line 15: *chata tsubkwakwatjoka*, "two rainbows." The reference is to the sharper
and fainter rainbows that often appear together in the sky.

bears and bear children might occur independently than that the entire complex would be traced to a single source, for example the Near East as Szoverffy (1956) suggests. The Kamsá materials propose a narrative matrix centered on seductive bears, with the maturation of the half-bear child a special case.

In fact, attending to the thematic possibilities developed in American Indian bear stories brings into focus the contrast between European and American prototypes. In *Haa Shuká: Our Ancestors*, Nora and Richard Dauenhauer (1988) provide the text of a remarkable Tlingit narrative by Tom Peters, "The Woman Who Married the Bear." The woman is carried off by the seductive bear, who in turn is destroyed by her brothers. But in a sequel to these events, the woman takes to putting on the skin of her bear husband and eventually she and her children become bears themselves. At last she too must be destroyed by her younger brother. In this broader context it is clear that the tales centered on the exploits of a bear-child represent only one strain in a highly productive narrative matrix.

"About the Bear" begins with the amusing antics of a festive bear, who appears as a man, gets the attention of a young woman, and carries her off into the forest. It ends with the bear's destruction at the hands of the soldiers, who have been sent to protect the woman when she returns to her original husband. The offspring of bear and woman is given very little attention in this narrative. The narrator mentions a year's captivity, some washing of children's clothes, and finally the destruction of the child, who is torn apart in one fell stroke. Taita Mariano's performance stays within the framework of Kamsá mythopoeisis, exploring the mystery of animal suitors and their interactions with human beings.

In this performance, the bear arrives and playfully enacts the festive scene in town, where the adults have gathered to celebrate Corpus Christi, formerly one of the great seasonal festivals of the Sibundoy natives. He prepares eggs in an unorthodox manner, breaking the shell on his forehead and sucking the raw contents into his mouth; then he dances with the seed rattle, singing the Corpus Christi celebratory song. His actions create a parity between *tabanok*, town, and *jajoy*, garden, two domains that are normally thought to be contrastive. These antics capture the interest of a young woman who had been left behind to look after the house; she responds to his advances and later travels with the bear to his forest home. The narrator tells us that such unions were common in the old days and that soldiers were routinely required to undo them.

In the forest the bear provides for the woman, making her a bench and pillaging and hunting for food, but she chooses to return to her husband when the opportunity arises. Stringent preparations must be made to contain the anger of her powerful bear consort: ten fences are erected around the home in the valley, and soldiers are on hand with their rifles at the ready. All of this is required to restrain the bear when he comes after the woman. Taita Mariano makes use of a striking metaphor in telling this final scene: at first the soldiers' bullets bounce off the approaching bear as if they were grains of corn. As the bear surges past one fence after another and defies the bullets that are showered upon him, he takes on a larger-than-life stature, though at last he is brought down and clubbed to death.

The narrator expresses some uneasiness with this plot, especially with its more lurid aspects. Twice he questions the possibility of the narrated events only to affirm that after all this is what the tradition asserts: *nyetxá nye chká jenakwentayana*, "but that's exactly how they always tell it" (line 16). Yet concerning the general setting of the story he is less hesitant, giving personal testimony in relation to the extended periods of festivity formerly associated with Corpus Christi day (line 4). From all accounts, the feast of Corpus Christi was indeed a wild one in the Sibundoy Valley; m13 tells that it was on this day that God descended to announce the destruction of the carnal world.

We are left with a parable stressing the inviolability of the natural order. The bear is admirable for his efforts to care for his family, yet he has doomed himself by mating with a human spouse. The woman has made a fundamental mistake by leaving home to follow "a beast." Their child must perish in the undoing of this unnatural relationship. I submit that this moral universe is central to the Amerindian narrative matrix involving seductive bears; in this light the Juan Oso story (see m26), in which the bear-child comes to maturity, is an abberation, perhaps under the influence of European prototypes.

osona anteona yentxá jobemana
In the old days bear could become a person.

anteo ch korobxekana korobxe[66]
In the old days on Corpus Christi day, Corpus Christi,

basenunga jtseshanyana btsetsanga tabanoye
the children would look after the house, the parents would go to
    Sibundoy.

i ko asta atxena chká tijoftsesenté
And there even I took part in it,

unga semana o asta shinye chká tabanoka jtseiñingana[67]   5
three weeks or even a month like that partying in Sibundoy,

[66]line 2: *korobxe*, "Corpus Christi Day." A Catholic celebration, falling in June; it was a grand feast in the Sibundoy Valley, a time of communal revelry.

[67]line 5: *unga semana o asta shinye*, "three weeks or even a month." To this day the Kamsá lifestyle allows for extended periods of festivity; adults will sometimes spend a week or more on the party trail.

basejemungna nye jaishanyanaka[68]
the poor children just looking after the house.

i chká inaishanyá
And like that they were looking after the house.

i chká ch oso btsana chká inetsashjajwana
And like that the bear, a man like that, came along,

ch basenga shanyangebentxe inetsashjajwana
where those children looked after the house, he arrived.

i shema kache ch basenga mamanaka inetsemna[69]   10
And a woman, those little mothers, were there.

bweno
Well.

**chora chana shmnebé twamnabe ushmemenaishañe chajasoye
    yojarepara**[70]
Then he went looking for hen's eggs in the nest behind the house.

nderado shmnebé tojinyena twambe shmnebé chbé jakana
Truly he found eggs, hen's eggs to gather.

**iye jawakana xkenana u platilluja jawakana ch mextomboka jwash-
    tebwajwana**
And he took down a plate, a small tin, he took it down and set it on
    that little table.

chorkokayé ntxamo inamanana   15
And then surely, what was he?

nyetxá nye chká jenakwentayana
But that's exactly how they always tell it.

ana fshenuxeka ch xubjaka jenantsakjwana[71]
So he would tie a seed rattle to his ankle,

ch fshenuxeka buntsuntsanuxe chká wabainuxe
that seed rattle makes quite a lot of noise, that's what it is called.

chuxe kanyexe jokiñana iye jenoxubjatsobwayana
One of those he took up to tie around his ankle.

[68]line 6: *jaishanyanaka*, "they look after the house." The Kamsá root, *shanyá*,
"caretaker," identifies a social institution of some importance in a community whose
members often tend fields, or attend parties, in distant areas.

[69]line 10: *basenga mamanaka*, "little mothers." This term refers to young unmar-
ried girls. The singular, *base mama*, is a polite term of address to a girl.

[70]line 12: *chajasoye*, "nest behind the house." Kamsá families keep nests hung
around the back of the house where hens sit and lay eggs.

[71]line 17: *fshenuxeka*, "seed rattle." The Kamsá make seed rattles which are used
in festive dancing. This is a delightfully onomotopoeic word; pronouncing it, one
cannot help but hear the sound of the rattle.

iye jontxana jatselantsana   20
And he began to dance about:

mntxasa tabanoka korobxstontxe korobxstontxe[72]
"Like this in Sibundoy, on Corpus Christi day, on Corpus Christi day."

imojtshekwana
He spun about:

tabanokase iye jajokna atxe kach lo mismoka
"As they are doing in Sibundoy, so I do here in the garden."

chká jtshekwanana chká waxubjuntsakwana
Like that he spun about, the seed rattle tied to his ankle.

iye shmnebé chora jokeñana iya jwentsaka jenaftsebana[73]   25
And those eggs then he took up and broke them against his forehead.

iye jobkwakwayana jatatsutxenana
And he sucked them dry and discarded the shells.

chore iye lempe yojtsosañe chora jijtiselantsana
Then when he had eaten his fill, then he returned to dancing:

a tabanoka imojtsesanga i jajokna lo mismo
"In Sibundoy they have eaten; the same in the garden.

korobxstontxe korobxstontxe
Corpus Christi day, Corpus Christi day."

chká jtsetsalantsayanaka   30
Like that he danced about.

bweno
Well.

chká inamna iye ajá kabaná ntxamasa inamanana
Like that it was, and, aha, finally, how did it work out?

i anye yojtisa orna ana shema shanyá ch mama shanyá[74]
And when he went there, so the woman caretaker, that mother who looked after the house,

como será atxe chkase tstatxumbo
how could it be? I know it like this.

---

[72]line 21: *korobxstontxe korobxstontxe*, "Corpus Christi, Corpus Christi." The narrator has the bear imitate the song of the Corpus Christi revelers in Sibundoy.

[73]line 25: *jwentsaka jenaftsebana*, "he broke them against his forehead." This is comic behavior on the part of the bear-man, who approximates but does not replicate human competence.

[74]line 33: *mama*, "mother." This term refers to a young married woman.

bweno xkwabkwentá   35
Fine, I will tell it.

chora chana ibojatontxa jaingeñana ch osona boyá oso inamna[75]
Then he began to fool around with her, that bear husband, a bear he
   was.

yojontxá jayingeñana shemaka
He began to fool around with that woman.

iye ch shema chkasa yojowena ch osoftaka
And that woman listened to that bear.

i chká ibojtsobwachjangwa ch umanidad[76]
And like that they came together to make love.

iye ch tjoye ibojtseitume ch osnaka ajá   40
And he hid her in the mountains, that bear, aha.

chokna yojá chokna yojaujotsunaye
There they went and he made her a wooden bench,

mo mwentxe tsetsetebemanaka kema entabladkwenta chká btsiñe
like here where I am sitting, of wooden planks with plenty of room.

a choka ibojtseyenaka baté ibojtseyena
Like that they were living, for a long time they were living together,

ya no mase watanaka
it was almost a year.

a chorna boyana jwesanaxaka inetsotajsañe   45
Then that husband wandered in the mountains with his blow gun.

ndeolpe buyesha inobujnaye
Suddenly, a stream ran by there,

iye ch buyeshoka yojtabokna orna
and when he appeared at that stream,

ase chorna xexonebe lachabetema inawashabiayika
then she was soaping a child's clothes.

bweno
Well.

i chora chentxe yojobekoná ch boyá ibojenakwenta   50
And then that husband approached there, they spoke to one
   another:

---

[75]line 36: *jaingeñana*, "to fool around." This Kamsá word comes from the Spanish
root, *engañar*, "to deceive, to fool." It is used to convey the notion of seduction and
sexual intrigue.
[76]line 39: *ch umanidad*, "to make love" (lit. "the humanity"). This Spanish root
serves as a euphemism for the sexual act.

chká tijtsepasá tijtsebomina tsbananoka
"Like this it happened to me, I came to live high in a tree.

ooh orna nye tokjisobokiñe nye tjoye tokjitsoñe pero ratose
Ooh, now he has just left for a while, he has just gone to the mountains, but only for a short time.

kochtashjangosna mejorna yibsa o nyeté koisaisaboye
You should return tomorrow, or come back the next day.

pero eso sí bnutsanasha kochjajetja
But be sure to put up ten fences,

pero de la warda cosa que duro   55
but heaven forbid, what a hard business.

kochjajetja bnutsana jetjanesha
Put up ten fences.

iye yebunentxa jtseshekona jtseshekona jetjanesha
And all around the house, all around, fences.

iye ase kochjashjango
And then you will come for me.

iye soldado chabiama soldado chamatseprontana jobowiyanama
And soldiers, those soldiers, have them ready to defend us,

nderada atxe iye kachká i basengna lempe jtsapochokañeka   60
or else truly he will put an end to me and the children."

i chkase serta yojtsemna
And that's truly how it was.

iye shemna serta yojtá oyenoye
And truly that woman went to her home.

iye yojasentia ch oso ara
And when that bear realized what had happened, damn!

iye xexona ibojtsebomina del viaje ibojetsebjatanaka
And they had a child, with one stroke he tore him in half.

iye yojotjajo yebunoye shema jtetsebjatanuka jtsobama yebunoye
                                                                        65
And he ran to the woman's home to tear her apart, he went to the home to kill her.

i chká jetjaniñe jetjanusha chká
And like that it was fenced, like that with fences.

ooh ch oso rabiaka pobre jetjanotemá eso sí
Ooh, that bear was angry, poor fellow, those fences, yes indeed!

jatasjanana altowal jwasjaná
He pulled them down, right there he pulled them down.

i kachke chabiamna santo dios soldadunga
And so those soldiers, saintly God, were waiting for him.

**chora eso sí cha nyetxá rabiaka aste balbé ndoñe bunstushejwana
nye kwerpuñe**   70
Then, yes indeed, he was so angry even the bullets could not enter
his body.

**nye jtsebtsanana ch balbé nye matse koftsatetchunjna kwenta
yojtsemna**
Those bullets just stopped there at the skin, it was like they were
shooting him with grains of corn.

i yenyengna bestxabé katoye imojtsejwesaye
And the others were shooting at the head from both sides.

iye ndayentxe imojeshache ch ena mntxena ndayentxe imojeshache
And when they got him in the pure flesh, when they got him in the
flesh,

chore ch sempra ibojontxa jorebajan
then they finally began to bring him down.

pero kanta jetjanshá impasa yojtachuwaye eso sí   75
But he completely tore down four fences, yes indeed!

a impase fxenubenache chká imojtseskopetayeyekna
Like that they aimed directly for the eyes.

a la finalna impas imojá imojarebaja imojautxenaka
In the end they brought him down, they made him fall.

cha imojautxenentxe garotiaka imojtsengarotiaye imojtsengarotiaye
Where they brought him down, they clubbed him with poles, they
clubbed him.

i asa katamonjanobenaye jobana i asa
And finally they were able to kill him, finally.

ooh jetjanishana mochnungwashá   80
Ooh, but he made it past four or more fences.

impase yojtsapochokaye kachká ndoñe skopetaxakana
They finished him off, he was without a rifle.

ooh pobre altowala jtsapochokama
Ooh, poor fellow, right there they finished him off.

ooh pobre mobuna cha yojotjajo
Ooh, poor fellow, right there he ran into them.

achká ch ante osona nye ndoñe borla
It's like that the bear of old, no fooling.

chká anteo kanjanatxembo ch osungna shemanga
ayingñayana   85
Those bears were like that in the old days, they liked to seduce
women.

chká wamaná wamaná osunga imenámena
Like that, that's how they were, that's how they were, those bears.

chká chijeka katunjanenobowiyana soldadungaftakaka
So that's how they were able to defend themselves, with soldiers.

chkasa tstatxumbo ch osobiama
Like that I know the story of that bear.

(m25) alegra osobiama
About the Lively Bear

As performed by Francisco Narváez in Kamsá, December 1978

In this permutation of the narrative matrix centered on seductive bears,
a flirtatious bear arrives where a young woman has been left behind to
look after the house, but the woman senses the bear's intentions and
proves to be resourceful in foiling them. She takes refuge in the attic
as below her the bear acts like the owner of the house, cooking some
eggs and, in imitation of the owners who have gone to a festival in
town, dancing with seed rattles around his feet. These activities mimic
and mock the ritual feasting and dancing that occurs at public celebrations in town. Notably, a plate of eggs with pepper sauce is often
shared among all present at these events as an embodiment of social
solidarity.

The bear gives away his one vulnerability: *nye koretsetse sebiawatjaka*,
"only the rattlesnake I fear." The clever young woman thinks to herself: *mejor nye txombiache* , "maybe with a woven belt (I can fool him)."
She readies a woven belt, attaching it to a needle, and drops it on the
bear's head, the belt presumably unraveling around him. This humorous oaf assumes that he has been attacked by his nemesis, the snake,
and runs off in panic, the sound of the seed rattles gradually retreating
into the distance.

This narrative defeats the familiar plot structure of the international
tale type. In this telling the bear's intended seduction never gets off
the ground, as the intended victim proves to be too smart for him. As a
consequence, there is no bear-child, no slaying of the enraged bear, and
no further exploits of his powerful offspring. Instead, we remain within
the Kamsá framework of animal suitors, though here the bear disdains
the conventions of trial marriage and attempts to lure or seize his mate
outright.

lansaité chtesena imojwabwache[77]
A day of festival it dawned that day.

btsetsanga tsoñengan tabanoy i ch fiestoy yibeta
The parents went into town to that festival in the evening.

kanya jokedan shanyá[78]
One remained behind to look after the house.

chorsa chká inaboye ch oso
Then like that along came that bear.

i tempo yojtsesentia na betsko tsemioye yojtsoxungwañaka[79]   5
And right away she noticed him, quickly she climbed into the attic,

tsemioye yojtsexungwan chorna chokna yojtsatobwatamé
she climbed into the attic, then she hid herself there.

chor chan nye yojabautsuntxeye yojabuntxa
Then he just began to push that door open.

chorkayé i chna limpe yojabontxa jutsereparanan chajasoika[80]
Then surely he began to look around behind the house.

shemnebé yojwinyin i twamba inoshemnaye chentxe yojwinyin
He found eggs, a hen was laying, there he found them.

i ch osona chbé yojtsaishniy   10
And that bear, he placed them on the fire,

chbene yojtsabweishniy como dueño yojtsabwañe chbé
those he placed on the fire, like the owner, he cooked those.

chorkayé platillajiñe o ndayiñé yojtsabotswamay
Then surely he placed them in a plate or in something.

i asna kubseroka yojtotbema yojwatebema shemnebé
And then he sat down in the owner's chair, he sat down with
    the eggs:

---

[77]line 1: *lansaité*, "festival." This word comes from the Spanish, *danza*, "dance."
It refers to the festivals that bring people from the different veredas together in the
town of Sibundoy, where typically they drink chicha, make music, and dance. Previously there were several of these, but the rigorous efforts of the Capuchin fathers
reduced this rich festival life of the community to only one, the carnival that falls just
before Lent.
    [78]line 3: *shanyá*, "to look after a property." Kamsá families customarily leave one
or a few children to look after the house when business or pleasure calls for travel
into town. The concept is so characteristic of the community that it has passed into
the neighboring Inga as a loan word.
    [79]line 5: *tsemioye*, "into the attic." Traditional Kamsá houses have pitched roofs
that are covered over with thatch. Often a platform is built in one corner to create a
kind of attic where various objects are stored.
    [80]line 8: *chajasoika*, "behind the house." Kamsá families keep baskets for hens
strung along the side and back walls of the houses.

i chor mntxasna tabanoka mojtsalkansanaka
And then: "Like this in Sibundoy they are eating."

yojwatsabaye i yojontxe jabateshakan   15
He broke the shell and began to remove it.

tstxá yojoboporma yojontxa chan jwasam
He prepared some sauce, he began to eat.

chká yojtsoshañe shemnebé
Like that he finished the eggs.

chorkayé mor kukayé xkoboijwaka
Then surely: "Now I will have some fun!"

achna fshenxa yojatinyen[81]
Then he found a rattle.

chuxa katatoy yojatenaxubjenay jatatsebunsentsenay tselansay   20
That he tied onto each of his legs, side by side, to make noise while
    he danced.

chká yojatasebunsentscnay tselansay orna
Like that he made a noise while he danced.

yojayana atxena tonday ketsatebiawatja
He said: "I fear nothing at all,

tonday ketsatebiawatja sino nye koretsetse sebiawatjaka[82]
I fear nothing at all, only the rattlesnake I fear."

i chká yojowena ch tsemiokana
And like that she heard him from the attic.

mejor nye txombiache[83]   25
"Maybe with a woven belt."

inajajon tsemioka bianatomba ntxayá wabiayetomba
They had stored in the attic a loom and some woven cloth.

ch tombañe yojandmanaye ch kach osjojnaye ch koretsetse[84]
On that loom it was wrapped, like that snake, that rattlesnake.

chiekna chká ch mtxkway chká inyna na txombiache inabwajon
And so like the snake, like that another woven belt was stored there.

---

[81]line 19: *fshenxa*, "seed rattle." This onomotopoeic word denotes the seed rattles that are strung on ankle bracelets to provide a rhythmic accompaniment to carnival dancing.

[82]line 23: *koretsetse*, a snake that "makes a noise." I have translated it as "rattlesnake," though it may not in fact be one.

[83]line 25: *txombiache*, "woven belt." Kamsá women produce long woven belts
with geometric designs that are used as articles of clothing and for swaddling babies.
Among the figures are two that would be especially pertinent here: "the snake" and
"the snake's belly."

[84]line 27: *osjojnaye*, the name of a snake that "drags itself along the ground."

chokayekna chká yojandemanay chká yojaporma
And so there like that she wrapped it around, like that she fixed it,

i chorkayé kushubja yojatetjo sebioka   30
and then surely she fixed it to the foot of the needle.

i ase chor chabe bestxoka yojatsatsatxeka
And then she let it fall on his head.

i aah, chorkayé chan kach fshenxak inetsaxubjenanka
And ah, then surely with that rattle tied to his foot,

yojateshachá mallajkta
he ran like crazy,

**yojtseteshachá wabonsuntsenayá yojawenatjumbañeka i kach
    fshenxaka**
he ran until the sound of that rattle was lost in the distance.

i ase chorkayé ndoñe mas yonjeshukonayekna yojtsatoñe   35
And then surely he never came around there again, he took off.

asna chor yojtastjango ch bemba
And so then she came down again, that daughter.

(m26) juan oso
John the Bear

As performed by Francisco Narváez in Kamsá, October 1979

As members of the *minga* or work crew gathered around, Francisco Narváez performed this story of a remarkable bear-child who overcomes the
stigma of his peculiar origins and capitalizes on his unnatural strength
to achieve success in war. The story begins in the familiar Kamsá milieu,
as a young woman is left behind to look after the house while her parents attend a festival in Sibundoy town. Along comes a bear, and without much ceremony he carries her off as his wife. The child of this union
already shows good judgment when he urges his mother to flee with
him, and the mother and son are eventually liberated from an outraged
husband and father. This much of the plot is close to the sequence of
events in m24, "About the Bear."

But this narrative picks up steam at this point, following with care
the fortune of the bear's son as he finds an uneasy niche in human society. He is baptized Juan Oso, dressed in human clothes, and sent off
to school. The other children make fun of him because he is ugly, half
human and half bear. Juan Oso tries to ignore the teasing, and the Catholic Brother warns them to desist. At last he swats one, leaving him
dead. The other children finally notice his tremendous strength and
leave him alone at that point. After his schooling, Juan Oso takes off
(with an unnamed companion) for a war, though which war it is im-

possible to say. There he distinguishes himself in a company of seven heroes. With the aid of a powerful weapon, a piece of Spanish artillery, this troop is successful against a far larger force. Their good fortune leaves them laughing at the end.

In the following tale, Francisco Narváez produces a sympathetic portrait of Juan Oso. This is not the rampant bear-son of the European parallels, strong and abusive, but rather a civil soul who strikes at others only after provocation. This bear-child fears the devastating effects of his own strength. Even as he enters his sketchy military career he remains a likeable figure, a hero who unites with a companion to triumph against all odds in battle. What we have here is a Kamsá incarnation of an international folktale celebrity and one particularly developed in the Spanish-speaking world. This narrative invokes the Sibundoy Valley milieu but departs from the familiar outlines of Kamsá mythopoeisis. It is the one instance in the whole corpus in which an animal suitor pursues with success the seduction of a human female and achieves with her a viable offspring that comes of age.

The narrative is striking also in regard to the degree of character development it encompasses. The narrator goes to some length in exploring the conscience and consciousness of the two protagonists whose lives have crossed paths with the unfortunate bear. These probes are accomplished through the transparent device of reported speech or self-address, a suggestive window into the person's inner self. Beginning with line 20, the mother explains to her son the sequence of events that has procured for him an animal father: *achkasna xjetsabokna atxebe btsetsangabioka ndoñe lisensia kenatsmena,* "For him I left my parent's home, there being no permission." Her statements convey an awareness of the role of volition in human destiny. Later, starting with line 50, the narrator employs a remarkable indirection, giving us insight into the mind of the young Juan Oso through the intuitive comments of the Catholic brother:

xmojtseborlana i el bueno,
You make fun of him, and he thinks:

atxena chantsawanta kexmuntatawanta atxebe añemna kach kuntxamo,
'I will put up with it, I hope I can stand it, my strength is too much.'

These narrative flourishes endow both Juan Oso and his mother with some depth of characterization, as we gain access to their reflections on their predicaments. In this least typical narrative within a vestigial mythology, the psyche of the protagonists receives incipient notice.

tempo chká inopasan tajayana inamna
In days gone by it happened that there was a festival.

kanye btsetsata nye tabanoy yojtsoñana tsotmoñama
The parents just went to Sibundoy to join in the drinking.

tobiaxna shanyá shanyá jokedan kanya
The girl stayed behind to look after the house, she stayed behind,
alone.

ndeolpna inaboy ch oso chentxe ibojabwache
Suddenly along came the bear, he payed a visit there.

ibojtseingañe ibojtsanbañe tsjwan ch betiyexoka tambo inabo-
prontán[85]   5
He fooled around with her and took her with him, climbing a tree
he prepared a shelter for her.

chata ibojtseneyen
Those two became established.

i ya pues achkas katakwente ibojtseyen
And then, well, like a married couple they established themselves.

chokna ya xokayujtsemena shembasa ya xoká xexona kukwatxiñe
Then she became sick, that girl, then sick with a child at hand.

yase ch boyá ch osna jtsanana ch familiangabenach jotbebama
twamba ndasoye
Then that husband, that bear, he went among the community to rob
hens or anything else,

i ch xoká jtsekwedanám   10
and he took care of the sick one.

i ya yojatetsebaná orna ch ch kachabe yentxayá tsabojabonám
And then she got up, then she went to wash his clothes.

i ch buyeshna mwentxe jtsabkukanám i ch tabanoye yojtsebo-
kanamna
And the water here gushed and flowed toward Sibundoy.

tonday lisensia shembasana nye kachentxe kachentxe jtsemenama
Without any permission that girl, alone, alone, she was.

i asna xexona mbuna yojtsobochaye
And then with the child, quickly she ran.

chana kanyoikna krischanka inyoikna kach oská   15
He was on one side a human being, on the other like a bear.

chká wabonaná i choroso ve
Like that, fierce and curly, you see? (laughs)

yojtsobochaye
She ran.

[85]line 5: *ibojtseingañe*, "he fooled her." The seduction scene is handled swiftly
here; compare m24 and m25. *tambo*, "shelter, camp." This word denotes a rough,
temporary abode.

i así chana nye bien jwesbomina yojtsejakán jwisio yojtseja-kanamna

And so he came of age, he gained judgment, he grew up fine.

chore ibojatjaye bebmaftaka ibojenekwentá

Then he inquired of his mother and she told him:

akabe taitana animal komna oso komna   20

"Your father is an animal, he is a bear.

chan ndoñe krischianika

He is not a human being.

achkasna xjetsabokna atxebe btsetsangabioka ndoñe lisensia kenatsmena

For him I left my parent's home, there being no permission.

atxena jtsanám akabe taitan bayuj

I went with your father, a beast."

chorna ch wakiñana bebmabioye txabá yojtsayañe bebmabioye yojtsayañe txabá

Then that son spoke well to his mother, he spoke well to her:

entonces atxebe taitan chaotsoñe saná tjayentxe jangwangán   25

"So my father has gone for food, he is looking for it in the mountains.

kejtsoñe ora chorna mamaftakna mwentxana boischañe

While he is gone, now with mother let's flee from here,

lijero tabanoy buchjetsebokna

quickly we must leave for Sibundoy."

i serto chká txamo ibojeniankana

And truly like that he spoke to her.

serto oso yojiyá ch bngabenache krischiangabenache jiyondebi-ayama saná

Truly the bear went among us, among us human beings, to steal food.

ya   30

Well.

i chora chatana betsko ibojtsachañika tabanoye ibojenakmiye ibo-jachá chatena

And then those two quickly ran to Sibundoy, they fled, they ran, the two of them.

i ch osna yojtashjango sanangaka

And that bear arrived with lots of food.

chor ndoknay shema ndokna xexon

Then there was nothing of the woman, nothing of the child.

chor ungetsetxenán chjena yojotjajo shukwatxe ibojwastoto
Then smelling them he ran, he followed the track.

i asta pronto tabanoka yojetsebokna   35
And before long he appeared at Sibundoy.

**chana chokna antes kaban ibundashjanga orna chokna limpe
    yojetsobwambaye**
There, before he finally appeared, she completely warned them,

a los soldados o que serán de ese skopetaxangak
those soldiers, or who were they with those rifles?

ibojatmanga imojwanyaye chbiama ch bebta juan oso
They waited, they protected them from that father of Juan Oso,

ch chan kabandonse wabayná
though he still hadn't been baptised yet.

ndayá ch oso ch bebta imojtsetabaye bebtaj imojtsetabaye   40
What, that bear, the father, they killed him, they killed that father,

ora cha skopetaxaka imojtsoba
then with their rifles they brought him down.

i chorkokayé libre ch wakiñatema bebmana libre
And then surely the son was free of his father, the mother free.

**i chorsa ch wakiñana tabanokna imojwabaye que llamó juan oso
    wakiña**
And then in Sibundoy they baptized that son, they called him Juan,
    son of the bear.

i chorna chentxana yojtsobochaye mobuna jwisio yojtsejakana
And then they had run from there, quickly he came of age.

skweloy imojomashingo tabanoy lempe imojabestia   45
He entered school in Sibundoy dressed completely like a person,

imojwabayentxana i skwele imojemashingo
he dressed in clothes and entered school.

**i ch kanyebé nyetxá podeskebé yojtsenajwabna nyetxá podeskebé
    yojtsenajwabna[86]**
And that fellow was very ugly, he was all mixed together, ugly, he
    was all mixed together.

lo de mase baseñamalunga ndoñe kas imentsebomina
The other little rascals didn't take him seriously.

kaftsoburlañika jtsoburlañingana
They made fun of him, they teased him.

[86]line 47: *yojtsenajwabna*, "he was all mixed together," human and animal that is.

i chorna ch ermanebeñe jombwambayana mntxá[87]   50
And then the Catholic Brother spoke to them like this:

xmojtseborlana i el bueno
"You make fun of him, and he thinks:

atxena chantsawanta kexmuntatawanta atxebe añemna kach kuntxamo
'I will put up with it, I hope I can stand it, my strength is too much.

atxe tstojatatxenana
I didn't lose my temper.' "

kaban nye ndoñe kaso imontsebomna
Still they didn't pay any attention.

asna yojobwambaye ndoñe kaso montsebomentxana   55
Then he advised them: "You'd better pay attention."

yojobwambay pronta ermanebeñe yojakastegakasa
He advised them, right away, the Brother punished them.

nye ndoñc ndojinyinga nye kaftsoburlañika chhé jtseborlanán
But they didn't have compassion, they just made fun of him, they teased him.

chentxan nemo erman ndoñe kaso imontsebomnentxan
From there they didn't pay attention to the Brother:

nye pronta jaoprobamna chabe añema
"Soon you will taste his strength."

tojanoprobay   60
They tasted it.

nye batatema chana jatsuntxana tempo chana obaná jaotxenamaka
He just gave one of them a little punch, right away he was dead, he struck one of them,

muerto con la fuerza de él
dead by the strength of his arm.

chentxana imojtsewatjanaka ndoñe mejor kachkay imojonyaye
After that they feared him, no, they had better let him be.

skweloye libre yojabokna i chorna chana inyana ndayá wabayina
Free from school, he left, and then with another, what was his name?

pero utatsa tsunditatxumbo   65
But I am sure they were two.

ibojá a la guerra ch juan oso y con el otro chbiama ndoñe tsutsa-bowinyna

---

[87]line 50: *ermanebeñe*, "Catholic Brother." Sibundoy schools have always been run by Catholic religious orders.

He went to war, that Juan Oso with the other fellow whose name I can't recall.

i otro tambien kantsubtay imojobema pero mayoralna juan osoka
And there were also seven others, but the oldest was Juan Oso,

mayorna mas mayorna ndayá podeskabé
the oldest, older, and so ugly!

i choka ch moikan kanya txamo soplomolina i kastellanamakanak[88]
And there they had some Spanish artillery.

**chiekna el otro i ch mayor i ch utata nyenga kansubta imojetsobu-
kañe**   70
Therefore the other fellow and that older one, those two, only those seven came out of there.

**choka imojtsanjanga mallajkta gente imojtsobatman skopeta-
xangak**
There they came against many people, they killed them with their rifles.

choka ch jenapelian ch con el juan oso
There they were fighting with that Juan Oso.

oh ch kastellanamakana yojtsangwebjoy
Oh, that artillery made them fly,

nyan nye twambebe plumashaka yojtsangwebubjoy la gente
just like the feathers of a hen the people were flying.

nye chan kansubta imojetsobukañamina   75
Only those seven came out of there.

**chorna nye grasia yojtsemna ch mallajkta imojtsemenungena gra-
sia yojtsemna**
Then they were just laughing, there were so many of the enemy, they were laughing.

kachká mujemungena imochjatsungana
Like that there were so many of them.

**pero chunga imojtsoganañe lempe chubta jente yojtsapochokaye
con soplomolina kastellanamakanak**
But they won, they completely finished those people off with the Spanish artillery.

---

[88]line 69: *soplomolina i kastellanamakanak*. The narrator was not certain exactly what kind of weapon this might have been; the word *soplomolina*, "windmill," suggests that it might have been some kind of automatic rifle, perhaps a large caliber machine gun.

7 Tales of the Spirit Realm

The Kamsá account of the evolution of civilization is founded upon a gradual taming of a protean spirituality unleashed at the dawning of time. The brute spiritual potency of the ancestral period is too volatile to nurture the steady cadence of social life in human societies. The potency that brought forth the precedents would instantly overwhelm them should it be left unchecked. But the pulsating spiritual power of the ancestral period cannot be entirely disarmed. Instead, it is pushed to the margins of human experience where it continues to exercise influence over the course of events. A realm of spiritual intrigue persists into the modern period, now removed from the center of human experience.

The mythic narratives gathered in this last section involve encounters with these marginalized spiritual forces. In ancestral times the first people would profit from such encounters, often coming away with knowledge that gained them stature in their communities. The protagonists in this set of myths are lucky to escape unscathed from their harrowing encounters with spirits. The bold woman heroine of "About the Water Birds" (m27) is pleased to find herself once again on a familiar path after her breathtaking excursion to the celestial realm. The lingering forces of the spirit realm are rarely friendly to human ambitions; most often they are downright hostile, as in the instance of the *antewelaj*, the principle of female malevolence who appears in m28 and m29.

John Bierhorst (1988, 206) speaks of a marginalization of female deities in the Central Andes, who occupy a more important role in the mythologies of other South American regions. Kamsá mythic narrative lends support to this thesis. Several female spirits make an appearance in the myths, but they are most often relegated to the status of witches, and typically they are destroyed by spiritually powerful males. The poor scabby girl (see m8) and the lively water-bird women of m27, who cavort in the lakes and then return to the celestial palace, stand out as a contrast to this trend in Kamsá myth. More common are the vicious figures in m11, m28, and m29, who muster spiritual influence in opposition to the goals of human society.

The ingenuity of the elders continues to preserve human communities from the onslaught of these ill-intentioned spiritual actors. In "About the Witch" (m28), a deadly vagina must be eradicated so that those traveling in the hills above the town of Sibundoy will no longer be attracted by its ethereal light. In "About the Earthen Witch" (m29) a remedy is sought for a witch who takes shape from loose earth and in that form preys upon children. It is the elders who devise solutions to these dilemmas, usually after partaking of the visionary medicines.

The final three entries in the section gravitate toward the morality tale; each focuses on a salient misbehavior and graphically explores its consequences. "The Tale of the Father-in-Law" (m30) finds poetic justice in the world as gluttony is punished by deprivation of food. "About the Thief" (m31) tackles the problem of avarice in connection with goods stored by a fierce gang of cannibalistic thieves. In these mythic narratives the tactic of moderation is advocated because excessive greed inevitably leads to calamity. Notably, in the final two mythic narratives, the pursuit of wealth becomes a major concern in its own right, a theme that is largely absent from the rest of the corpus.

The historical reality of the native people of the Sibundoy Valley enters the scene in "The Gold Mine" (m32), which can be read as a parable of the relationship between Indians and non-Indians in this region. A thesis emerges, with these tenets: that outsiders covet any good thing an Indian has, that some confused members of the indigenous communities can be duped by unscrupulous outsiders, but at last that Indians have access to spiritual resources that might allow them to persevere and eventually triumph over their aggressors.

Tales of the Spirit Realm invoke the eerie presence of alien forces and the need for constant vigilance if the project of human civilization is to succeed. They conduct us from the ancestral period, in which the Sibundoy Valley appears as an undisturbed laboratory of cosmic process, to the heart of the modern period with its awareness of the broader political context of the Sibundoy indigenous peoples.

(m27) ngwebubebiana
About the Water Birds

As performed by Estanislao Chicunque in Kamsá, May 1979

The narrative portion of "About the Water Birds" opens and closes in the mundane reality of the Sibundoy peasant family, hard-pressed to find adequate food supplies during the "hunger months" just prior to the initiation of the corn harvest in the valley. But within this framing scenario the story takes us on an imaginative journey into another, quite different, domestic scene, the celestial home of the bird-people spirits. In fact, as the depiction of this cottage and its inhabitants unfolds, it seems possible that we have been transported to the home of Wangetsmuna, or to that of his grandfather, the thunder deity, though the narrator never confirms this possibility.

In any case, "About the Water Birds" provides a striking portrait of the spirit world, with its playful water birds, a long snake that serves as a bench, a powerful liquid that is consumed from small cups, and the familiar birds of the valley who go about sweeping and preparing chicha. The adventurous heroine gamely enters this curious environment but in the end lacks the spiritual force to profit from her experience; instead, she finds herself abandoned in the high mountains and only through the offices of an enterprising hawk manages to find her way back to the valley.

The story is launched as a poor woman "from here" undertakes the trek to Aponte, a full day's walk through the mountains, to ask for corn from the people in that place. Aponte is a town of Inga-speaking Indians across the border into the state of Nariño, apparently settled in a previous century by members of Sibundoy families. In Kamsá it is called *tambillo*, "little settlement," a word that likely derives from the Quechua *tambo*, meaning *rancho* in Spanish; a rancho is an isolated, primitive settlement, and this name recalls perhaps the initial status of Aponte as an offshoot of the Sibundoy stock. To this day residents of the Sibundoy Valley look to Aponte, with its staggered growing season, for a supply of corn in the months and weeks before the corn harvest begins in the valley. It is a familiar pattern in the Andes to exploit variations in the micro-ecology of the region.

The woman is surprised to hear the sound of laughter high in the mountains. She approaches and finds young women bathing in a mountain lake. Her curiosity gets the better of her:

chokna biena yojtsenyayaka nye yojtsexnajem
From there she had a good view, she just stared at them.

a vera ntxamo biyanga bemna
"What creatures are these, what language do they speak?"

They speak to her in a language that she can understand, in the casual variety of Kamsá, suggesting familiarity; in these tones they invite her to accompany them to their home. One word of caution is offered: "Be careful not to sit down."

The next episode takes place in the high-mountain home of the water birds. Numerous transformations mark this house as a spiritual headquarters: the long pole that turns into a snake; the greenish liquid that provides spiritual vision (a *yagé* prototype); the birds of the valley going about their domestic chores, sweeping and preparing chicha much as Sibundoy women routinely do. We are told that "in the old days there was a power in those small cups." The water birds disappear after their experience with the liquid. When the protagonist tries a sip, she completely loses her senses. She "comes to" in a lonely perch surrounded by cliffs, with none of the familiar bird friends in sight.

Our resourceful heroine catches a fish in a small stream that passes by these cliffs, and as she eats it a large hawk arrives. He offers her a ride to the valley in return for the fine hen that she and her husband are keeping. On the back of the hawk, the woman disobeys orders and opens her eyes. She fights off the dizziness this brings about and manages to hold on until the hawk deposits her where she had left her basket. A significant lapse of time is suggested by the fact that the corn she had obtained in Aponte is now entirely rotten. The story concludes as she is reunited with her husband. She tells him what happened, and they take note of the missing hen: the hawk has already settled the bargain.

Tales of a human being who journeys to the sky world are common throughout Amerindian mythology, and this mythic narrative appears to be a Sibundoy adaptation of this familiar mythical prototype. The episode at the top of the cliff (starting with line 59) is reminiscent of the bird-nester complex, in which a culture hero is abandoned on a cliff or at the top of a tree and eventually rescued by a large bird. The beginning point of Lévi-Strauss' *mythologiques* (his M1, a Bororo myth) contains this element: the hero is abandoned on a cliff, he kills lizards; vultures come along and fly him to the ground (Lévi-Strauss 1969, 35-37).

"About the Water Birds" is internally coherent, but it contains a number of tantalizing details that are left unexplained. The long pole or bench that turns out to be a snake is reminiscent of the *amaru*, a spiritual patron of Kamsá native doctors, often associated with lightning and the thunder deity and recognized on earth as the anaconda. The hierarchy of birds presented in this mythic narrative—the free water birds, the birds of the valley who tend to domestic chores—reminds us of the prominence of birds in Kamsá cosmology, and of Wangetsmuna, the culture hero whose name contains the Kamsá root for "beak." This evidence, admittedly incomplete, raises the possibility that the water birds have led our protagonist to a kind of Kamsá spiritual headquarters in the sky, the abode of the thunder deity, his grandson Wangetsmuna, and their many bird companions.

diosbe lwarna bida jiisebomenana pobre jiisemenana[1]
In God's world we are born to live in humble circumstances,

trabajosa kwanetsemna
surely life is not easy.

mwentxajema yojá tambelloye bida jongwamgwama
A poor woman from here went to Aponte in search of food,

[1]lines 1,2: The narrator opens with a lament employing the formulaic vocabulary of Kamsá ritual language, which portrays human destiny as a tenuous affair made possible only through God's kindness. The double vowel, /ii/, is an expressive device associated with ritual language speeches.

matsetemama jobwamiñama tambelloye²
to buy a little corn in Aponte.

i chokna yojonyena granotemna   5
And there she found a few grains of corn,

**chjemna karidado imojabema apartena partena ana imojakarida-
    dojema kachká**
some of it they gave to her out of kindness, some of it she bought,
    like that.

ya yojtsataboyajema chokana tambillokana
And so she was returning from there, from Aponte.

inataboyajema tja tsuntsokna yojowenayajema
As she came walking through the mountains, she heard them,

imnenatajtsebiajwayeka
they were laughing among themselves.

yojiiswenana orna chjemna yojatuwena mase tsmanoika   10
When she was hearing them, she heard them a little ways below,

nyetxá kwatenabiajwa
how they laughed.

chorna chjemna yojoftsaitume wasmanatema
Then that poor woman hid her load,

xbwachanatema yojaftsatajtseitume
she hid her load of corn.

chorna yojoftsá jaftsentjexiyama
Then she went to look around.

ndayentxe chká imenebiajwaka   15
Where were they laughing like that?

chora bejayoka waubjajonaye inetsomiñe
Then in a river, in a pond, there they were,

choka ch tobiaxunga yojanyena betsshubkjañika
There she found those young women, just splashing about in
    the water.

chokna biena yojtsenyayaka nye yojtsexnajem
From there she had a good view, she just stared at them.

²line 4: *matsetemama jobwaminama tambelloye*, "to buy a little corn in Aponte." Due
to changing conditions of soil and climate at different elevations, the corn harvest
arrives at different times in the environs of the Sibundoy Valley. This narrative
makes reference to a form of economic interdependence linking communities into a
regional network of food distribution. Aponte, a day's walk from the Sibundoy Valley, might be the source of a corn supply during the "hunger months" in the Sibundoy Valley.

a vera ntxamo biyanga bemna³
"What creatures are these, what language do they speak?"

i kwatenabiajwaka   20
And they certainly were laughing among themselves!

chorna imojatsaye ndomoykaka⁴
Then they spoke to her: "Where are you going?"

kach atxebioye tsutá
"I am just going to my home."

chorna chngana serta yojowenajemana
Then she really heard them speak to her.

yojetsastjonajema mwentxa xmochjatianaka
She remained still: "Now what will they say to me?"

tempo ch tobiaxungana ngwebubungaka⁵   25
Right away those young women were water birds.

chngana biyanga biyajemunga imenetsomiñeka
They could talk, they were able to speak.

imojoftsobebiya i imojoftsekonvida
They bathed themselves and they invited her:

morna atxebe oyenoye kwayika
"Now you will surely come to our home."

iye chjemna yojowena yojauseto⁶
And she listened, she followed them.

i chabukna jashjango bekonanokna imojabwayena   30
And as they approached closer to the house, they told her:

ojala chakotsotebiamnaka
"Be careful not to sit down."

i chora chjemna serto ch tsoye imojaumashingo
And then truly they bid her enter the house.

chokna ch tobiaxunga imojatotebiama
There those young women sat down.

---

³line 19: *ntxamo biyanga bemna*, "what language do they speak?" The speech
identity of mythological figures is of primary importance in Kamsá mythic narrative.
    ⁴line 21: *ndomoykaka*, "where are you going?" Note that the water-bird women
address the protagonist in a familiar mode, as if they were members of her family or
close friends.
    ⁵line 25: *ngwebubungaka*, "water birds." According to don Justo, "these are small,
silver birds, who come down to the valley for a month or so, where they fly around
at night stirring up the air."
    ⁶line 29: *yojowena*, "she listened." This verb is used to indicate that the recipient
of speech has been persuaded by the act of speech.

imojontxá jalkansan bejayetema
They began to partake of a liquid,

imojontxá jobxiyana kopatemiñe   35
they began to drink from a cup.

anteona inetsomandañe ana bashetemiñeka⁷
In the old days there was a power in those small cups.

yojtsunyaye ana niñuxka inetstebeñika ch posadentxna
She noticed a long pole stretching all the way across the floor.

i bien kontjexe orna chana ndoñe banguxa yendowamena⁸
And when she looked closely, it turned out not to be a bench,

bayujema inamna inawabaina mtxkwayika
a beast it was, the one called "snake."

**chana jwatseboka chana jutsatsanungana ch tobiaxungena uftsote-
   bemañika**   40
They were standing on top of it, those young women, it seemed
   they were seated on it.

i tojalkansaye i fshantsoye jutsentjachkayana
And they drank and they all fell backward to the floor.

i achká lempia yojanye iya chngena lempia fshantsoye
And just like that she saw them, and they all fell to the floor.

chorna ch jajashloftxe ch pikanke chngena tsjajwayungaka⁹
Later that sparrow and that *pikanke*, they went about sweeping.

iye chjemna chká imojwaprobá batatemana
And so they let her try a little of the drink.

i chjema ibojtsatmena i yentxama jutsemanana¹⁰   45
And she completely lost her senses, she didn't know what to do.

---

⁷line 36: *anteona inetsomundañe ana bashctemiñeka,* "in the old days there was a power in those small cups." The verb is a Spanish borrowing, from *mandar,* "to order," and it retains a kind of biblical, or fateful, quality in this expression. The notion is that the deity put a special power into this liquid, which appears to be a mythical prototype of *yagé,* the visionary medicine.

⁸line 38: *banguxa,* "bench." Many Kamsá houses are equipped with long plank benches where visitors are received with "a drop" of chicha.

⁹line 43: *jajashloftxe,* "sparrow." According to don Justo, "a small bird that announces the dawn; it bothers corn plants when they are branching." *pikanke,* "pikanke." According to don Justo, "a rather small bird, dark brown with long legs; it lives above the valley though it is occasionally seen there. Its song is pi-kun kc." It seems likely that this bird has provided the family name for one of the main Kamsá lineages, the Chicunques.

¹⁰line 45: *i chjema ibojtsatmena,* "and she completely lost her senses." The verb root here *-tmena-,* translates literally as "to be drunk," but carries a more positive, spiritual sense, a kind of "blessed intoxication."

kwatobxena orna tsañena tsañe konporma
When she awoke in the room, the room was just the same.

pero ibsana chjemena lempia yojtsenyaye
But the next day she saw the same thing,

lempe imotsetsujajo lempe ch baserushe lempe bnoka imojautxena
they swept it very clean and threw all that trash far away.

iye ntxamo jutsemanana ch wabonshna tobiaxungena imojtsatoñe
And what could that poor woman do? The young women had gone.

ch pikankena ibonawabwatema jajashloftxena
    ibonetsabwatemiñe   50
That *pikanke* knew her, the sparrow also knew her.

iye ch kakjanana chiwako chana ibonetsabwatemiñe[11]
And the one who makes chicha, the *chiwako*, she also knew her.

chngena lempe kamokunga imenetsomiñe
Those are native to the valley.

iye ch tobiaxungena ndokenunga ndomoye kwatoñana
And there was nothing of those young women. Where did they go?

ndoñe yenjutsotatxumbo ntxamo jutsemanana
She had no idea what she should do.

chentxana chngena imojtsatskedañe ch ngwebebungena
    imojokedá   55
They stayed away from there, those water birds stayed away.

i ratotemasa chngena ndokenunga
And after some time there was no sign of them.

i ch jajashloftxena ndokná ni ch chiwakona ndokná
And no sign of the sparrow, no sign of the *chiwako*,

lempia ndokenunga
not a sign of any of them.

tjaka betiye techitxaka ndeolpena jwisio kwatskaka
In the mountains, at the foot of a tree, suddenly she came to.

iye ntxamo jutsemanana ndomoy jutama ndoñe
    yenjutsotatxumbo   60
And she didn't know what she should do, where she should go.

yojtsonamana ndmwajana juteshacham ndmwajana jutama ndoñe
    yenjutsotatxumbo
She wondered which way she should go, which way to go, she
    wasn't sure.

---

[11]line 51: *chiwako*, "chiwako." According to don Justo, "a rather large black bird
with yellow feet and beak; by dawn he is singing. He also calls just before it rains."

chorna yojatserepará moknoya atxe kabuntjeshache[12]
Then she was looking around: "Which way should I go?"

yojontjexiyeka moina peñuxe mwanyoika peñuxe
She peered about: here, cliffs, over there, cliffs,

inyoikna peñuxe ibetsomiñeka
there were cliffs on all sides.

i bejayetema chentxa inobujna chentxe beonatema
    ibojoshbwañe   65
And a small creek flowed by there, there she caught a little fish,

ndetxebebioka ibojobwajo ibojanktatema
she placed it on a rock, it dried.

inasayajema orna ndeolpna ibojatsbwache ana ngavilana[13]
As she was eating it, suddenly a hawk arrived,

ch btsa ngavilan ch bwitreka kwawabaina
that large hawk, the buzzard hawk surely it is called.

chana biya ndoñe morna ndoñe sino biyay inamna[14]
He was able to speak, not now, no, but in those times they
    could speak.

kekmojtsengemena akabe lwaramaka ibojawiyanaka   70
"Aren't you lonely for your home?" he said to her.

aiñeka xunjtsengemenaka
"Yes, I am lonely for my home."

pero asna kondabobonshana kanye twambajema kondawamena
"But then, you have a fine thing, one hen you have.

cha jutatxetayan asna kbuntjiisebetxe kbuntjatseboshjonaka
If you would give me that, I could take you, I could leave you at
    your home.

i mo ndoñe chká knanesna asna ndayama chká mwentxna
    kwatapadesenajema
And if you don't like it this way, then you will have to remain
    stuck here."

chorna yojtsangwamiya nya chká pabor jutsebemanasna   75
Then she said to him: "If you will just do me this favor,

[12]line 62: *moknoya atxe kabuntjeshache*, "now where should I go?" The narrator delivers this bit of self-address in a stage whisper, simulating the protagonist's likely state of mind at this juncture in the adventure.
[13]line 67: *ndeolpna ibojatsbwache ana ngavilana*, "suddenly a hawk arrived." Delivered in a dramatic stage whisper, with a slower pace of speech.
[14]line 69: *chana biya*, "he was able to speak" (literally "he was a speaker"). Note the narrator's absorption in the curious fact of a speaking animal, a definitive feature of ancestral times.

kbatjatatxetayajema stutsayimjanaka
I will give it to you, I will leave it with you."

bweno trato ibojenabemajemata txabá ibojwawenana ch krischiana
Well. They struck a bargain, he understood that human fine.

entre krischianajemata o ngavilana ch bwitre chana biyá inamna
As among human beings, the hawk, that buzzard hawk, he was
    able to speak.

iye ch tobiaxna biyá lempia inabiya
And that young woman, she could speak fine,

ndoñe ndokna iyetemená lempe ena biyajemunga
    imenetsomiñe   80
she had no speech defect, they were both able speakers.

chká yojopodia jenakwentana
Thus they were able to converse.

iye ntxamo chjema ntxamo jutsemanana
And what else, that poor one, what else could she do?

nye jutayinjanana nemoria yojobokakaye
She could only give it to him, she thought to herself.

asna mntxaka asna pero atxebe tantxaka kochotsubtxiye
"Now like this, now, just grab ahold of my shoulders,

katoika botamán pero ojala ndmokna chakotsantjetxana   85
a good grip on each, and be careful not to be looking down,

koisobshetayajemaka
just close your eyes."

pero bngabe nemoria bngabe jwabna ketsomñikana ndokenentxe
But our memory, our judgment being what it is, she didn't obey.

chjemna chká ibojatsebana iye lomo jwatseboka
Thus he lifted her to rise over the hills.

ibojtsanbaye orna chjemna kwaisuntjexe[15]
As he lifted her, she dared to open her eyes.

la warda peñuntxe mallajkta tabwayema ibeisobinyniye   90
God forbid, she was seeing great cliffs, deep chasms.

betsko serta jutsebiatamenka ibojebionana
Right away she really started feeling dizzy.

ndoka remidio yojtotobshetayika
Without remedy she quickly closed her eyes again.

iye ch pobre wabonshna ndayentxe sebarotema yojaftsaitume
And that poor person, where she had hid her basket,

[15]lines 89, 90: Delivered in a high-pitched, sing-song voice.

i choka ibojaisatsaye yojoyijwajema
there he left her standing, she became very happy.

morka mwentxana kochtobenayajema bndatabe pwesto jatse-
    boknanaka 95
"Now from here you should be able to find your way to your
home.

pero trata tbonjenebema chká koisemna
But a deal we have made, and just so it must be,

ako nye chkasa koisemna
remember, just so it must be."

i chora ch pamillena moikana yentxajemana[16]
And then that native of the valley, that poor person,

sebarotemama yojaftsatajtsamengo kboisakiñeka
she went to look for her basket: "I will take it with me."

chora chtemana tonday lempe inetsajangwaka del todo
    perdido 100
Then that day she found it all rotten, everything was ruined.

ko nye yenajema yojtá kompañerna ibojatsebwach
She just emptied it there and went on her way.

kompañerna ibojatsebwach mntxá tsepasa
She returned to her husband: "This is what happened to me.

mntxá sentido joperdian mntxase tentación
Like this I lost my senses, like this I was tempted.

ndayá serta ndayá bemenana ch ajentajoka
What, really, what are they in that mountain?

chká xuntsoborlá ana mntxá palabra 105
Like that they confused me, just as I said.

a vera ndayá chká bemenana
Just what might they be?

a vera ndamwana bememana serto krischiana ndayá bemena
Who are they? Are they human beings or what are they?

ndoñe chkañe kwandemunaka
No, they couldn't be human beings.

trato tebjenebema kema pamillaftaka
I made a deal with that fellow.

ntxamo jutsopasanaka yojanotisia 110
Did he stop by to inform you of it?"

[16]line 98: *pamillena moikana*, "native of the valley" (literally "family person from
here"). This is one of several labels used to identify members of the Kamsá community, which is conceived of as a large family in ritual language speeches.

ako mo ntxamsa kopasajemasna bndatabe bonshana twambena
"So that's what happened to our fine hen."

impas ngavilana tbundabisokuñika ibojtsobwetxe
The hawk had already come by to collect, it was gone.

chiye shemjenena chana boyana ya yojenojwaboye
That poor woman and her husband understood,

chká trato tkojabema tempo kwatukjabisokuñika
like that the deal was made, he surely had already come by to
    collect.

ndoka remidio mwentxana ntxamo masesna   115
"Without remedy, here what else could we expect?

nye chká trato betsokedañe nye nyetxasa kwatenokedá
Just like that was the deal, and just so it must be between us.

ntxamo mase remedio chaisebemas
We could expect nothing else."

ndoka remidio nye nyetxasa atxajema respeto tijatenoperdey[17]
So be it just so much with all due respect I have told you,

nyetxase tstatxumbo
that's all I know of it.

nye nyetxá sindutatxumbo   120
Just like that as I know it.

(m28) welajbiana
About the Witch

As performed by Mariano Chicunque in Kamsá, December 1978

This mythic narrative describes the removal of an evil spot, a spot
charged with spiritual power and believed capable of inflicting spirit
sickness, through the application of holy water blessed by the Catholic
priests. It has affinities, then, with myths portraying the triumph of
Christianity (or some other world religion) over a localized religious
substrate. Such myths often describe the replacement of indigenous
spiritual shrines with imported ones; in this formulation, an indigenous
forest spirit is vanquished by resources drawn from the Catholic church.
But it is significant that the two heroes also arm themselves with traditional Kamsá remedies: the bear medicine, a greenish liquid (very likely
a vision-producing substance akin to the modern *yagé*), and portions of
a medicinal tree. The holy water removes the evil spot, but a larger spir-

---

[17]line 118: *atxajema respeto tijatenoperdey.* This closing contains elements of Kamsá
ritual language: the empathy marker *-jema,* "my poor self," and the formula, "without losing respect."

itual armature is implied. The holy water is named both in Kamsá and in Spanish, marking the confluence of cultures in this myth.

Evil spots are capable of producing *binyea*, "evil wind" or "spirit sickness." Their evil aura can infect people, ruining their luck and leaving them susceptible to sickness, misfortune, even death. The mythical geography of the Sibundoy Valley is sprinkled with these evil spots, some of them associated with topographical features, others at political boundary points, still others implicated as sites of mortal happenings. This mythic narrative identifies the source of evil at this particular fold in the mountains west of the Sibundoy Valley as a light emanating from a sprawled witch, the dreaded *welaj* or "old hag of the mountains." Her evil aura appears in the distance as a bright light, something like the glare from a kerosene lamp. From a closer distance the light is finer and more beautiful, like the glow of a candle. It turns out that the light emerges from her vagina, projected outward as she lies on the earth with her legs spread wide open.

The *welaj*, or *antewelaj*, the old hag of the mountains, is a prominent figure in Kamsá mythic narrative, a vestigial force of destruction that lingers on in the mountains and forests surrounding the Sibundoy Valley. She appears in many different varieties but always in the form of a weird and destructive female. The present mythic narrative reduces her to a luminous vagina; in m29 she is the suckling witch, luring young children to their death. "The Tale of the Two Little Children" (m11) features a more humanoid witch figure who (like the witch in "Hansel and Gretel") fattens children so that she may eat them. Each of these witches is viewed as a particular expression of a multifarious supernatural entity, a pernicious female spiritual presence, part of the spiritual substrate that must be swept to the margins if civilization is to prosper.

We find that this witch has been "bringing people down," giving them spirit sickness, killing them with her evil wind. A traditional Kamsá corrective is initiated. To begin with, two younger men show courage in tracking down the source of the problem. Once they have reported their findings the elders speak among themselves (line 29) and devise a strategy for combating this threat to the collectivity. We know from other myths and from attested practice that the elders generally imbibed the visionary medicines to conduct these spiritual diagnoses. In this instance they elect to call on the priest with his holy water, actually sending to far-off Popayan for a *padre* who is ferried on the shoulders of Indians across the rugged Andes to the Sibundoy Valley.

As is usual in this corpus of myth, the measures devised by the elders prove effective; once the holy water has been poured on the source of the weird light, the menace is removed and travelers are no longer threatened as they pass by this spot. We have in this mythic narrative a model for the integration of Christian elements into the indigenous belief system. The holy water, blessed by the priest, eradicates this evil spot, but the entire procedure is designed and implemented through traditional channels. In a similar fashion, the Kamsá Indians have incorporated Catholicism as a powerful resource within a broadly animistic spiritual system.

ana mwana kach welabiana
So here is the one about the old hag.

pero kamwentxa tjañika bu̱tsa tjatxe kanjanemuna a vera kem tabanoka
But hereabouts in the mountains, high in the mountains, it was, near the town of Sibundoy.

ndayá chana chjatsparla ultimoka
What was she? I will tell you about it at last.

i ya btse tjatxe inamna
And so there was a high cliff,

imnawabánasna benache inetsemna   5
they passed by it, there was a trail.

asna lwarokna jitsebinynana
Then in the distance it could be seen,

konporma mora ch kerosina ch lamparoshá intsajajoñika
like one of these kerosine lamps nowadays it was shining.

jiitsebinynana btseñe chká inawabana
They would always see it like that as they passed by.

bweno
Fine.

ana kachká ndoñena choikana tojobonjo ntxamona   10
So if it happened to move from there, then what?

nya inobainaisa ana inobanaiye
It could be deadly, it might kill.

i asna utatna brillata ibnamena
And then there were two hardy souls,

more chká ch osunga tempo chká ndaytema binyeama imojiso-kiñe[18]
now like that they took with them some bear medicine and something to protect them from spirit sickness.

ibojá ibojeniana a vera a vera jaftsereparama
They went, they said: "Let's go have a look around,

---

[18]line 13: *osunga*, "bear medicine." It isn't clear what this might be, but Kamsá curers use grease from various animals, and also body parts such as feathers, claws, etc. *binyea*, "spirit sickness." Once again we encounter this preoccupation with spiritual power and danger.

a vera ntxamo nya taibochjobanaka   15
I wonder if we will die."

nyetstxá ngubshnushe yojtsasmana[19]
They took with them some of that green medicine,

i chana ch bayungesheka ibojataka
and they cut down that bayunge tree.

aray asa chokna ndayá bejtsebinynana
Damn! So what made it shine like that?

ase mas choye ibojá orna chora ch kerosinka binynoyuna
Then as they went further on, then it shone like a kerosene lamp.

yojarepara orna ana nye iñe fwerte botamana ftseyiñe botamana
   iñeka yojtsinynaka   20
When he looked around, a strong, beautiful fire, a fire beautiful like
   that of a candle, appeared.

bweno
Fine.

ana nya jobanana taibochatobana a vera bochjá
"So as for dying, this isn't going to kill us, let's go."

ibojataka asa ndoñeka iñe yendomanasna
They went, but it wasn't a fire after all.

ch bayujbe owatjaka tkanana[20]
A woman's vagina, her legs spread open,

mntxá tkanana betsobinyne uwatja   25
thus with her legs spread open, the vagina was shining.

chká aiñeka ininynaka uwatjaka
Like that, yes, they found a vagina,

chkaye chká ibojaftsinyeka
like that they found it there.

iye chama yojobwambaye tijinye chká
And they came to report: "This is what I saw."

ch tangwangebeñe imojenekwentaye
The elders spoke among themselves.

ch tangwa ch welá Jarebaja chká yentxanga   30
That elder: "That hag has been bringing people down."

---

[19]line 16: *ngubshnushe*, "green medicine." Possibly the ancestral *yagé*, the traditional medicine that induces spiritual vision.
[20]lines 24-27: Spoken in a subdued tone of voice for dramatic effect.

obana yoja inamna
She had been killing them.

ndoka remidio tempona ana bachnana
So be it right away for a priest,

bastokna tondaye bachne yendemuna[21]
in Pasto there was no priest,

ana popayana inawachwana
but in Popayan they knew there was one.

hasta choye semanana imojaka iye bastoka ndayentxe[22]   35
From there they carried him on their shoulders to Pasto.

ana asta mora chká mundenakwenta ch agua benditaka
Even now they speak like that of that holy water,

ch wabwinyetxiye bnga jayanama
that *wabwinyetxiye* as we call it.

i chyitema botamana yojtsabaye yojtsabaye
And he blessed that beautiful drop of water, he blessed it.

**iye chiye imojtsabwiyebo i chiye chabe tkanentxe imojetsab-
wakushe**
And they brought the water, and they poured it between her legs.

basta impasa ana impasa ndoknajuka   40
That did the trick, forever, just forever she was gone,

ni welá jtutsjajonan nye tonday nye impasa nye binyea
there was no old hag stretched out there, forever no evil wind.

ana nye impasa katunjana kabá
So forever it was finished, entirely.

pero chká ch trabajwentxe
But like that they took care of it,

bastante yentxanga tojoftsapochoka yojoftsobaye chojaka
enough people had perished, she left them dead there.

achká ch anteona yojanamuna mwentxa tjañe mwentxa tjañesa 45
That's how that old one was, here in the hills, here in the hills.

ajá chana kache welajbiana
Aha, that's the one about the old hag.

[21]lines 33-34: Pasto, capital of the adjacent state of Nariño, is the nearest city of any consequence, but Popayan, far to the north of Pasto, was a major administrative center of colonial and ecclesiastic authority. This detail places this story into the early colonial period, when Pasto was still too remote from centers of Hispanic settlement to have its own priest.

[22]line 35: It was indeed the custom in the Andes for Indian bearers to carry European "dignitaries" across the rugged terrain (see Taussig 1987).

(m29) tondor welajbiana
About the Earthen Witch

As performed by Mariano Chicunque in Kamsá, December 1978

Kamsá mythic narrative has quite a variety of witch or old hag figures that pose a serious threat to human well-being. The earth witch is a shadowy figure who takes human form from the clay or mud of the earth, and in this form entices very young children to suckle at her breasts, only to destroy them. The story is set in an earlier historical period when people lived far apart from one another and there was presumably less supervision of the children. The witch would arrive urging the children to come and suckle, *moftsotondó, moftsotondó* (line 4), and here the narrator imitates the deadened (and deadly) monotones of her voice.

As in many of these myths, it is an elder, a *tangwa tatxumbwá* (line 10), an elderly native doctor, who tackles the problem and finds a solution. In much the same manner as the modern native doctors of the valley, he ingests *borracheru*, a vision-producing remedy prepared from the bark of the Datura tree (G. Brugmansia), and he becomes "very drunk," that is, he enters a visionary state. In this condition, the native doctor sees the witch arising from mud and settles on a cure as well. By touching a heated shard of pottery to her teat, he is able to return her to mud, so that she can never again bother the children. The remedy seems appropriate enough, since the witch arises from loose mud, but without human intervention. The heated shard also originates in loose earth, but takes shape through the exercise of human design. The remedy, then, can be seen as an assertion of human control over this natural element, and by extension, over the spiritually charged natural environment.

kach welajbiana
About that old hag.

ana ch basenga imenamna yebunatementxa imenamna
So there were those children, they were in these little houses.

i ar tempna ndoñesa bañe utañe ungañe bnoka imenoyena
And in those days there weren't many, two or three, they lived far apart.

i chorna chká jtsashjajwanana motsoftondó motsoftondó[23]
And then like that she would arrive: "Come and nurse, come and nurse."

chuchu jtsawambwambayana jawambwambayana   5
She would offer them her teats, she would offer them.

---

[23]line 4: *motsoftondó motsoftondó*, "come and nurse, come and nurse." Spoken in an eery, repetitive monotone.

i ch tontajemungna jochochanaka
And those poor little fools would suckle,

i tojochocho i obaná i bwetatemungena
and they suckled and they died, many of them.

ftsoshanyañe tuwatabo ch btsá
She was of the earth, that person.

orna lempe obanjemunga jtsatokjañunganaka
Then they were all laid out in death.

bweno chorna tangwa tatxumbwa inamna   10
Well, then there was an old native doctor.

choye cha yojayana a vera a vera bwenosna ar
There he spoke to them: "Let's see, let's see, fine."

nya chká ndayuja yomna
That's just how he was.

a ver atxa chajobxiye ch boracheraka²⁴
"Let's see, I will drink that *borrachera*."

borachera serto yojobxiyeka
Truly he drank that *borrachera*.

iye chiñe ibojatemena   15
And he became very drunk.

ora serta ko̲ ngweche chká ngwechoikana
Then truly from this mud, like that from mud,

chja chká jobemana ngwechi chká konforma yentxajka
like that she came from the mud, like that just like a person,

welaja jobemana i cha̲ obuntxe chká jobemana
she became a witch, and very weird, like that she became.

bweno kach ibojauyana
Well, he said to them:

bwenoka a ver ch basenga metsaishanyaye i atxe tijinye   20
"Fine, let's see, leave those children behind and I will keep an eye
    on them,

a vera atxe cha ch tachnungwaka
let's see if I don't get even with her."

---

²⁴line 13: *boracheraka*, "vision-producing medicine." Known by the Spanish
word, *borrachera*, implying something that can cause intoxication, this medicine is
derived from the Brugmansia plant (Datura) and used by the native doctors to obtain
access to the spirit realm. It is particularly valuable in combatting serious cases
of sorcery.

aray de la warda imojtsoñika yojabo yibetata[25]
Damn! Heaven forbid, they left, dusk arrived,

ch orasiona ko ch sinko ora[26]
that prayer for around five in the evening.

ko serta yojashjangoka btse btse welayema yojashjangoka
Then truly she arrived, a large large witch, arrived there:

tsoftondó tsoftondó tsoftondó chká yojtsamojaka   25
"Come nurse, come nurse, come nurse," like that she did.

chora ch btsá eso sí btse jwako yojtseboxinyemena
Then that person, yes indeed, he had hidden there a large earthen
    shard,

ch iñoye yojtseboxinyemena
in that fire he had it hidden.

iye ch oftondayubja
And that suckling witch.

chore ch btseka yojwantxabujatse ndayusheka yojwantxabujatse
Then that person picked it up with something, he picked it up.

iye chentxe ibojetsa jatsuntxiye ch aftonday ch weláj   30
And there he went to place it against that witch's teat.

**basta ch ena ngweche ena ngwechetxa bejtsatsatsutabontsana
    komna**
That did it, she collapsed into pure mud, pure mud she was.

i impaseka ana cha ch jwako jwinyinyeka katunjanabwowinyana
And forever thus with that burning shard he defended them,

chuja katamunjanitana chuja tondo welá ajá
she came to an end, that suckling witch, aha.

(m30) wamben taitabe parlo
The Tale of the Father-in-Law

*As retold by Justo Jacanamijoy in Kamsá, from an original Kamsá performance by Fran-
cisco Narváez, December 1978*

Francisco Narváez performed this mythic narrative, among others,
as the other members of his *cuadrilla* or work crew gathered around.
My small Sony tape recorder, which had served me so well, misfired (or
was it human error?), leaving me without an audio record of this

---

[25]line 22: The narrator animates this juncture in the story by uttering this line in
a high-pitched voice.

[26]line 23: *orasiona*, "prayer." This line shows how pervasive was the influence of
the missionaries, who structured the Indians' day around hours for specific kinds
of prayers.

performance. When we returned to vereda San Felix and I made this discovery, my host don Justo informed me that he remembered the story very well and would be pleased to provide a replacement performance. The text presented below is thus mediated through an additional procedure, a retelling by a native consultant who was present at the original performance. In any case, as Justo explained, the narrative is well-known in Kamsá communities. I cannot say how closely Justo follows the original narrator in this retelling, but I do know that we are left with a mythic narrative text of considerable interest in its own right.

This mythic narrative involves the transportation of a motif associated with Our Lord in other myths into a domestic morality tale. This detachment of mythic narrative material from its original source illustrates another facet of the diversity inherent in mythologies and perhaps represents a step in the evolution of myth into folktale. This myth, to a greater extent than any other in this collection, takes the form of a morality tale. It cautions against greed, confirms the importance of respecting the elders, and asserts that poetic justice is the way of the world. Gluttony, specifically the unwillingness to share food, is punished by a most fitting curse, the eternal presence of a second mouth insisting on its portion.

Professor Warren Roberts has suggested to me that this tale has the feel of a medieval exemplum, a morality tale at the service of popular sermonizers. I have not found any exact equivalent for it in the standard indices, though some fairly close parallels exist in Latin America and elsewhere. Américo Paredes (1970) includes a version of Type 779 C*, "The Hard-Hearted Son," wherein a son who refused to share corn with his parents is punished: "a serpent came out and wound itself about his neck and strangled him" (Tale #40, p. 125). Paredes (1970, 219) observes that "tales of this sort are much more popular in Mexican oral tradition than published reports indicate."

Kamsá ceremonial life dramatizes the ideal of sharing, as large portions of food and chicha are systematically partitioned and ritually distributed from one person to another until even the smallest child has been included. These rituals always enfranchise the elderly first; the goods gradually work their way down through a social hierarchy determined largely by age, gender, influence, and wealth. If these ceremonies display the official values of the community, then the behavior of the young man in this mythic narrative can be seen as highly deviant. Not only does he refuse to share, but he denies an elder who is moreover his father-in-law. At weddings young couples are sternly advised to be generous with the parents of their spouses. These ceremonial statements argue that the integrity of the community depends on the exercise of generosity within the established social channels.

Naturally, the very existence of such arguments indicates the presence of an underlying social problem, and in this light the punishment visited on the self-serving young man is exemplary, carrying a clear warning to one and all that elders must be respected and food must be shared. All of this is reminiscent of Christian morality, and the episode revolving around the snake's refusal to enter the church provides further evidence of a European connection.

wamben taitá yojabwacham bebinkbioy
The father-in-law went to visit his son-in-law.

chentxe twambian inawabwanay
There they were cooking a hen.

ch bembe tsoy imojobjase pero ndoñe imojojwatxe
That daughter invited him inside the house but gave him nothing to eat.

sino que boyá ibojamandá metsakashá itsabjoka
Instead that husband ordered her: "Take the pot into the kitchen,

metsabwajo kejtetoñe ora mochjwalmorsar   5
keep it there until he leaves, then we will have lunch."

ch wamben taitá chká inatebeman i ndoñe jwajwatxiana
That father-in-law sat down like that and they brought him nothing to eat.

i ch bembe yojtsechan i ch boyá ndoñe
And that daughter wanted to but the husband didn't.

i rato chká inabtsetebemana ch wamben taitajema
And for quite a while that poor father-in-law was sitting there.

después ya yojtsatoñe
Finally he left.

chorkokayé ibojamandá morkokayé betsko xmawatxeka   10
Then sure enough he told her: "Bring me food right away,

ya xojtseshuntsán
I am very hungry."

i shem yojatsabjoy jautsukama ora
And when the woman went into the kitchen to take the lid off the pot,

ndoñe yonjopodey jutsukama yojtsanjo stapush
she was not able to remove it, the lid was stuck.

i asna chor boyá yojatschembo
And then the husband shouted:

ndayá knetsam betsko xmajwatxe   15
"What are you doing? Serve me the food right now!"

ndoñe kenatopoden jutsukama
"I can't get the lid off."

i as kach boyá yojamashingo tsabjoy yojtsautsokaye
And then that husband came inside the kitchen to open the pot.

ndoñe yojobenaye
He was not able to do it.

ungarotebey yojwak i yojwangarotiay ch jutsukama
He grabbed a piece of kindling and struck the pot to open it.

y chorna yojutsuka ora mtxkwaye animalok inetsatswamiñe   20
And then when he opened it, a large snake climbed out,

yojonsunja ibojtso tamuxundiamana
it leaped up, it wrapped itself about his neck.

i chteskana ch mtxkwaye nye chká wayaxentxe uta wayaxá
And from that day that snake, like that by the mouth, two mouths,

i ch mtxkwaye bewayaxá i ch yentxá bewayaxá
and that snake's mouth beside that person's mouth,

chká kanyeñe tsesayana
like that eating as one.

mor mexama jamna kachujabtaka   25
Now to go to mass, that thing came along with him.

i diosbe bxaka jastjangwán jobatman
And at the church door it would get off and wait.

i ch mexe tojopasa ora jututontsunjan ch tutondumanán
And when the mass was over, it would jump up again and wrap
    itself around him.

ch yentxá yojajwaboy jojwanán
That man thought to escape,

yentxangabe tsuntsaka yojtsotjuxa
he placed himself in the middle of all those people.

pero pronto ch mtxkwaye animalna achká er ya ibojtsabwatema
                                                                     30
But right away that large snake like that would know him,

pronto ibojtatobondamanaye inye
right away it wrapped itself around him again.

ch kach jaftaka vida inabomna asta jojenachentskoñe
It stayed with him as long as he lived until death might take him.

nye nyetxá tstatxumbo
That's all I know of it.

(m31) salteadorbiama
About the Robber

As performed by Mariano Chicunque in Kamsá, November 1978

This mythic narrative takes us out of the Sibundoy Valley and into the adjacent *páramo*, a cold Andean wetlands lying to the west on the way to the city of Pasto. Even today with the gravel road that traverses this zone, it is an eerie stretch with ghostly shapes of low-lying shrubs emerging and disappearing into the mist. Taita Mariano, who knows this zone from the old walking days, describes it well:

nde la warda susnana ndoñe borla susniñe
Heaven forbid, it's cold, no fooling, in the cold,

iya binyea nye kachká batxatema wabtema
and the wind blowing, it's just drizzling like that.

ooh ana jutxena jutxena nyetxá jabwache binyea
Oh, that wind hits so hard as to almost throw you, throw you right off that mountain.

The trip by foot to Pasto must have been very difficult indeed, and it is not surprising that this peripheral zone, transitional between the indigenous valley and the mestizo Andean corridor, has acquired a legendary status in Kamsá thinking. Taita Mariano relives his own experience of this inhospitable stretch as a means of enlisting his listener's interest in the story.

The motif of a black man and his crew, robbers and cannibals, who maintain a hideaway in a mountain cave, belongs to European narrative. The door that opens on command is a tip-off that we are dealing with a reflex of Type 676, "Open Sesame," known from Ireland to India and beyond and preserved in a South American version. Robe (1973) reports fifteen variants from Mexico and Central America alone. Indeed, this story has a European feel to it, yet the setting remains thoroughly Kamsá in spirit. The plot follows the familiar program fairly closely, though we do not have here the moral element of rich versus poor as in Grimm's "Semsi Mountain" (142), nor does the greedy brother-in-law perish at the hands of the robbers. The man and his son who make a camp in the shelter of Black Man's Gulch are believable travelers from the valley, equipped with an earthen jar and a flint device to make fire. If the coveting of money stands outside of the mainstream thematics of Kamsá mythic narrative, the badgering wife who covets what her brother's family has obtained is indeed familiar in the corpus. The motif of a cannibalistic clan of black marauders resonates equally in the European and Amerindian imagination (see Blaffer 1972).

anteo atxena serta basajema tijoftsabwatmana jashajanaka bastoy[27]
In the old days, truly as a child I knew the high wetlands on the way
to Pasto.

bweno
Well.

santo dios ndoñe bnuniñe kenatsemuna pobloikana[28]
Saintly God, it isn't far after Santiago,

jachnungwana sombush sombushentxana yaskoyeka[29]
you pass the point called Sombush, there by Sombush and a point
called Yaskoy.

i tempo jaboknana jashoye   5
And right away the high wetlands appear,

ooh chesiyajta jftsayana[30]
ooh, you go walking through the mountains all the morning,

ena jashañe ena jashañe ena jashañe
nothing but wetlands, nothing but wetlands, nothing but wetlands.

nde la warda susnana ndoñe borla susniñe
Heaven forbid, it's cold, no fooling, in the cold,

iya binyea nye kachká batxatema wabtema
and the wind blowing, its just drizzling like that.

ooh ana jutxena jutxena nyetxá jabwache binyea   10
Oh, that wind hits so hard as to almost throw you, throw you right
off that mountain.

basto choye atxe tijoftsabwatemana
I experienced that place on the way to Pasto.

**i choye serta anteona ana wakiñá beka btse wakiñaftaka ntaftse-
tebemana**
And there truly in the old days a child, a man was resting with
his child.

[27]line 1: *jashajanaka*, "high wetlands." A special ecological niche in the Central
Andes, known generally by the Spanish name *páramo*, itself derived from the Quechua *para*, "rain."
[28]line 3: *pobloikana*, "from Santiago." The narrator describes a trip over the rough
terrain between the Sibundoy Valley and a nearby provincial capital, Pasto. The town
of Santiago lies at the western edge of the Sibundoy Valley, and is thus the taking-off
point for Pasto.
[29]line 4: *sombush, yaskoy.* These are named points along the way up the
mountain.
[30]lines 6–10: *ooh chesiyajta jftsayana*, "ooh, you go walking through the mountains all the morning." Throughout these five lines the narrator's voice is an icon of
human agony: a high-pitched, chantlike tone of lament.

ch wakiñaftaka ch bebtá yojá bastoye
That father was going to Pasto with his child.

bweno
Well.

**chore chatena choka kwanabaina ftsengujibe tbokaka ftsengujibe
tboka** 15
Then the two of them, there in Black Man's Gulch as it is called,
Black Man's Gulch.

**atxena kanye soye tsuwabwatema tsonyá ndayentxe ch ftsengujibe
tboka**
One time I happened to go there to that place, that Black Man's
Gulch,

ftsengujibe tboka btse tamboshe atanuñe
Black Man's Gulch, a large camp where you could sleep.

**i chentxe more kaldero anteo ndayá matebá ch fshantsa mata-
batema chká jtsambayana**
And there now in the old days they were carrying like that a jar, an
earthen jar,

susna lware ndayentxa joitanusa
in that cold place looking for some shelter.

buyeshtema jtsobobunyayama inawambayena 20
They brought along a little water for boiling.

a chtemiñe ch wakiñá ibojauyana
He spoke to that little one, to that child:

xkoniñesna
"I will make a fire."

anteona tonday posporana ana selebonatombaka[31]
In the old days there were no matches, only the flintstone,

jaiñana a la fuerza selabonatombaka
to make fire, nothing but the flintstone.

**chká yojoftseniña i anye batxana niñá yojoftsekjaye jwashameb-
wama** 25
Like that he made a fire and there was only a little bit of firewood
left to cook with.

iye bweno
And fine.

yojtsabwanaye ch wakiñana i ch bebtena
And so that father and that child cooked with that.

[31]line 23: *selebonatombaka*, "flintstone." A memory of what was a conventional
artifact before the days of matches is preserved in this narrative.

yojoftsayana a ver ch jashoye keka peñuxo bekonana xkwetsá
He said to him: "Let's see, I will go to that wetland area over there by the cliff,

xkwaftsengwango txabe niñatema
I will go for some good kindling.

bndata kachusena ndayana bochisebmwaná   30
We two will have to eat something in the morning.

bochjiyá bastoye beka bayetema mas ke inye pamillabiamana chawatokedaka
We will go to Pasto and there will be wood left behind for another person from the valley."

i serta yojá i ch wakiñá yojtsabwanaye
And truly he went off and that child started cooking.

bweno
Fine.

bna ndoka ase impas jashame jetakna orna
Then not long after that it began to get dark.

ch bebta yojtashjango niñatemaka aray nyetxá btamana ojon-wamna[32]   35
That father arrived with the wood, damn, just tucked inside his *cusma*.

ibojutsebwache chentxe ase chana chentxe niñá yojtsengway orna
He went back there, and then when he went to look for more wood,

ch ftsenga tsoykana chentxa impase peñuxe inetsomiñena
that black man from there inside, it was quite a cliff,

tsoikana ndeolpe yojotseyebwambaye abra la puerta[33]
from inside suddenly he spoke: "Open the door."

kayé nye yojotubjoka yojotseboknaye
Right away it just opened, he came out.

i ch bxaka kachká yojisoyebwambaye   40
And that door, like that, he spoke those same words.

yojatoñe iye chkase cha ch bakashe
He went off like that, that ugly fellow.

cha atxe kboma kachká kboma
"As he did, so will I do."

---

[32]line 35: *cusma*, "men's kilt." At the waistline in this traditional outfit there is a space that can be used as a large pocket.
[33]line 38: *abra la puerta*, "open the door." Note that the black man speaks Spanish.

i serta chká yojoyibwambaye cha yojopodia ch tsoye yojoftsa-
mashingo
And truly like that he spoke, he could do it, he entered the place.

ooh tsoka nyetxá buxenana inakjana ralunga matse eso sí[34]
Oh, inside there were all good things, coins, corn, yes indeed!

wasmana ch bultanga nyetxá inawakjana nye kosa
yentxayunga   45
Sacks of these good things, all stored there, even human clothing.

nye bweno
And so, fine.

ndoka remidio chana nye ch rala tsatxa yojopodia nyetxana
yojokniye
Without remedy he grabbed some coins, as many as he could hold.

i ch lachabia presadia tsebonjaniya kobija yojweshachiniye
And he gathered some clothes, and blankets, blankets to keep
warm with.

i sanatema yojoftsojakniye
And he took a little food from there.

yojtá ch tamboye yojtashjango yojobwambaye mntxá   50
He left and returned to the camp, he spoke like this:

bweno betsko bwetsesaye rala tojotxe ndayá
"Well then, let's eat quickly or we might lose this money.

mo derada mandajna botsayshekoñe kachkoye bwaishekona
We had better move along, let's head on back."

iye inye tambo komna jashatsuntsoye
And there was another camp in the middle of this bleak region.

asta choka chuntskoñe klaro boisenakmiye
"To there we will move, yes we must flee,

asta choka chuntskoñe boisachá mwentxe reso   55
let's move over to that place, let's hurry, here there is danger."

ibojisosañata ibojishekona
They ate some food, they retraced their steps.

iye chata eso sí el otro día ana ibojtsaishekoñe
And those two, yes indeed, the next day they returned,

bastoye ndoñe ibonjá ibojtsushjango
but not to Pasto, they walked, they arrived here,

btska medio iya yentxayá chká yojtsushjango
with plenty of money and clothes, like that they arrived here.

[34]line 44: *ralunga,* "coins." From the Spanish *real,* worth one-quarter of a *peseta.*

i esa chabe kuñado ibsana chká ibojatsekwentá   60
And he told the story to that brother-in-law of his:

mntxá tijapasaka
"This is what happened to me."

a nye yojtsafxnaka
And his eyes opened wide:

malayatxe nyetxá pobrejema malayatxe xkatewanatseka
"Please, we are so poor, please, take me there with you."

wantado jtsemenanasna
He just remained silent.

**diosa jtserwanana diosa rwanana tal vese a vere nya tabwatapo-
    choka**   65
"For God's sake," he begged him, "for God's sake, please, like this
    we might just waste away,

a vera buntjaka bwena nya diosmanda
let's just go, fine, just for God's sake."

chká ibojwanatse i choka serta chká silencio inamna
So he took him along, and there truly it was silent like that.

chká yojoyibwambaye ko serta chká yojopodia
Like that he spoke and there truly like that he was able to do it,

**utata kwaishachiñe ralunga i ch chore tsechamaka yentxayunga
    mntxenatema**
a second time they were able to take some coins, and then as I said
    before, clothes and meat.

a ibojtachá txabana txabá ibojoshkona txabá   70
And they left there fine, they returned just fine, fine.

bweno
Well.

**a chorna shemanga ketsomñikana yapa kodisia podeska jwa-
    bunkausna**
And then women are sometimes very greedy, they have ugly
    thoughts.

ch yojatayana shema
That woman said to him:

araye wabtxe mo ndoñe tbuntisanatsa wabtxe
"Damn! My brother won't take you there again, my brother,

aray malaye nye kanya kata choye   75
damn, please just alone go there,

mejor kanya ya i kojtsabwatemana
its better to go alone, since you already know the way."

i choka palabra ntxama yojtsemna
And there she spoke just these words.

i chká koisejwabnaye a vera katjaka
"And like that you know the way, so go there."

nya mal taistapasaka
"I hope no harm will come to me."

ne ndoñika anya jatana betsko xkopormá   80
"Oh no, I'll just quickly fix you some provisions."

a lo de que mas pueda tambwatema ibojobá betsko ch jatana
As fast as she could she killed the hen to quickly make him a
    snack,

i ase ibojechumwa
and then she sent him on his way.

ibojechumwa orna sertoka nye jamashingwamuna ibojolisensia
When she sent him along, truly he was able to enter there,

chká txabá yojoyebwambaye txabá
like that, fine, he spoke well.

orna de la warda iye jitiseboknamena ch abra la puertakana
    ndoñe   85
Then, heaven forbid, when it came time to leave, that "Open the
    door," nothing,

ibojtsebnatjumbaka ndoñe injenojwaboye ndoñe
he had forgotten it, he couldn't remember it, no.

more ngemenaka txamo jayanana
Now, worried, how to say it?

a la warda bekoña jwenaña skopeteyema ah bekoñe tabatenana
Heaven forbid, nearby he heard a rifle shot, nearby another
    sound.

a nde la warda tonday mas remidio
And heaven forbid there was nothing else to do,

chore kostallemunga inawakjana bachexa uftsastjonaka   90
there they had sacks stored, standing like large bowls,

choye moche ngufshenjemakwenta yojtsojwé
there rather like a frog he hid himself.

bweno
Well.

tondayan inetsabwawañe yentxabe pechubjunga[35]
Like nothing, they were calm, boiling people's breasts,

[35]line 93: *yentxabe pechubjunga*, "people's breasts." These men are cannibals as
well as thieves.

imenetsabwexniñe yentxabe pechana kutsetsakunga jasama
they placed human breasts on the fire, and took them off to
eat them.

ibetsosañe bomoka ch yentxabe mntxena   95
They ate that human flesh with potatoes,

mo twambianka bngabe mntxena ininyna
like hen here, our flesh was to them.

imojisosañungaye iye ajá jetisasangamaka
They finished eating and aha, they were ready to leave.

ah ch mayora ah ndayeka ndayeka
"Ah," that elder, "ah, what's this, what's this,

mwentxa pulga tawantsemnaka ndayeka pulgaka
there might be a flea around here, what's this, a flea?"

**chinya yojayana eh ndayá uchatsemuna pulga kwaisajnunga
    betskoka**   100
Another one spoke: "Eh, what do you mean, a flea? Let's go,
quickly."

ne ndoñe nya pulga mwentxa kutsemna
But no: "There is surely a flea around here."

ndoñe inyenga imojtatsebana jatangana
No, the others stood up to leave.

ah chorna txabá tonjayana morepará ch ch mayorotxeka
Ah, then he said it firmly: "Have a look around," that big elder.

de la warda chora chana kada bulto ch bultañe
Heaven forbid, then each sack, inside the sack,

ch yojontxá jtawachebayana jtawachebayana   105
he began to lift them off the floor, to lift them off the floor.

nday
Nothing.

ultimokna ah ibojetsenyena choka chentxe ibetsotbemañe
In the last one, ah, he found him there, there he was sitting.

ah ngayé sundechamo pulga
"Ah, I told you there was a flea."

ah tempo ibojeshache nyets utatxeka iye ibojtsatsutxenaka
Ah, right then he grabbed him with both hands and threw him
against the floor.

iye kwateshachiye kwatatsutxene   110
And again he grabbed him and threw him down.

chká pronto pelotebekwenta ibojtsepelotiaye pelotiaye
Like that, just like a ball, he kicked him about, kicked him about.

impase yojadesmaya obaná
He fainted completely, dead.

chorkokayé ch taboye imojoftsokutsá iye choye imojisabentá
Then surely they carried him outside and threw him into a hollow.

ajá mora kwatajnunga
"Aha, now let's go."

imojatoñungaka   115
So they took off again.

i chana kaba inetsoiñe
And he was still alive.

bweno
Well.

bnoka yojtatenano skopetaxanga
In the distance a rifle sounded.

yojtaye impas temiakwenta
He moved, but like a drunkard.

inye ntxamo mase inye nye yojobenaye nyetxá jashatsuntsoye 120
Again, but how? Again, but he was completely broken.

yojtachá choka
He got away from there.

ibojaté inye ibsana impasa xoká nye yojtá
He awoke the next day, very sick, but he kept going.

cha chore xokana sersa pobloye sersa
Then, very sick, truly, he came, truly, to Santiago.

ndoñe bnoka kenatsamunana
It's not so far to there.

i chokana yojtashjango moye xoká yojtashjango   125
And he arrived here, sick, he arrived.

asa ibojatenaye ch kachabe kuñado
Then he spoke with his brother-in-law.

cha mntxá tijtsepasaka
He, like this: "So it happened to me."

ah ibojwakakana ndá tkmunjamandá chká
Ah, he scolded him: "Who sent you like that?

chká jana nye sin permiso amase atxebe sin permiso
To go like that, only without permission, without my permission?

nday milagro ndoñe tkonjobana   130
Its a miracle they didn't kill you.

mo matkmuntsepeká o matkmuntsejwesá impase makojtsemena
Here they could have cut you with a machete or they could have
   shot you, they could have finished you off.

mora nya ndoñe masa choye kwatutsayika
Don't be going there, now, not any more.

**impase katanjanoperdia ch ibonatjumbay kausa yapa batebomen-
   kausa**
Listen to me, since you forgot yourself, because of your greed,

ndoñena entre katxatasna mase tijatonyen
we cannot return, even the two of us, to find things there."

palabrasa inamna   135
That was the word.

chiekna nyetxá salteadorbiamna tijuftsekwentá
And so I have told you the whole story about the robber.

pero lo demasna chabojakwenta
But the other ones I will tell you as well,

ar señor
by Our Lord.

(m32) la mina de oro
The Gold Mine

As performed by Bautista Juajibioy in Spanish, 1976

This narrative performance emerges one afternoon as I ply taita Bautista
for stories of the old days. He complies, grudgingly, amused that this
young visitor is so intent on hearing things that he terms *cuentos pajosos*,
"foolish tales." At one point he muses, *ahora, iqué vamos a inventar?*
("now what should we invent?") yet, as cups of chicha pass from hand
to hand, the elder's voice fills one and then another cassette tape. This
performance is remarkable in that I am the primary audience, though a
secondary audience of Kamsá listeners wanders in and out as the afternoon progresses. Since he is talking to an outsider, taita Bautista tells
his story in Spanish, in the colloquial dialect of Colombia's southern
highlands.

   This particular narrative evokes a prologue, a moment of reminiscence in which taita Bautista recalls (and thereby credits) his sources,
the elders of his own youth who would spin tales of the old days
through the dark Sibundoy evenings and nights. Taita Bautista pictures

himself, listening in, paying close attention, for only in that way does one learn these things. And so this narrative is preceeded by an implicit claim for authenticity; it is framed as a genuine token of Kamsá tradition, as a tale that has been passed along the chain of elders. Here is a man who clearly values what he has gathered at the indigenous hearth; even so, he is vulnerable to the stiff posture of renunciation imposed by his devout Catholicism. A few years hence he will refuse to talk to me about these things, preferring to relate the story of Adam and Eve and other biblical episodes.

"The Gold Mine" features intriguing glimpses into the Kamsá mythic world, yet it illustrates myth at the service of historicity as the indigenous community seeks understanding of its interactions with the surrounding national society. The narrative plot draws upon important cosmological resources keyed on the "little white dog" that guards the gold high in the mountains. This dog, we are told, is the lightning, and it convincingly destroys all those who approach with impurity. To successfully extract this gold, it is necessary to diet on a wild grass and to refrain from sexual congress for one week prior to making the journey. Once at the mine, one should take only a small quantity of gold and then quickly move into the shelter of a nearby boulder.

These ritual prescriptions are familiar in the spiritual life of the Kamsá Indians, especially with reference to the use of the visionary remedies (see McDowell 1989). A relationship between gold and the thunder deity is established in the Wangetsmuna cycle (see m2 and m3). The association of a mountain spirit with canines is developed in m6, with its "dogs of the volcano." These elements suggest that this narrative develops a mythical framework for the placer mining that has occupied Kamsá Indians since before the arrival of the Spaniards. We know from ethnohistorical sources that the natives of the Sibundoy Valley exchanged gold found in their region for goods produced in other regions of the Quillasinga federation (Uribe 1977–1978) and that this practice continued into the colonial period (Bonilla 1972).

But "The Gold Mine" is not merely a mythopoeic treatment of the ancient custom of placer mining. It is situated in the contentious present, where indigenous peoples must somehow manage a detente with city people whose greed threatens to devour every material benefit an Indian might have or acquire. The mythopoeic elements in this narrative take on special potency as components of a spiritual code advantageous to the knowledgeable Indian, but devastating to the ignorant "whites." A political message (and indeed, a parable) can be discovered in this plot: a wise Indian prospers in a rarified spiritual zone, a foolish Indian inadvertently draws the whites into this zone, the whites perish there because of their greed and ignorance. This message complicates the ready assignment of blame by bringing in the collaborating Indian, who mistakenly provides whites with access to Indian goods.

The cosmological setting for this narrative is indigenous: the association of gold with the thunder deity emerges in the Wangetsmuna cycle, and the presence of a white dog as a spiritual guardian occurs in Chibchan oral tradition (Pittier de Fábrega 1905-1907, 325). Alberto Juajibioy (1987, 39) describes the thunder as owner or master of gold mines in Sibundoy tradition: "sometimes he would appear to the miners, during a full moon, as a beautiful little white dog, jumping on the rocks that emerge from the rivers . . . in the place where he disappears, they find the mine."

Stories of buried treasure, lost mines, and other sources of gold are widespread throughout Spanish America (Miller 1951; Foster 1964), and they retain a historical poignancy in this setting: it was, after all, a hunger for gold that drew Spanish adventurers into the New World in the first place. Briggs (Briggs and Vigil 1990, 193) notes that in Latin America, "legends of buried treasure . . . are frequently concerned with the supernatural" and that "spirits can either guard the treasure or aid the hunters in recovering it." He notes further that "the position a spirit adopts . . . is often tied to the moral disposition" of the seekers. The interaction between Native America and Europe is explicit in many of the Spanish-American variants. In the story that Briggs analyzes in detail, "the difficulty involved in recovering the treasure emanates from its enchantment by Pedro Cordova's Indian servants prior to interment."

"The Gold Mine" can be seen as an attempt to redefine the plight of the indigenous people through the creative use of traditional resources. It holds out hope that the Indian, through superior awareness of spiritual reality, may eventually triumph over the encroaching whites. As such it belongs to a class of valiant attempts by the dispossessed to wrest from their unkind destinies a modicum of hope and self-respect.

los viejos que celaban por las noches
The old people who kept vigil at night?

ellos sabían estar sentados, así conversando
They would often be sitting there, talking like this,

y uno de muchachito así, uno está oyendo
and oneself, a small boy, oneself just listening.

de ese modo se aprende, si no, no
That way you learn something, otherwise, you don't.

hay un cuento, no   5
There is a story, see?

había una indígena tenía vista la mina en una loma, y una gran peña
There was an Indian who had spotted a mine on a hill, and a large cliff.

y allí stilaba un poquito de agua y bajaba el oro así
And there a little bit of water dripped and the gold came down like that.

pues así entonces caía, reboteaba así el agua, reboteaba
So like this then it fell, the water splashed like this, it splashed.

y allí a lado había un perrito blanco bien enroscadito
And there at the side was a little white dog, with very tangled hair.

bueno   10
Well.

perros como antes había
Dogs like there used to be.

el iba ayunando casi una semana
He would be fasting almost an entire week,

comiendo esta, que una yerba que hay aquí
eating this, a grass that we have here,

no hay aquí, allí barato los ipialeños lo llaman[36]
we don't have it here, there it is cheap, the people from Ipiales call it,

cómo es que lo dice, mmm ni me acuerdo   15
what do they call it, mmm, I don't even remember.

es de comer, en nuestro dialecto llama tsebajusha
It is a food, in our language it is called *tsebajusha*.

antes lo comíamos
Previously we ate it.

cuando mi mamá señora vivía eso comía todos los días
When my mother lived we ate this every day.

ahora ya de eso no se come y allí barato nadie come
Now people don't eat this any more, and it's there so cheap, nobody eats it. (laughs)

este ya está comiendo una semana, de eso alargarba   20
This fellow is eating it for a week, then he took off.

un día, dos días y llegaba vuelta
One day, two days, and then he returned.

puñadito de oro
A fistful of gold.

---

[36]line 14: *ipialeños*, people from Ipiales, a city that lies on the high plateau just north of the Colombia-Ecuador border.

lo guardaba y llevaba a Pasto pero eso con medida
He saved it and took it to Pasto, but in small quantity.

entonces el traía todo lo que el quería de Pasto
Then he brought everything that he wanted from Pasto.

comida, pero lo que el quería tenía todo   25
Food, but whatever he wanted, he had it all.

**un hermano le dice, por qué sería que usted ni trabaja como yo y
usted tiene todo, nada le falta**
A brother says to him: "Why is it that you don't even work like I do
   but you have everything, you lack nothing?

haceme el favor avíseme
Do me a favor, tell me,

cómo es que hace usted las platas
how is it that you come by your money?"

que él sabe no
He knows about it, see?

**a la final en la ultima hora de tanto que lo molestaba lo
convenció**   30
Finally, at the end after so much pleading, he convinced him.

dijo bueno yo te voy a llevar pero con esta condición
He said: "Well, I am going to take you with me, but on this
   condition:

cuidado con dormir con mujer, aparte tienes que dormir
Be careful about sleeping with a woman, you have to sleep apart,

**y una semana tienes que comer de esta yerba que llamamos tsebaj-
wasashe bngabe palabra kwabaina**
and for one week you have to eat this grass that we call *tsebajwasashe*,
   that's how it's called in our language,

huacamullo llaman en castellano, huacamullo
huacamullo they call it in Spanish, *huacamullo*.

bueno   35
Well.

ya había completado
He had already complied.

dijo bueno le voy a llevar
He said: "Fine, I will take you."

y el avío era la misma yerba, cocinada
And the provisions were the same grass, cooked.

mira, allá en el camino cuando el nuevo que lo iba a llevar
Look, there on the path, when the new guy he was going to take,

había llevado una gallina bien preparado con arracachas   40
he had brought along a hen well prepared with edible roots.

y allá dijo que comamos ya que es medio día vamos siguiendo
And there he said: "Let's eat, its already midday, and we can
   continue."

y el otro agarró eso y allá lejos lo mandó[37]
And the other guy grabbed all that and threw it far off. (laughs)

y no habido querido seguir, se regresó
And he refused to continue, he went back. (laughs)

después de un tiempo vuelta llegó molestando
After a while he came pleading again,

de tanto molestar que dijo bueno pero con cuidado   45
with so much pleading he said: "Fine, but be careful."

y cierto dijo bueno
And truly he said: "Fine."

a la mina es que lo llevó
He took him to the mine.

bueno
Well.

llegaron a una loma, todos esos árboles blancos de nieve, no
They arrived at a hill, all those trees white with snow, see?

todo blanco, bueno   50
Everything white, fine.

y llegaron a la peña
And they came to the cliff.

le dijo, le dijo, bueno aquí es
He told him, he told him: "Well, here it is.

pero usted tan pronto como yo saco y usted saca
But just as soon as I take some and you take some,

nos vamos a una piedra abierta en una quebrada
we will go to an exposed rock in a stream."

---

[37]lines 42, 43: Here the narrator breaks into an extended round of laughter, with
a prolonged interlude of some ten seconds between these two lines; the poignant
detail of discarding a delicious meal, and the traveller's greed as an omen, are perhaps the cause of this hilarity.

fueron a meter allá adentro   55
They went and hid themselves inside there.

dijo bueno ten cuidado calladito calladito
He said: "Fine, be careful, quiet, quiet."

cuando en un ratico pon pon pon pon
When in just a moment, pon pon pon pon,

de eso truenos y relámpagos y rayos
all that thunder, lightning, and thunderbolts.

ese rayo había sido el perrito
That thunderbolt, it turned out, was the little dog.

ese rayo es que cuida el oro   60
The thunderbolt, it looks after the gold.

y así despues de un buen rato ya calmaba
And so after quite a while things calmed down.

entonces sí ya, no les pasaba entonces
Then it was safe, nothing happened to them then.

entonces tenían que salir de la piedra y sale a llevar
Then they had to come out from behind the rock, and they took the
     gold with them.

y así bajaron, llegaron al valle, y lo aconsejó
And so they came down, they arrived in the valley, and he advised
     him:

cuidado con estar llevando, tanto harto, no, poquito no mas   65
"Be careful about carrying it around, not so much, just a little bit."

el otro tonto sale llevando todo
The other foolish guy goes out carrying all of it.

**anduvo en la ciudad de Pasto y no hubo nadie que fue capaz para
     poder comprar con todo caso[38]**
He went about in the city of Pasto and there was no one like him
     able to buy just about anything he wanted.

como tanta maldad hay en esta vida
Since there is such evil in this life.

a la final unos dijeron
At last some of them said:

cojámoslo preso, que nos vaya a amostrar a donde es   70
"Let's take him prisoner, so he will show us where it is."

---

[38]line 67: Pasto, capital of the neighboring state, Nariño, is a center for regional
commerce.

pobre tonto trajeron amarrado que llegó onde el hermano
Poor fool, they took him tied up, he arrived at his brother's,

que lo acabó de regañar
who gave him quite a scolding:

no ves, animalote[39]
"Don't you see, you big idiot.

buenamenta te fuí a mostrar
In vain I went to show you.

ora no te escapas, ora te mueres, allá vas a morir   75
Now you won't get away, now you will die, there you are going
    to die.

pero pueda que dios se compadezca de ti[40]
But maybe God will have mercy on you.

tal como yo vi vas y esta gente va, no
Just as I saw it, you will go and these people will go, is that
    right?

pero eso sí, sacás pero te vas a esconder inmediatamente
But for sure, take some but go and hide immediately.

y esta gente que va a seguir, ooh[41]
And these people who will come after you, ooh."

llego la gente allá así como hormigas   80
The people arrived there thus like ants.

sacar el oro peleando, dando puños, y así costales llenando
To remove the gold, fighting, exchanging blows, and like that filling
    sacks with it.

bueno
Well.

ratico a esos peleones sale relámpagos y truenos y rayos ffffttt
In a moment lightning and thunder came down upon those queru-
    lous people, ffffttt.

se acabó la gente
The people were finished off.

[39]line 73: *no ves, animalote*. Note the shift to informal second person as the speaker takes to scolding his brother; previously he addressed him with the formal *usted*. *Animalote* is literally "big animal," thus "brute," "idiot."

[40]line 76: *dios se compadezca*. Note how easily the Christian God fits into this pantheistic system.

[41]line 79: *ooh*. This is a very expressive interpolation, prolonged and contoured with musical effect.

**después de un buen rato que ya se había calmado todo el se
    sale**   85
After quite a while when everything had calmed down, he
    came out.

a ver, qué será, qué ha pasado
"Let's see, what's going on? What has happened?"

entonces se salió
Then he came out.

buscaba ellos, allá encima de los árboles
He looked for them, there at the tops of the trees.

la gente ni uno, nadie
Of those people, not a single one, nobody.

por ahí es que dejalos, no estarase reparoso, que se va ligero   90
Over there just leave them, don't stand there looking, just get out of
    there quickly.

se acabó
It's over.

8 Aftermyth

We have now completed our survey of mythic narratives gathered through access to a social network that radiates outward from the Jua-jibioy family and their base in the vereda of San Felix, activated for my benefit by my Kamsá partner, Justo Jacanamijoy. I returned to San Felix in June 1991 to find that don Justo had passed away some months previously. My hostess during that earlier period, doña María, was much smitten with this loss, and she had also lost one of her sons, Lucho, shortly after Justo's death. But she was in the company of her daughters, Carmen and Clemencia, who themselves had babes in arms, and the garden was green as ever around the house, so I departed with a sense of continuity in the face of these terrible losses.

I have stressed already the signal contribution of Justo Jacanamijoy to this project, as field coordinator, as storyteller, as aid in the processes of transcription and translation. Perhaps most remarkable was Justo's unequivocal commitment to the project, not so remarkable after all since my fascination with the myths coincided with his own. I see now that my arrival provided him with the occasion to do something he had always wanted to do, and he soon set about rounding up the good performers of mythic narrative within his ken. As I stated in the introductory section of this book, it is this group of verbal artists assembled through Justo's diligence that have created the present corpus of mythic narratives.

Had there been time and opportunity to canvass other social networks in the Kamsá community, no doubt other myths and other versions of these same myths would have materialized. What we have in this collection is merely a sample, a specimen frozen in time, of an evolving narrative tradition. Now that we hold it in our grasp, what can we make of this specimen? I believe that these stories leap forth as powerful imaginative creations in their own right; they possess the inherent aesthetic qualities of what is generally referred to as literature. I know that they have haunted me since I first encountered them some fifteen years ago; they have entered my consciousness and worked on it over the years, emerging as my own when I needed stories for my children or coming to mind when I was confronting personal moments of crisis or intrigue. In this sense, they have annexed me to the expansive dominion of Kamsá tradition and placed within my reach the wise counsel of the Kamsá elders. The remarkable transmutations of the ancestors conveyed in these mythic narratives have forever enriched my perception of life's possibilities.

As "literary" creations, these mythic narratives hold a universal appeal to human sensibilities. They provide a direct channel to the wellsprings of the human imagination with their tantalizing rationales to match the basic enigmas of human existence. Their accounts of human ambition and its effects deliver a trenchant analysis, coded in narrative discourse, of the tug between the self and society. It may be that we necessarily receive these stories as indigenous South American reflexes of the universal themes, but we nonetheless find in them a power beyond the reach of the merely exotic or quaint.

But it is clear that these tales cannot be severed for long from their point of origin; they starkly bespeak the personalities of those who perform them as well as the ethos of the community in which they have persisted over the years. More than that, they can be read as indices of a particular historical moment in the experience of this community. In returning this literary legacy to the arena of those who cultivate it, we must inquire exactly what it means to them and how it reflects this particular crossroads in their destiny. It is a thesis of the present effort that only through grounding in the indigenous language and worldview can oral literature be fully appreciated.

I recall don Justo's advice to taita Mariano Chicunque as we initiated our narrative sessions: "Tell it with a beginning and an end; make a story out of it." This advice seemed superfluous once taita Mariano got underway, for it soon became obvious that he was a gifted and much practiced narrator who knew very well not only how to structure a coherent narrative but also how to bring it to life through dramatization of selected episodes. But Justo's advice conveys a degree of reflexivity, an awareness of genre and a sense of responsibility to an audience, that immediately locates this corpus of mythology in the evolution of mythopoeisis. It indicates a mythology that is valued for aesthetic as much as for instrumental properties. This is not myth in service to ritual or myth as theology, but rather myth as "literary" entertainment.

I have tried to show that Kamsá mythic narrative, as a transitional or vestigial mythology, possesses both sacred and secular dimensions. Viewed as a communal heritage, these stories constitute an indigenous theory of culture evolution, a Kamsá account of the emergence of human society in the Sibundoy Valley. They index the regulation of natural forces, the removal of substrate populations, and the establishment of proper mores, all essential to the flowering of civilized life. Although there is some overlap with historical fact, it makes sense to characterize the work of these myths as a *theory* of history rather than as history itself. In this capacity they lay down a framework for interpreting events that have shaped the history of the region, a framework that remains efficacious as people continue to wrestle with the meaning of their lives.

This essentially religious orientation is complemented by a coded analysis of social structure and agency that relocates the thrust of narrative intent firmly within the societal realm. The myths are savored as imaginative castings and recastings of recurrent dilemmas endemic to social life in the Kamsá community. Myth protagonists face the same temptations that lure the modern people astray; they exhibit strengths and flaws of character ringing true to the people one encounters in the veredas. The mythic narratives assembled here concentrate on moments of tension, conflict, or ambivalence in social relations. They address key issues in the maintenance of the social contract: securing an appropriate spouse, reconciling personal ambition and social obligation, applying traditional wisdom to novel problems. The myths give play to these matters in striking journeys of the imagination featuring celestial bodies, the first people, animals masquerading as people, and a range of uncouth spirit forces. But these exotic personages deliver models for the conduct of human life, models that are judiciously interpolated into the lives of narrators and their audiences.

Another theme that I have developed in commenting on the corpus is the scope for personalization of mythic resources, especially prominent in a mythology that is evolving toward folktale. The mythical substrate holds great potential for reframings of the familiar prototypes according to personal whim or fancy. Narrators cannot help but identify with particular story protagonists, and they respond to perceived characteristics of the audience as well. These incidental features of the performance setting can greatly inflect a standardized plot. We have seen that taita Mariano, himself an elder, foregrounds the wisdom of the elders in his narratives. In parallel fashion, doña María, herself a renowned planter of corn, features women who contribute to the persistence of civilized life through planting and careful surveillance of the spiritual frontier.

The mythical substrate is far more malleable than one might have suspected, at least in the instance of a mythology no longer tethered to organized religious praxis. At the extreme, narrators extract mythological episodes from their cosmological environment and present them as autonomous vignettes. At this moment in its trajectory, Kamsá mythology encompasses both elaborated and restricted versions of the myths. It may be that general familiarity with the place of the owl or the sparrow in the cosmology frees narrators from the need to provide extensive cosmological grounding. In any event, an aura of the sacred clings to even these personalized versions, which highlight the presence of literal belief in reported supernatural occurrences. We are still at some remove from the deliberate suspension of disbelief that characterizes folktale traditions.

Myths in the Sibundoy context, as elsewhere, are instruments for thinking about the world in both its natural and its social aspects. Myth is an intellectual tool fashioned from empirical observation but freed to enter the realm of the conceivable, where gaps in human comprehension can be scrutinized through the lens of imaginable relations. Kamsá mythic narrative entails, as we have seen, an indigenous theory of history that moves largely within the context of of the traditional worldview and lifestyle. As the Sibundoy Valley drifts toward assimilation into the national culture, the myths become disembodied reminders of a largely inactive worldview in spite of the best efforts of the elders to convey the wisdom of the past to the emerging generations. Signs of this transformation are prevalent in the corpus itself as it moves in the direction of fable, legend, and folktale.

But there is a vitality to this narrative tradition that keeps it present in the minds of even those who aspire to another lifestyle. The children of Justo and María, who heard more than a few of the narrations represented in these texts, developed an interesting routine during the interminable games of marbles played on the patio of the Jacanamijoy house: when one of them made a particularly fine shot the others would remark, *cha ndoñe krischian,* "He is not a human being!" In this manner a formula occurring as denouement in so many of the mythic narratives found an application to the mundane scene at hand. I believe that the mythic tales recorded in this volume retain this ability to link the past with the present, even in the altered circumstances of the Sibundoy Valley today. Wangetsmuna's name may no longer resound throughout the valley, but his example still lies at the heart of an ethos that for the time being separates the Kamsá indigenous community from its non-Indian neighbors in this stretch of the Andes.

As long as this ethos persists, mythic resources can be drawn upon to make sense out of the disparate currents of history affecting the region. "The Gold Mine" offers a palpable example of the continuing potency of the tradition by presenting a parable of Indian persistence in the face of unfavorable social and political conditions. As we have seen, this tale suggests that the Indian, by drawing on superior spiritual awareness, can finally triumph over the heavy-handed mob of whites, but only if the temptation to adopt white values can be resisted. It is evident that the whole corpus of Kamsá mythic narrative, with its charting of indigenous values, must play a key role if this project of cultural survival is to have any chance of success.

References

Basso, Ellen. 1985. *A Musical View of the Universe*. Philadelphia: Univ. of Pennsylvania Press.

Bastien, Joseph. 1978. *Mountain of the Condor: Metaphor and Ritual in an Andean Ayllu*. American Ethnological Society Monographs, no. 64. Minneapolis: West Publishing.

Bierhorst, John. 1988. *The Mythology of South America*. New York: Morrow.

Blaffer, Sarah. 1972. *The Black Man of Zinacantán: A Central American Legend*. Austin: Univ. of Texas Press.

Boas, Franz. 1891. "Dissemination of tales among the natives of North America." *Journal of American Folklore* 4:13–20.

———. 1912. "Notes on Mexican folklore." *Journal of American Folklore* 25:204–60.

Boggs, Ralph Steele. 1930. *Index of Spanish Folktales*. Helsinki: Folklore Fellow Communications.

Bonilla, Victor Daniel. 1972. *Servants of God or Masters of Men: The Story of a Capuchin Mission in Amazonia*. London: Penguin.

Boydstun, L. C. 1947. *The Classification and Analysis of the Spanish Versions of the "Tar Baby" Story*. Masters thesis, Stanford.

Briggs, Charles, and Julián Vigil. 1990. *The Lost Gold Mine of Juan Mondragón: A Legend from New Mexico Performed by Melaquías Romero*. Tucson: Univ. of Arizona Press.

Brinton, Daniel. 1901. *The American Race: A Linguistic Classification and Ethnographic Description of the Native Tribes of North and South America*. Philadelphia: McKay.

Bristol, Melvin Lee. 1968. "Sibundoy agricultural vegetation." In *Actas y Memorias: 37th Congreso Internacional de Americanistas*. Buenos Aires: Librart S.R.L.

Brown, Michael. 1985. *Tsewa's Gift: Magic and Meaning in an Amazonian Society*. Washington, D.C.: Smithsonian Institution Press.

Buchwald, Otto von. 1919. "El Sebondoy vocabulario y notas." *Boletín de la Sociedad Ecuatoriana de Estudios Históricos Americanos* (Quito, Ecuador) 3:205–12.

Castillo y Orozco, Padre Eugenio del. 1877. *Vocabulario Paez- Castellano, Catechismo, Nociones Grammaticales i dos Pláticas* [1755]. Collection Linguistique Américaine, vol. 2. Paris.

Clifford, James, and George Marcus, eds. 1986. *Writing Culture: The Poetics and Politics of Ethnography*. Berkeley: Univ. of California Press.

Cobo, Bernabe. 1956 [1653]. *Historia del Nuevo Mundo*. Biblioteca de Autores Espanoles, vol. 92. Madrid: Atlas.

Dauenhauer, Nora, and Richard Dauenhauer. 1988. *Haa Shuka, "Our Ancestors:" Tlingit Oral Narratives*. Seattle: Univ. of Washington Press.

Demarest, Arthur. 1981. *Viracocha: The Nature and Antiquity of the Andean High God*. Monographs of the Peabody Museum, no. 6. Cambridge: Peabody Museum Press.

Dover, Robert. 1992. "Introduction." In *Andean Cosmologies through Time: Persistence and Emergence*, ed. R. Dover, K. Seibold, and J. McDowell. Bloomington: Indiana Univ. Press.

Dundes, Alan, ed. 1988. *The Flood Myth*. Berkeley: Univ. of California.

Edmonson, Munro. 1971. *The Book of Counsel: The Popol Vuh of the Quiché Maya of Guatemala*. New Orleans: Tulane Univ.

Emmons, Louise, and Francois Feer. 1990. *Neotropical Rainforest Mammals: A Field Guide*. Chicago: Univ. of Chicago Press.

Faron, Louis. 1963. "The magic mountain and other origin myths of the Mapuche of Central Chile." *Journal of American Folklore* 76:245–48.

Foster, George. 1964. "Treasure tales and the image of a static economy in a Mexican peasant community." *Journal of American Folklore* 77:39–44.

Friede, Juan. 1945. "Leyendas de nuestro señor de Sibundoy y el santo Carlos Tamoabioy." *Boletín de Arqueología* (Bogotá) 1:315–18.

Gayton, A. H. 1935. "The Orpheus myth in North America." *Journal of American Folklore* 48:263–86.

Graham, Joe. 1981. "The *caso*: an emic genre of folk narrative." In *"And Other Neighborly Names": Social Process and Cultural Image in Texas Folklore*, ed. R. Bauman and R. Abrahams. Austin: Univ. of Texas Press.

Graham, Malbone. 1925. "Some folktales of the Chibcha nation." *Publications of the Texas Folk-Lore Society* 4:68–79.

Greenberg, Joseph. 1960. "The general classification of Central and South American languages." In *Men and Cultures: Selected Papers of the Fifth International Congress of Anthropological and Ethnological Sciences*, ed. A.F.C. Wallace. Philadelphia: Univ. of Pennsylvania Press.

Guallart, J. M. 1978. "El mito de Nunkui." *Amazonía Peruana* 2:7–8.

Guaman Poma de Ayala, Felipe. 1980 [1615]. *El primer nueva corónica y buen gobierno*, ed. J. Murra and R. Adorno. Trans. J. Urioste. Mexico: Siglo XXI.

Hansen, Terrance. 1957. *The Types of the Folktale in Cuba, Puerto Rico, the Dominican Republic and Spanish South America*. Berkeley: Univ. of California Press.

Harrison, Regina. 1989. *Signs, Songs, and Memories in the Andes: Translating Quechua Language and Culture*. Austin: Univ. of Texas Press.

Hartmann, Roswith. 1984. "Achikee, Chificha: Mama Huaca en la tradición oral andina." *América Indígena* 44:649–62.

Horcasitas, Fernando. 1988. "An analysis of the deluge myth in Mesoamerica." In *The Flood Myth*, ed. A. Dundes. Berkeley: Univ. of California Press.

Howard, Linda. 1967. "Camsá phonology." In *Phonemic Systems of Colombian Languages*. Lomalinda, Colombia: Summer Institute of Linguistics.

———. 1977. "Esquema de los tipos de párrafo en Camsá." In *Estudios en Camsá y Catio*. Lomalinda, Colombia: Summer Institute of Linguistics.

Hymes, Dell. 1989. "Tlingit poetics." *Journal of Folklore Research* 26:236–48.

Isbell, Billie Jean. 1978. *To Defend Ourselves: Ecology and Ritual in an Andean Village*. Austin: Univ. of Texas Press.

Jara, Fausto, and Ruth Moya. 1987. *La venada: literatura oral quichua del Ecuador*. Quito: Abya-Yala Press.

Jijon y Caamaño, Jacinto. 1938. "Las naciones indígenas que poblaban el occidente de Colombia al tiempo de la conquista, segun los cronistas castellanos." In *Sebastian de Benalcázar*, vol. 2. Quito: Imprenta del Clero.

Juajibioy, Alberto. 1987. *Relatos y Leyendas Orales*. Bogotá: Servicio Colombiano de Comunicación Social.

Juajibioy, Alberto, and Alvaro Wheeler. 1973. *Bosquejo Etnolingüístico del Grupo Kamsá de Sibundoy, Putumayo, Colombia*. Bogotá: Imprenta Nacional.

Kane, Stephanie. 1988. "Omission in Emberá (Chocó) mythography." *Journal of Folklore Research* 25:155–86.

Labov, William. 1972. "The transformation of experience in narrative syntax." In *Language in the Inner City: Studies in the Black English Vernacular*. Philadelphia: Univ. of Pennsylvania Press.

Ladd, D. Robert. 1978. *The Structure of Intonational Meaning: Evidence from English*. Bloomington: Indiana Univ. Press.

Lammel, Annamária. 1981. "Historical changes as reflected in South American Indian myths." *Acta Ethnographica* 30:143–58.

Laughlin, Robert. 1988. *The People of the Bat: Mayan Tales and Dreams from Zinacantán*. Ed. Carol Karasik. Washington, D.C.: Smithsonian Institution Press.

Lévi-Strauss, Claude. 1963. *Structural Anthropology*. Garden City: Anchor.

———. 1969. *The Raw and the Cooked*. Vol. 1 of *Introduction to a Science of Mythology*. New York: Harper and Row.

———. 1973. *From Honey to Ashes*. Vol. 2 of *Introduction to a Science of Mythology*. New York: Harper and Row.

———. 1978. *The Origin of Table Manners*. Vol. 3 of *Introduction to a Science of Mythology*. New York: Harper and Row.

Loukotka, Cestmír. 1967. *Classification of South American Indian Languages*. Los Angeles: Latin American Center of University of California at Los Angeles.

Lowie, Robert. 1940. "American culture history." *American Anthropologist* 42:409–28.

Marzal, Manuel. 1985. *El Syncretismo Iberoamericano*. Lima: Pontificia Universidad Católica del Perú.

Mason, John. 1950. "The languages of South American Indians." In *Handbook of South American Indians*. Vol. 6. Ed. J. Steward. Washington, D.C.: GPO.

McDowell, John. 1973. "Performance and the folkloric text: a rhetorical approach to 'The Christ of the Bible.'" *Folklore Forum* 6:139–48.

———. 1981. "Towards a semiotics of nicknaming." *Journal of American Folklore* 94:1–18.

———. 1982. "Beyond iconicity: ostension in Kamsá mythic narrative." *Journal of the Folklore Institute* 19:119–39.

———. 1983. "The semiotic constitution of Kamsá ritual language." *Language in Society* 12:23–46.

———. 1985. "The poetic rites of conversation." *Journal of Folklore Research* 22:113–32.

———. 1987. "The Kamsá musical system." In *Andean Musics*, ed. R. Dover and J. McDowell. *Andean Studies Occasional Papers*, vol. 3. Indiana Univ. Bloomington: Center for Latin American and Caribbean Studies.

———. 1989. *Sayings of the Ancestors: The Spiritual Life of the Sibundoy Indians*. Lexington: Univ. Press of Kentucky.

———. 1990. "The community-building mission of Kamsá ritual language." *Journal of Folklore Research* 27:67–84.

———. 1992. "Exemplary ancestors and pernicious spirits." In *Andean Cosmologies through Time: Persistence and Emergence*, ed. R. Dover, K. Seibold, J. McDowell. Bloomington: Indiana Univ. Press.

Miller, Elaine. 1973. *Mexican Folk Narrative from the Los Angeles Area*. Publications of the American Folklore Society, 24. Austin: Univ. of Texas Press.

Morote Best, Efraín. 1957, 1958. "El oso raptor." *Archivos Venezolanos de Folklore* 6, 7:135–79.

Mosquera, T. C. de. 1853. *Memoir on the Physical and Political Geography of New Granada*. New York.

Mukarovsky, Jan. 1964. "The esthetics of language." In *A Prague School Reader on Esthetics, Literary Structure, and Style*, ed. and trans. P. Garvin. Washington, D.C.: Georgetown Univ. School of Languages and Linguistics.

Niles, Susan. 1981. *South American Indian Narrative: An Annotated Bibliography*. New York: Garland.

Ortiz, Sergio Elías. 1954. *Estudios sobre lingüística aborigen de Colombia*. Bogotá: Ediciones de la Revista Bolívar.

Paredes, Américo. 1968. "Folk medicine and the intercultural jest." In *Spanish-Speaking People in the United States*, ed. J. Helm. Seattle: Univ. of Washington Press.

————. 1970. *Folktales of Mexico*. Chicago: Univ. of Chicago Press.

Parsons, Elsie Clews. 1945. *Peguche—Canton of Otavalo, Province of Imbabura, Ecuador: A Study of Andean Indians*. Chicago: Univ. of Chicago Press.

Pittier de Fábrega, Henry. 1905–1907. "Ethnographic and linguistic notes on the Paez Indians of Tierra Adentro, Cauca, Colombia." *Memoirs of the American Anthropological Association* 1: 301–56.

Propp, Vladimir. 1968. *Morphology of the Folktale*, 2d ed. Austin: Univ. of Texas Press.

Rael, Juan. 1939. "Cuentos españoles de Colorado y de Nuevo Méjico (primera serie)." *Journal of American Folklore* 52:227–323.

Rappaport, Joanne. 1980–1981. "El mesianísmo y las trasformaciones de símbolos mesiánicos en Tierradentro." *Revista Colombiana de Antropología* 23: 365–413.

Rasnake, Roger. 1988. "Images of resistance to colonial domination." In *Rethinking History and Myth: Indigenous South American Perspectives on the Past*, ed. J. Hill. Urbana: Univ. of Illinois Press.

Reichel-Dolmatoff, Gerardo. 1971. *Amazonian Cosmos: The Sexual and Religious Symbolism of the Tukano Indians*. Chicago: Univ. of Chicago Press.

Rivet, Paul. 1912. "Les familles linguistiques du Nord-ouest de l'Amerique du Sud." *L'Année linguistique* 4:117–54.

————. 1924. "Langes Américaines." In *Les langues du mond*, ed. A. Meillet and M. Cohen. Société de Linguistique de Paris, vol. xvi. Paris: Librairie ancienne Edouard Champion.

Robe, Stanley. 1973. *Index of Mexican Folktales*. Chicago: Univ. of California Press.

Rocha, Joaquín. 1905. *Memorandum de viaje—Región Amazónica*. Bogotá: El Mercurio.

Salomon, Frank, and George Urioste, eds. *The Huarochirí Manuscript: A Testament of Ancient and Colonial Andean Religion*. Austin: Univ. of Texas Press.

Sañudo, Jose Rafael. 1938. *Apuntes sobre la Historia de Pasto*. Pasto: Imprenta Nariñense.

Saussure, Ferdinand de. 1959. *Course in General Linguistics*. New York: McGraw-Hill.

Schultes, Richard Evans, and Albert Hofmann. 1979. *Plants of the Gods: Origins of Hallucinogenic Use*. New York: McGraw-Hill.

Segal, Roberta. 1989. "The Jealous Potter (review of Lévi-Strauss)." *Journal of American Folklore* 102:207–210.

Seijas, Haydee. 1969. "The Medical System of the Sibundoy Indians of Colombia." Ph.D. diss., Tulane University.

Sherzer, Joel. 1990. "On play, joking, humor and tricking in Kuna: the Agouti story." *Journal of Folklore Research* 27:85–114.

Sijindioy, José Chasoy. 1983. *Calusturinda Yaya: El Patrón de Carnaval*. Editorial Townsend.

Simón. Fray Pedro de. 1953 [1625]. *Noticias Historiales de las Conquistas de Tierra Firme en las Indias Occidentales*. Bogotá: Biblioteca de Autores Colombianos.

Swann, Brian, ed. 1992. *On the Translation of Native American Literatures*. Washington, D.C.: Smithsonian Institution Press.

Szoverffy, J. 1956. "From *Beowulf* to *The Arabian Nights*." *Midwest Folklore* 6:89–124.

Taggart, James. 1986 " 'Hansel and Gretel' in Spain and Mexico." *Journal of American Folklore* 99:435–60.

Tandioy, Francisco. 1988. *Iscay Huagchucunamanda Parlu: Los Dos Huérfanos*. Editorial Townsend, Comité de Educación Inga de la Organización "Musu Runacuna."

Taussig, Michael. 1987. *Shamanism, Colonialism, and the Wild Man: A Study in Terror and Healing*. Chicago: Univ. of Chicago Press.

Tedlock, Dennis. 1972. *Finding the Center: Narrative Poetry of the Zuni Indians*. New York: Dial.

———, trans. 1985. *Popol Vuh*. New York: Simon and Schuster.

Thompson, Stith. 1955–1958. *Motif-Index of Folk Literature*. 6 vols. Rev. ed. Bloomington: Indiana Univ. Press.

———. 1961. *The Types of the Folktale: A Classification and Bibliography*. Helsinki: Academia Scientarum Fennica.

———. 1966 [1929]. *Tales of the North American Indians*. Bloomington: Indiana Univ. Press.

Toelken, Barre. 1969. "The 'pretty language' of Yellowman: genre, mode and texture in Navajo coyote narratives." *Genre* 2:211 35.

Triana, Miguel. 1951. *La Civilización Chibcha*. Bogotá: Biblioteca Popular de Cultura Colombiana.

Turner, Victor. 1967. "Betwixt and between: the liminal period in *rites de passage*." In *The Forest of Symbols: Aspects of Ndembu Ritual*. Ithaca: Cornell Univ. Press.

Uribe, María Victoria. 1977–1978. "Asentamientos prehispánicos en el altiplano de Ipiales, Colombia." *Revista Colombiana de Antropología* 21:57–195.

Urton, Gary. 1981. *At the Crossroads of the Earth and the Sky: An Andean Cosmology*. Austin: Univ. of Texas Press.

Vogelin, Erminie. 1950. "Myth." In *Dictionary of Folklore, Mythology, and Legend*, ed. M. Leach. New York: Funk and Wagnalls.

Whitten, Norman. 1976. *Sacha Runa: Ethnicity and Adaptation of Ecuadorian Jungle Quichua*. Urbana: Univ. of Illinois Press.

Index